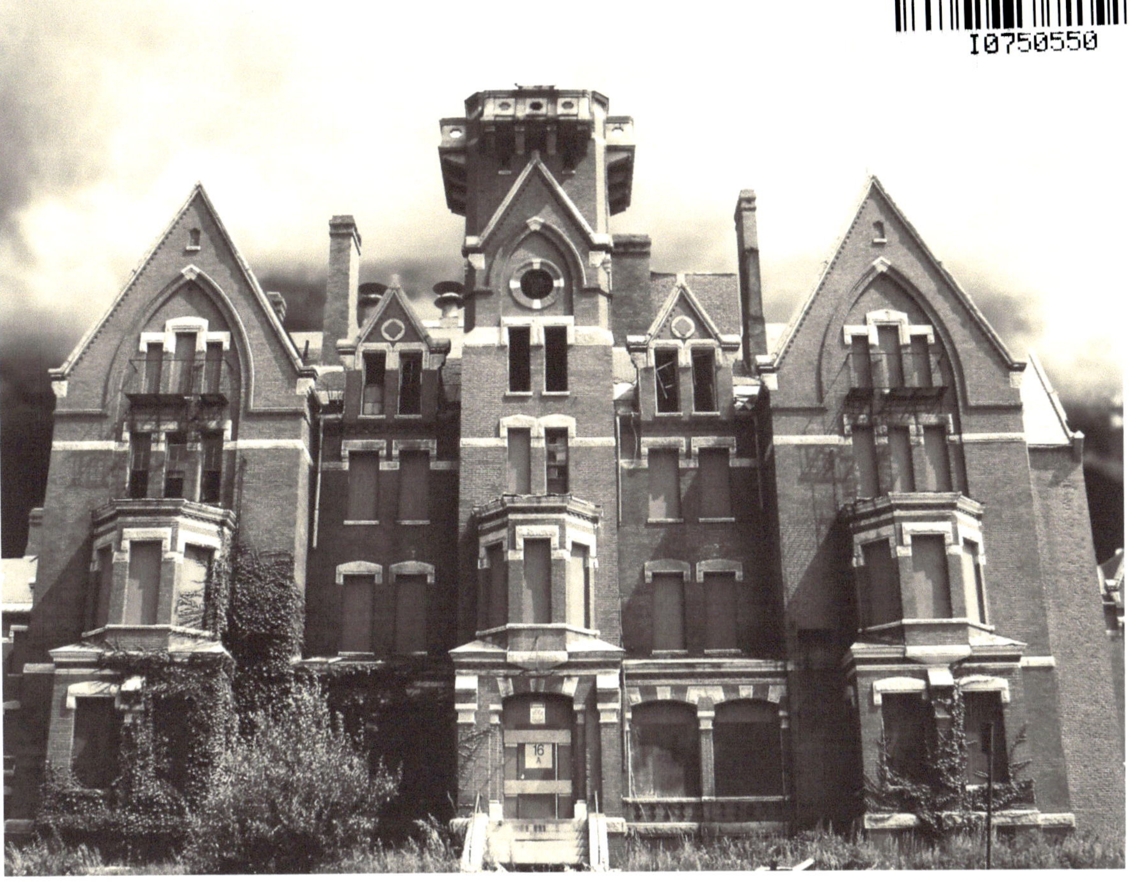

The Forbidden Tourist

by Fred Szabries

The Forbidden Tourist

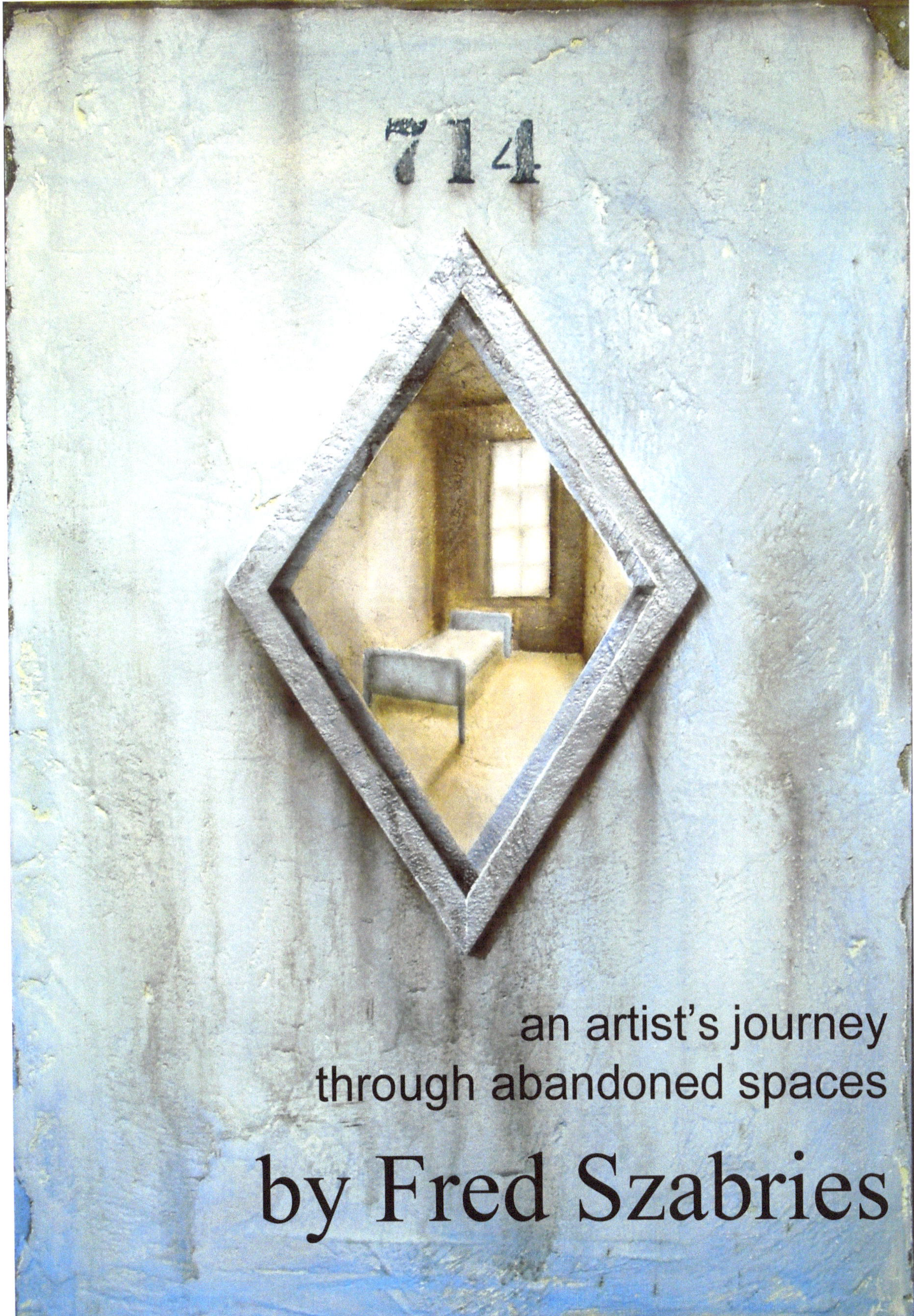
714
an artist's journey
through abandoned spaces
by Fred Szabries

The Forbidden Tourist
Second Revised Edition

The Art Of Szabries
www.szabries.com
www.theforbiddentourist.com
E-Mail: artist@szabries.com

ISBN-13: 978-0-9791352-1-7
ISBN-10: 0-9791352-1-4

Published by Studio Szabries
Printed In The United States Of America

Previous Page:
"714"
original oil on board
Fred Szabries
2005

This book is for everyone who believes in their dreams and has the courage to relentlessly pursue them.

ITINERARY

Arrivals

This is not a travel guide. You will find no reviews of restaurants, local entertainment or shortest possible routes. There is no mention of quaint and cheery shopping districts because the only way I ever see that sort of thing is passing through on my way to someplace I'm probably not allowed to visit. This is an account of my obsession with the abandoned and forgotten. If it's rotting in the woods and the paint is peeling off the walls, then that's the place for me. If it contains vintage medical ephemera, or rusting industrial machinery, then even better. I will drive for hours to spend even more hours inside of a building on the verge of collapse. I will willingly walk through dark, dank forests, pouring rain, two feet of snow or brave sub freezing temperatures. I will risk a possible trespassing violation, toxic chemicals and dangerously unstable structures. There are times that I've had traveling companions, which is safer, but no matter, I will go alone when necessary. Whatever it takes is what I will do to enter a world that is on one hand timeless, quiet and poignant and on the other almost palpably frightening.

There is no doubt that these ventures carry a fair degree of risk on many levels. I try to reduce the risks as much as possible through preparation. Extensive research and study is conducted for each location including historical documents, maps, modern aerial surveys and newspaper accounts. Through this research I've learned that our society has abandoned virtually every type of institutional building and complex from hospitals to schools to factories to hotels to theme parks and even moon rocket facilities. The most shocking discovery is that there are millions of square feet of abandoned mental institutions in this country. Some are so old they were called lunatic or insane asylums when they were built. Some were massive enough to have buildings that spanned a half a mile in length. I also learned that almost all of these abandoned asylums were the scenes of horrific forms of arcane treatment. Electroshock therapy, lobotomies, insulin shock therapy, restraints and hydrotherapy, among others, were used on mental patients all the way up to the closure of many of these places in the 1990's. I can tell you that no amount of foreknowledge can prepare you for observing the remnants of these horrors firsthand. To see seclusion rooms no larger than eight by ten feet with bars on the windows and small portholes in the doors makes you realize that these places were more prisons than places of healing. To see the actual table where lobotomies were performed rusting in a dark tunnel is a sobering sight. When you turn a corner in a pitch black basement and enter a morgue with the examination table, autopsy tools and body freezers intact it also makes you understand with cold, stark reality that real people suffered and died in these places.

I should mention that while it's true that these mental institutions probably hindered more patient's recovery than they helped, they were never intended to be that way. When they were built they were the pinnacle of treatment for the mentally ill. Dr. Thomas Story Kirkbride, one of the most celebrated authorities on care of the mentally ill during the latter 19th century, believed in the "building as a cure" method. He felt that exquisite architectural details, soothing colors and well-landscaped grounds would provide the patient a calming space in which to recover. He also designed a building with staggered wings, which was intended to allow as much light as possible in each ward. It also provided each patient room with sunlight during a portion of each day. All buildings that prescribed to this plan were referred to as Kirkbride Buildings and were typically the largest and most central structure of the asylum campuses. Despite his imminence, he evoked wildly diametric reactions in mental patients. One tried to kill him, while another ended up marrying him.

Unfortunately, the noble intentions of the early architects and doctors eventually collapsed under the weight of overcrowding and under-funding. The entire concept of state funded mental health itself eventually collapsed and the once intricate temples of healing, and in some cases their contents, were left abandoned to rot.

So if all of this is so fraught with risk and unpleasantness, you might ask why in the world I do it. The answer is as complicated and convoluted as the places themselves. The buildings alone make it worthwhile. The architectural triumphs such as huge curving wood balconies, soaring spires and incredible details in wood, metal and stone at every turn are something that simply cannot be found in today's boring utilitarian construction. The architectural oddities are an attraction too. One institution has a morgue distastefully located under the cafeteria. Another converted their morgue into a cafeteria. Some have cemeteries with only numbers on the grave markers, no names or dates of passing identifying the interred. Almost all had extensive tunnel systems connecting the buildings. These tunnel systems aided in moving patients and staff amongst the various buildings in inclement weather. They served to move me about in much the same way. They also, at times, made me hopelessly lost since I've yet to find a map or diagram of any tunnel system. The items left behind are compelling too. Some places are nearly empty, some seem as if they went from full operation one day to abandoned the next leaving everything behind. I've seen medical instruments, entire operating theaters, beds, furnishings, and even patient belongings and records. The records were supposed to be kept confidential and stored securely or destroyed, but they too were left behind in the seemingly haphazard closings. There are other oddities too. An old foundry littered with rat skeletons, a sign in a hospital warning of an animal head in the freezer, a weed-strewn theme park near a more famous park, a full size, formerly operational moon rocket rusting in a swamp and a turn of the century insane asylum right next to a contemporary, active psychiatric center.

The human experience is what compels me the most. To walk empty corridors and stand in rooms where a steady stream of patients suffered for over 100 years creates tremendous mental reflection. The fact that people were committed, lived their confused lives, and then died forgotten within these grounds without even the decency of a headstone gives me pause. The pause turns to sadness which turns to anger at the state governments who allowed abuse through apathy then allowed the decay of these buildings through neglect and then ultimately profited, both financially and politically, through their sale to developers. The fact that these structures have been, or will be, bulldozed into oblivion with total disregard for the National Historic Register on which many places were supposedly listed for preservation is bad enough. To offer no respect or memorial for the memory of the former inhabitants is unconscionable.

The atmosphere of an abandoned space is itself compelling. In this book you will visit, through my eyes and experiences, mental institutions, hospitals, a hotel, a school, a factory, a space age test facility and cemeteries. Some are completely abandoned, some partially. I wondered in each one, why were places of such scale and purpose left to the elements? Why was money and profit more important than the needs, desires and dreams of real people like you and I? I wonder still to this day if we will learn from history, or will we be forever bulldozing our future potential enlightenment.

Someone once said that a secret told loses its power. These abandoned spaces hold fast to their secrets and powerful they are.

A technical note from the author:

This book contains a selection of photographs taken at the various locations along with a journal of my travels to each. They are not presented in chronological order, but rather in the order of architectural interest and historical importance. Additional unpublished photographs and videos can be viewed on the optional CDROM in slideshow format. The CDROM is 100% compatible with PC based computer systems. The video segments are purely my artistic vision and are not intended for profit, nor to portray any persons, living or deceased, nor any specific building, actual corporation or entity.

Where possible, I have provided a bit of history for the location. These histories are from my memory and research and are by no means complete. Sources and references are not provided because this is not intended to be a textbook or reference manual. The histories are only intended to pique your interest. I invite you to research places of interest more thoroughly on your own.

Some locations referred to have been demolished since publication and some are still standing. The names have been changed on many locations to protect the property and to prevent this from being a field guide to abandoned buildings. Most are not open to the public and are dangerous and illegal to enter. I was granted permission to enter these locations. Please do not attempt to enter any place that is listed in this book as it could result in bodily harm, death, arrest or worse.

Journeys

Places that merited several visits. All the sites in this section have since been demolished. Remnants of some can still be seen incorporated into condominium developments.

CHAPTER ONE

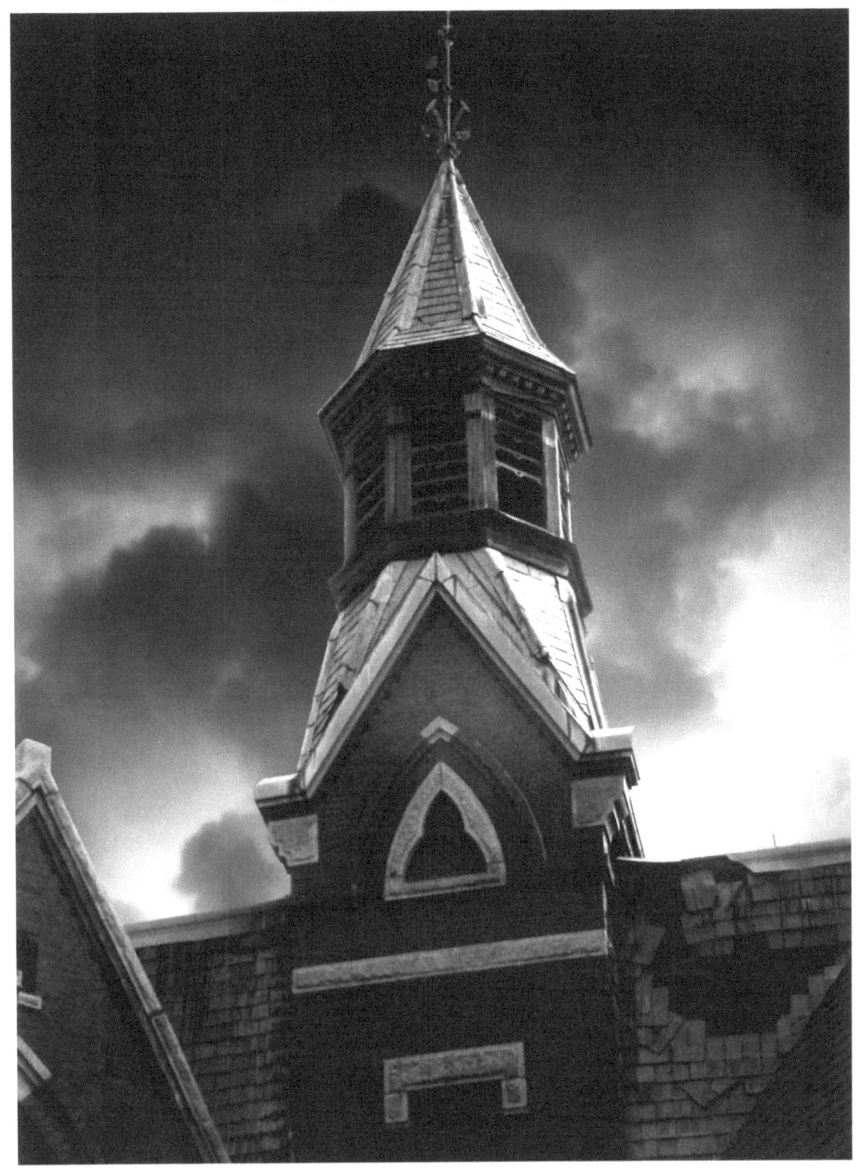

DANVERS STATE HOSPITAL

Massachusetts

Danvers State Hospital

Welcome to the Scariest Building in the World

The first time I visited Danvers State I drove past an open gate and onto the grounds of the hospital. It was a short drive up Hathorne Hill through the woods and past a few smaller boarded up structures. You would have to drive with your eyes closed to not see the old hand painted signs indicating that this was state property and visitors were no longer welcome. Since no security or police officers were present, I simply continued on with the intention of feigning ignorance should I be approached. I doubted that ruse would work, but it didn't matter because for all the dire warnings and promises of prosecution I saw no one. The entire grounds seemed vacant and devoid of human life.

The approach to the main hospital complex itself was shrouded in what appeared to be old growth forest. It was thick and initially offered no hint of the Victorian behemoth perched atop the hill. As I continued up the hill, I peered through the woods looking for my first glimpse of the building. Before I had my first view of what was known as America's Scariest Building I noticed a drop in temperature and a general darkening. The area just seemed dim. It was as if it was too much effort for the sun to penetrate the gloom that permeated the approach road. It was only the thick canopy of woods, of course, but it made for a classic horror movie atmosphere.

When I finally glimpsed the main building, known as the Kirkbride, through the woods, gooseflesh broke out on my arms and I'm pretty sure the hair on the back of my neck stood straight up. Red brick, green slate roofs and rusting spires that only Edgar Allen Poe could conjure squatted like some medieval castle on the edge of the wood. As I rounded the last corner of the road and into the large plaza and parking area in front of the main building I felt an overwhelming sense of awe. This building was simply like nothing I had ever seen. First of all, it was huge. The Kirkbride building was over a half a mile long. The staggered shape made it appear even larger and confused the eye as to where it began and ended. It was topped with spires in a seemingly random way and the very center was crowned with a huge square tower that obviously had a very large spire attached to it in the past. Whether that structure was amputated purposely at some point, or simply fell off due to neglect was not apparent.

The overall sense of decay and neglect was very apparent. Vines climbed the building and insinuated themselves into the boarded up windows. Roof slates were strewn about on the ground and there were piles of the building lying where they presumably fell off and were never collected.

I parked the car right at the front door, grabbed my camera and started walking around. Upon closer inspection, those piles of debris were amazing in themselves. They contained doors made of mahogany and walnut, intricate moldings and even an antique wheelchair along with piles of the green roof slate. I picked up a roof slate and walked back to put it in the car. I felt like I really needed to have a piece of this amazing place. I guess I didn't feel that strongly about it because I ended up leaving it in the rental car when I turned it in. I wish I still had it today.

As I headed back to the building a security patrol came speeding up to me. The guard jumped out of his little white car and approached me.

"What are you doing here?," he said. "You're trespassing."

"I thought it was ok since the gate was open. I came all the way from Florida just to photograph this building."

He said, "Really? You came all that way? Well, ok…I guess you can take some pictures but stay out of the buildings".

"Great! Thanks," I replied and the moment he drove away, I started looking for a way in. This proved more complicated than the dilapidated state of the building indicated. The windows were boarded and screwed shut. All the old wooden doors were retrofitted with commercial metal doors and frames, which were securely locked. Or so it seemed. I later learned that the metal doors didn't fit the openings very well and could be easily opened by simply pushing on the frame. The process didn't even leave a mark. But, on this trip Danvers held fast to her secrets and refused my entry. That is, until I noticed a board that was removed from a window under a stairwell. I moved the board aside and peered into the gloomy interior. I crouched through the opening and stood there staring at a dark corridor. I snapped one picture with the flash and it gave me a sense of the scale. The hall was long and had many doors off to each side. Just then, I heard tires crunching in the parking lot and I knew the security detail was back. I climbed out the opening and pretended to be taking pictures. The guard called me over to his car and said my time was up and I needed to leave so he wouldn't get in trouble. I thanked him and left the way I came in. I was disappointed at not being able to spend any time inside but, to be honest, I really don't know if I would have had the nerve. I had no flashlight and no real idea of the building layout at the time. I knew one thing: I would be back. Danvers was not a place I could easily forget.

Walking Into a Nightmare

This time I was prepared with a traveling companion named Xavier, my camera and flashlights with extra batteries. Xavier knew the building and grounds and knew an easy way in. What he didn't know was an easy way to actually approach the building. It was a sweltering morning as we walked up Hathorne Hill in waist deep summer grass and I thought I might have a heart attack or heat stroke or both. We walked past the cemetery on the way, with its numbered head stones, but didn't linger there for fear of being seen by security. There would be no feigning ignorance this time. Not equipped as we were with flashlights and backpacks containing water and snacks and cameras, so stealth was the rule. After clearing the hill, we entered the woods and were shortly at the road that circled the building. We sprinted across the road and up to a door. Xavier worked the door and in seconds we were in the part of the asylum that housed the most violent and mentally ill patients.

Entering the asylum was such a stark contrast to the bright summer day outside that I can only describe it as walking straight into a nightmare. The stairwell we were in was dark and smelled of rot and mold. The paint was peeling off the walls and the iron banister was cold and wet and from an era long past. When we walked into the ward it was as if time had stood still. The air seemed to be holding its breath and the darkness pressed in from everywhere. Our flashlights could only penetrate the gloom with a narrow spear of light. Down the hall, in the center of a dayroom, sat a lonely chair with wheels. Not a modern wheelchair as you might envision, but an upholstered contraption with small wheels, restraints and a handle on the back for pushing. This chair would be for someone who was unable, or unwilling, to move themselves about. Lying on the dusty floor in front of the chair was a newsletter from when this ward was alive with the criminally insane. I could imagine a former patient sitting there with the newsletter, blank staring eyes seeing not the words but his own personal visions of hell. We left this forlorn sight to its timeless seclusion.

Xavier indeed knew his way around and headed straight for the center of the building which was the part that housed the Administration offices. Along the way, we saw isolation rooms no larger than 8' x 10' with bars on the windows, ward dayrooms with glass blocks instead of windows and, between each ward, metal grated doors to keep the more dangerous patients separated from the rest of the population. We also traversed a portion of the basement along the way and saw hydrotherapy tubs appropriately filled with rainwater that had dripped into the building, electroshock machines and a myriad of other medical artifacts like beds and constraints. There was also a strange fog in the basement due to the condensation of all the moisture trapped down there and while I knew what it was and why it was there, it was still very creepy.

As we made our way towards Administration, we started hearing voices. The building, as I mentioned, was huge and it relayed sound in a strange way, so it was difficult to tell where the voices were coming from. The shroud that wrapped the asylum in secrecy for over a decade was slowly lifting and the state had offered the entire property for sale to the highest bidder. The voices could have been potential buyers, developers or workers preparing the place for it's imminent demolition. They also could have been people like us: some of the last visitors those ward floors would ever see. We decided to continue on since the building was so big and offered so many dark places to hide and avoid being seen.

The closer we got to the center of the building the more apparent the voices became. Finally, while in the movie projection booth, the people we were avoiding walked right into the theater below us. We decided it was time to go. We made our way back into the Administration hallway, which was the only part of the building with no boards on the windows, and therefore well lit, when we noticed a briefcase sitting by the stairwell. It happened to be one of the very stairwells we needed to use to exit the area. We headed towards another stairwell in the opposite direction and the people started coming up. We backtracked, trying to make as little noise as possible, which is hard because the floor is strewn with broken glass and all sorts of other things that crunch under your feet. We were basically trapped in the brightly lit hallway with only small rooms on either side to hide in. The room we chose unfortunately had one of the only locked doors in the whole place. We were forced to flattened ourselves against the door in a small alcove while the other group of what we now suspected were executives of some description chatted no less than fifteen feet away from us. They started back down their stairs and we were finally able to slowly make our way down the hall to the other stairwell after ten minutes of holding our breath and trying to be invisible. After such a close call, we decided to not press our luck and further and made our way out of the building.

My time inside and around The Lunatic Asylum at Danvers was brief on both trips, but it left an indelible mark on my psyche. I doubt the bland, generic condominiums that now inhabit Hathorne Hill will last a fraction of the 110 years that the original building stood. I'm certain that architectural historians will look back with horror on the destruction of this once magnificent and unique building. Its demise will likely be compared to the loss of The Pennsylvania Station in New York to make way for the architecturally insignificant Madison Square Garden. A small portion of the outside walls of Administration and two wards have been preserved and new condominiums have been built inside the shell of the old building. I guess you could go up there and see a shadow of the former building, but it will never give an idea of the true scale and personality of the original. I know I won't go back. I prefer to remember Danvers as I saw it: decrepit, malevolent, lonely, fraught with dark memories and yet the most spectacular and unique example of American Victorian Architecture I have ever seen.

A Brief History of Danvers State Hospital

Its imposing Gothic spires rose above Hathorne Hill just a few miles north of Boston. Dark and malevolent, even on faded denim blue-sky day, Danvers had an epic presence. Formerly known as the Danvers Lunatic Asylum, this complex of buildings witnessed the most horrific treatments of the mentally ill. Lobotomies, insulin shock treatment, hydrotherapy and prison like restraints were just some of the horrors visited upon the "lunatics" who unwillingly called this snake pit home.

Designed by Dr. Thomas Kirkbride, a pioneer of mental health, Danvers was actually a revolutionary design in asylums for its time. The main building opened in 1896 and was later referred to as the "Kirkbride". It was constructed in a staggered shape that allowed the maximum amount light into each section and separated the most dangerous patients through a series of wings. Kirkbride had the notion that ample windows giving onto landscaped grounds and the flood of sunlight would help the mentally ill. He also thought it prudent to keep the most dangerous patients as far from the Administration wing as possible.

The hospital complex fell victim to state deinstuitionalization in the 1980's and the Kirkbride building was closed. The entire grounds were closed for good in 1992 and the few remaining patients were moved to nearby facilities.

The Kirkbride building sat neglected and decaying for years, a sad testament to nearly incomprehensible suffering of the patients. The water supply to the building was left on, but the state refused to heat it. The result was frozen pipes that burst causing catastrophic water damage. Vandals and trespassers further aided the destruction by spray painting graffiti and setting fires inside the structures. One odd note in this institutions storied history is that a horror motion picture "Session 9" was filmed there in 2001. Hardly painting a positive picture of Danvers it did capture a moment in time in which the decay of the buildings is hauntingly beautiful in it's varied hues of peeling paint, rotting wood and solitary loneliness.

This amazing building, alternately called "America's Only Castle" and "The Scariest Building on Earth", has since been mostly demolished by developers planning to build condominiums on the site. Preservationists have pushed to save the Kirkbride building, which was listed on the National Historic Register, but their efforts have resulted in only a small, gutted portion being incorporated into the development plans.

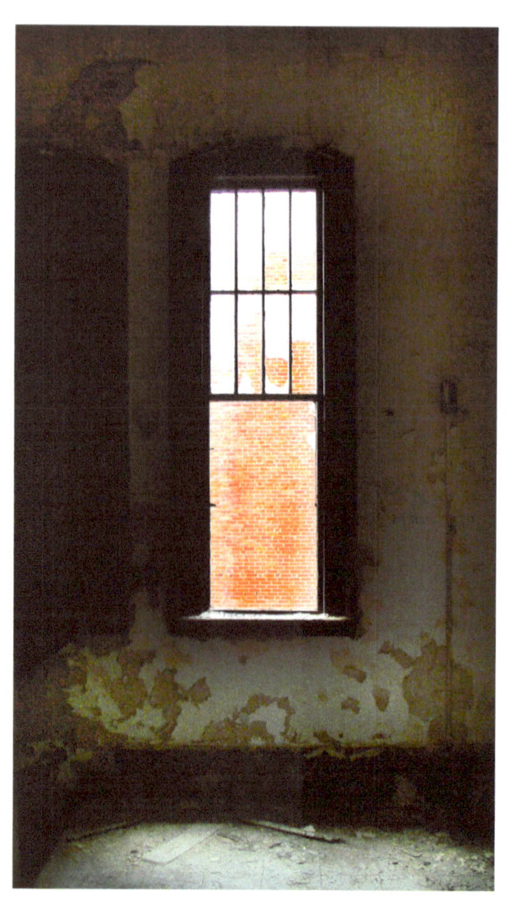

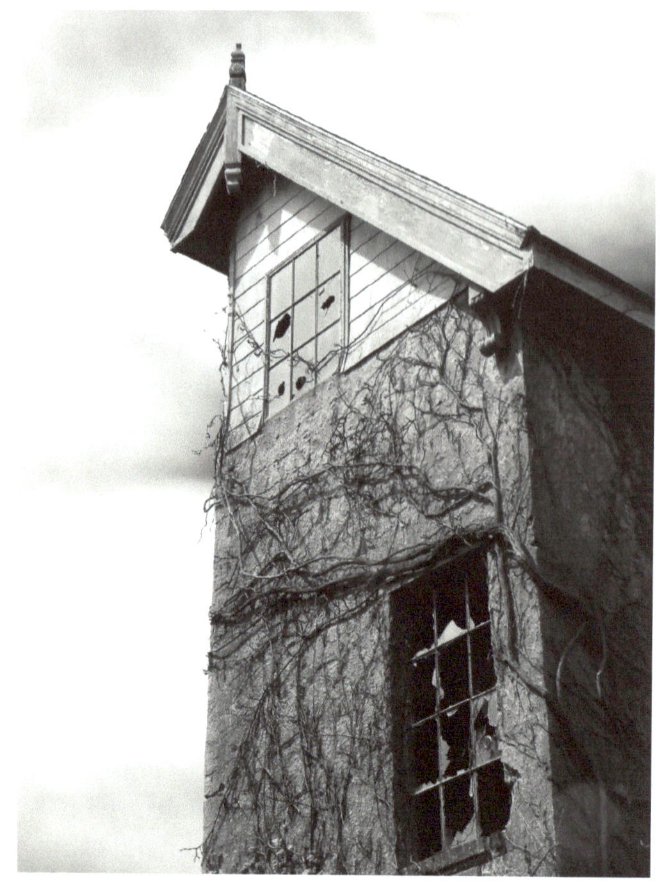

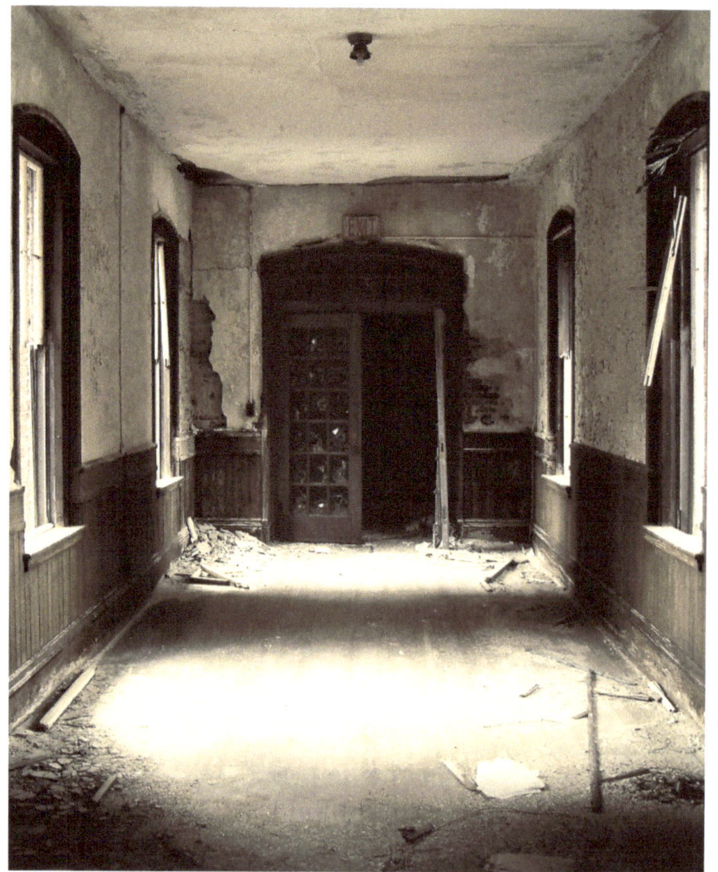

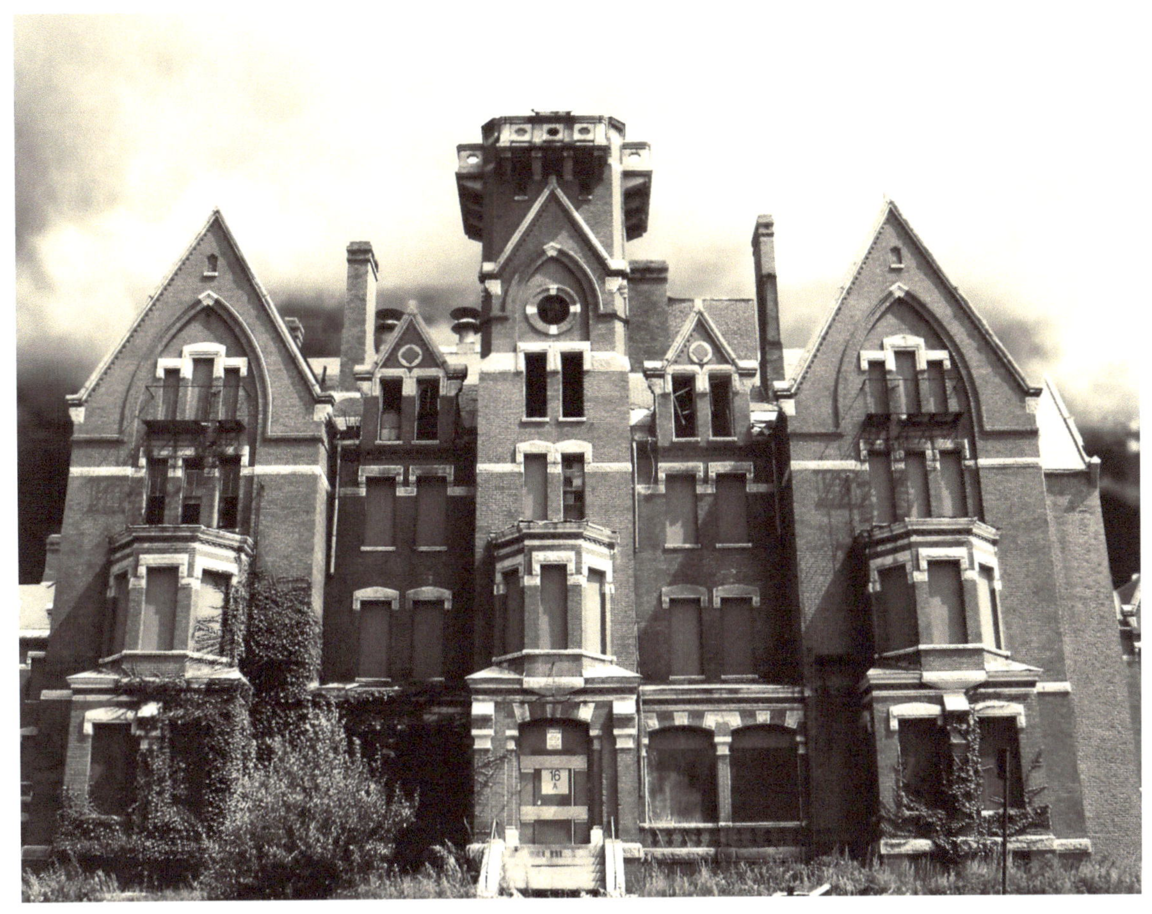

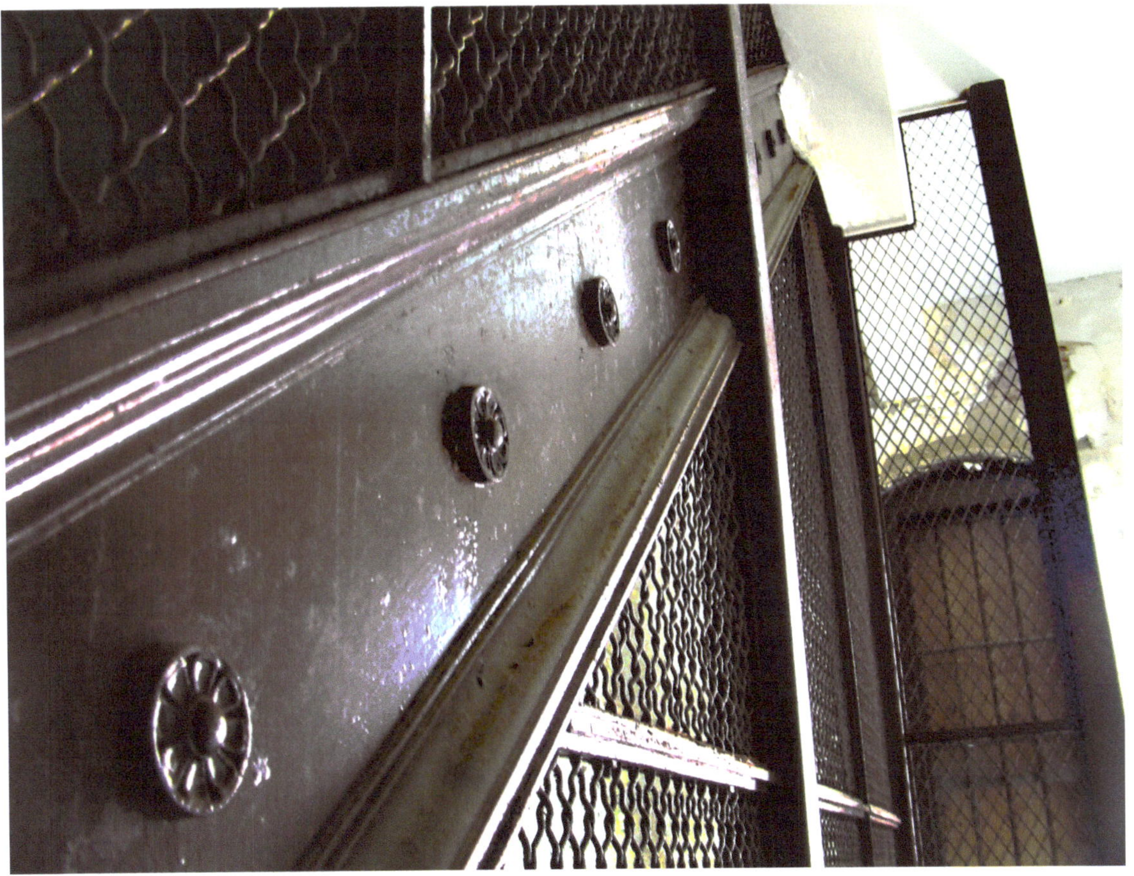

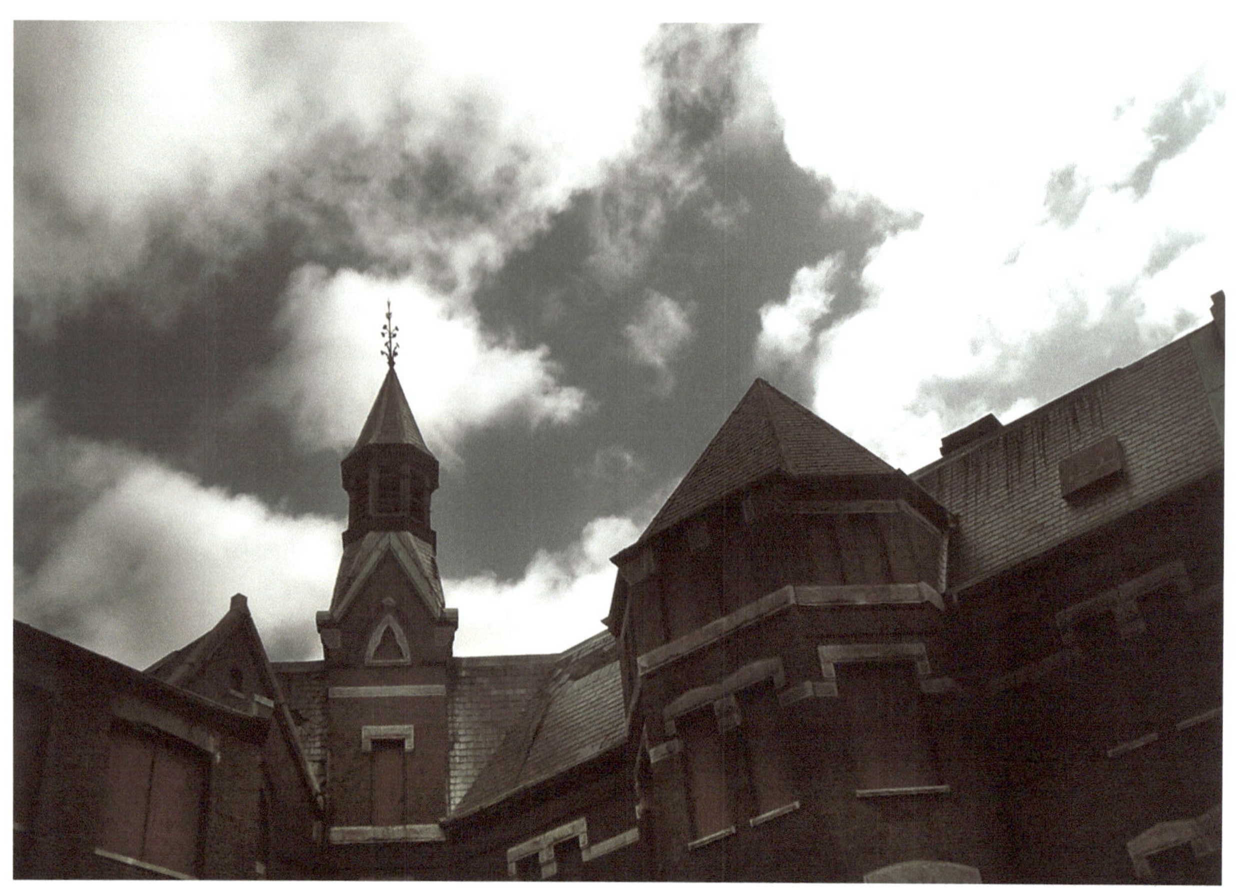

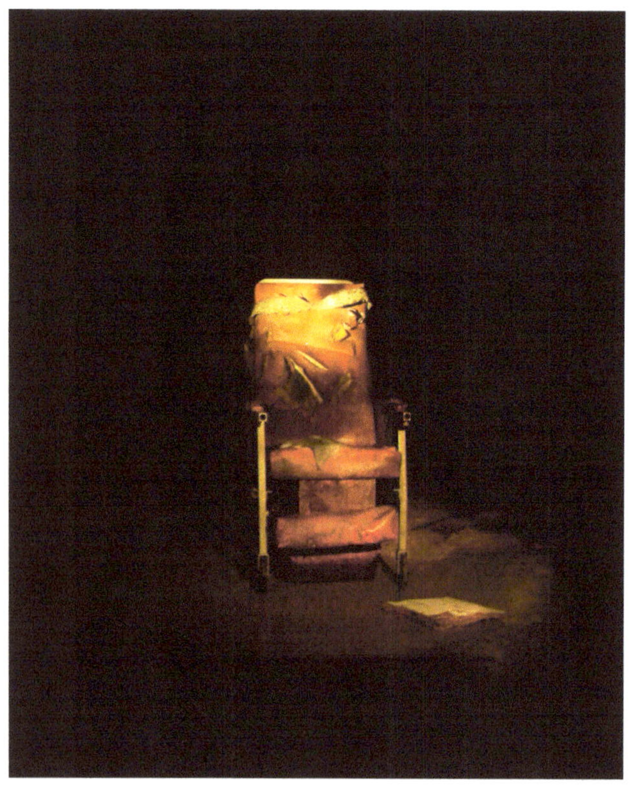

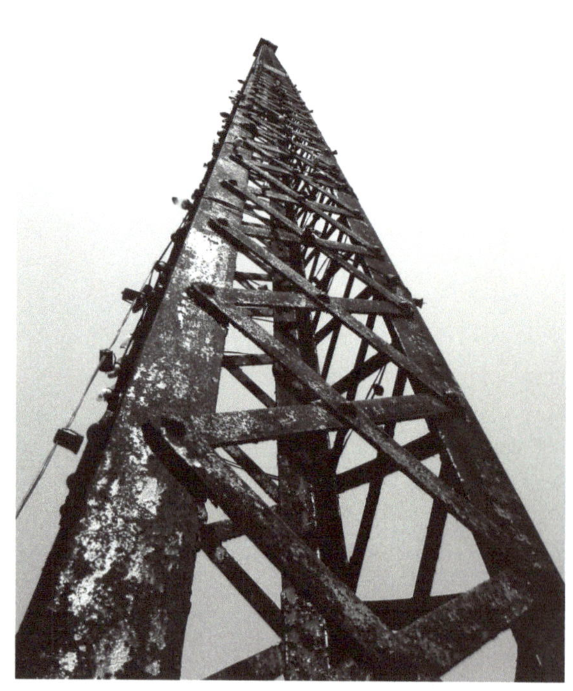

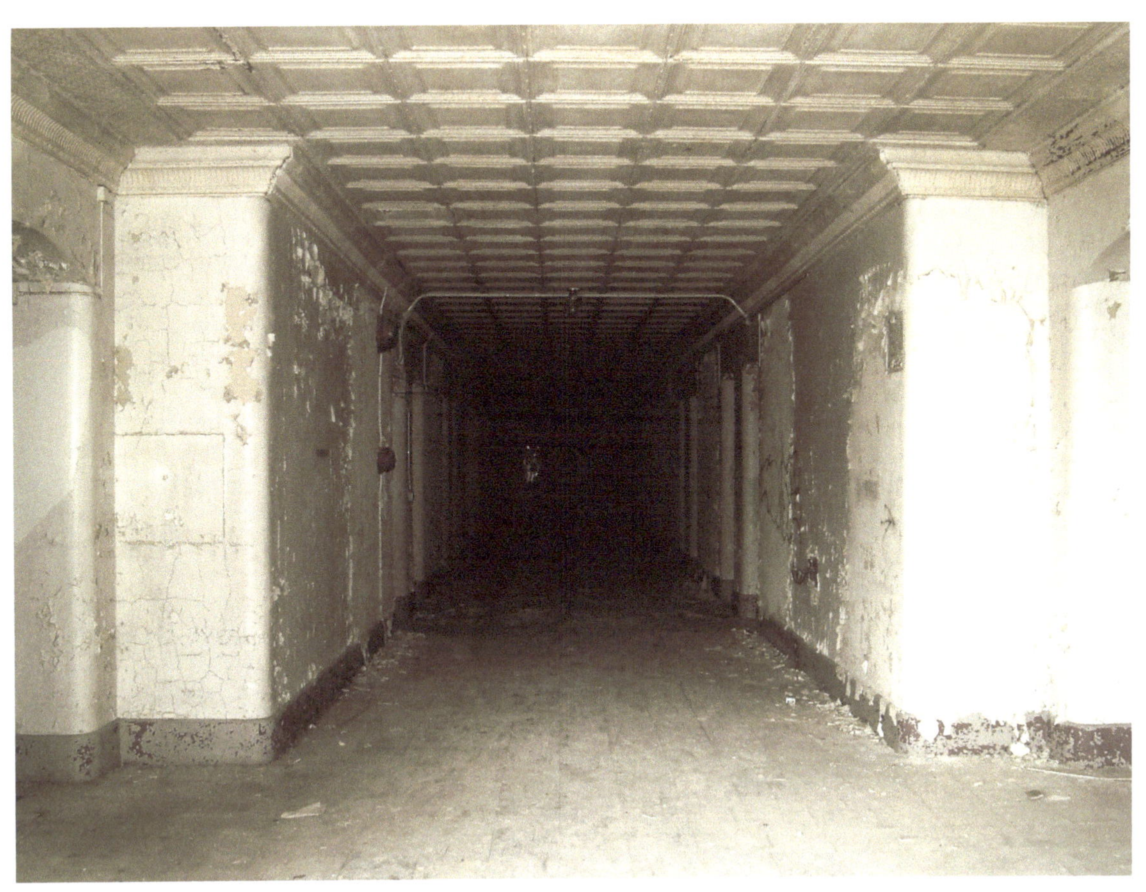

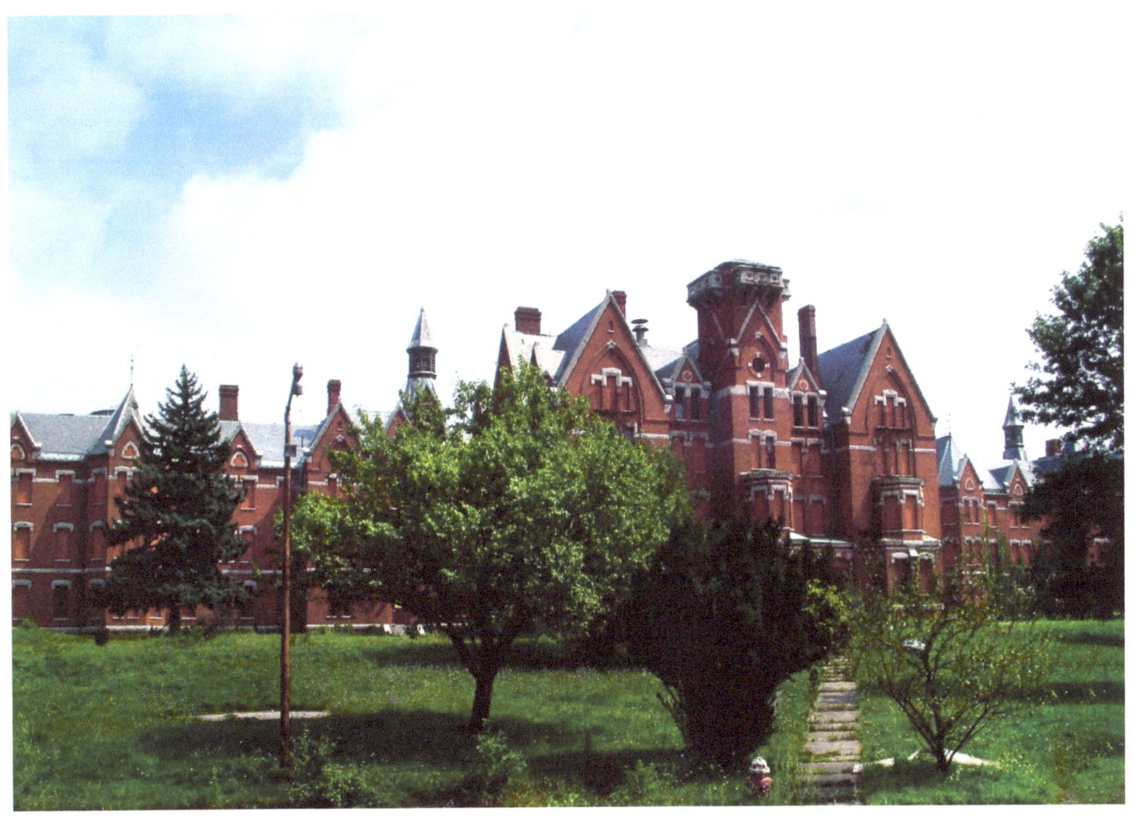

CHAPTER TWO

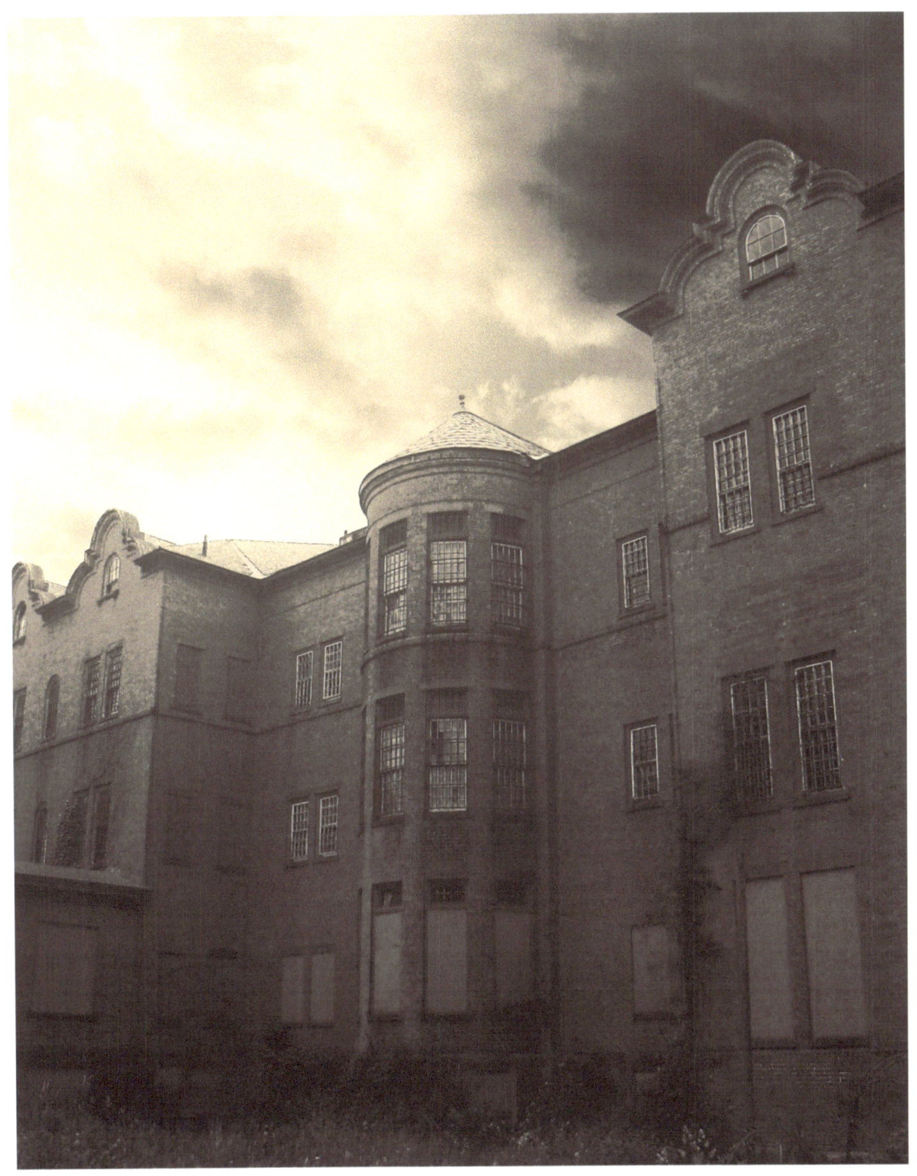

Northampton State Hospital

Massachusetts

Northampton State Hospital

Lost In The Tunnels

Northampton was the place that initially got me interested in asylums. I had been fascinated with this place ever since seeing an internet photo essay about it in 1999. It was more interesting to me at first than Danvers, which was overtly Gothic and almost patently scary looking. Northampton was a sophisticated and elegant place to house the insane and had some very unique architectural features. To finally experience the place in person was a tremendous and unforgettable experience for me. I met my traveling partner, Xavier, near the Northampton property at a.m. on a Sunday. It was legal to stroll the path in the woods near the hospital grounds and many people did so, walking their dogs and jogging. It was still early, so we didn't see anyone that day on our way into the woods and we approached the building with impunity. My first glimpse of the main structure brought a chill. I knew the structure was not as large or imposing as some other asylums, but it still had a dark and grim appearance. We entered an overgrown courtyard and were presented with the now familiar Kirkbride layout of staggered wings. The Northampton architects added a unique detail in semi circular dayrooms that gave the building its unusual shape on the outside.

Unlike some other abandoned structures I've been to this building only had boards on the ground floor windows, which would later prove to be very conducive to photography. I've found through subsequent trips that Northampton was, by far, the most photogenic abandoned structure I have ever seen.

We entered the building through a wide open door that placed us in the wing of the building that housed the most violent patients. We found ourselves in a stairwell with a choice to go up to the main wards or down to the basement and tunnels. We chose up, saving the basement and extensive tunnel system for later. The first floor was dark and gloomy, due to the boards on the windows, and was in such a state of decay that I was momentarily disappointed that the place had deteriorated drastically since the last photos I had seen. Xavier assured me that this area was among the worst and that it got better the further we went up. This proved to be true, but there were still dangerous areas with collapsed floors. We had to carefully watch our step. We went up another stairwell and onto the second floor, which was in better overall condition. The stairwells alone were incredible. They were constructed of an intricate, open latticed iron unlike any I had ever seen used for such a simple feature as a stairway. That type of detail in a relatively unseen area was repeated throughout the building and we were surprised by architectural treatments and oddities at every turn.

As we made our way through the wards, I was mesmerized by the seclusion rooms. Some still had beds with sheets on them. Some actually had grass growing on the floor and others had no floor at all; they had collapsed into the next level down. The rooms were so small that there was barely space for anything but the bed. Some rooms had a small, slotted diamond shaped window from which orderlies and doctors could peer in at the patient. The patient could of course peer back out the window, but he, or she, would not see much more than the wall across the hall. The rooms all had windows. Some looked out onto the grounds and some had a view of the next ward over. I'm not sure if the view of huge brick walls was very soothing or produced more of a feeling of claustrophobia. The most poignant thing we found in the seclusion rooms was a stanza of a poem by Algernon Charles Swinburne literally scratched in to one of the walls by a former patient:

From too much love of living,
From hope and fear set free,
We thank with brief thanksgiving
Whatever gods may be
That no life lives for ever;
That dead men rise up never;

That even the weariest river
 Winds somewhere safe to sea.

We made our way towards the middle of the structure where the Administration Wing was located. This building had many changes and additions of the years, some of which were not exactly improvements. One example of this was the large, soaring rotunda that used to grace the very center of the building. The rotunda was, at some point, removed and replaced with a rather bland set of square, undecorated rooms, which served as the nexus of the hospital. Beyond this area was an original feature of the hospital that was by no means bland. We entered a grand auditorium through a set of double doors that also had diamond shaped windows, but these diamonds were horizontal rather than vertical like the ones in the seclusion rooms. Maybe they were placed that way to subtly remind the patients that were still in a lunatic asylum and not an opera house. The auditorium indeed did resemble an opera house. It contained one of the more impressive examples of woodworking that I have seen. Vaulted arches soared over a cantilevered and curved wooden balcony encrusted with molding and trim. That feature alone would have made the auditorium spectacular, but the architects didn't stop there. They also added huge stained glass windows surrounded by columned pediments. The dramatic and awe-inspiring effect was even greater given the state of disrepair. As will be the case many more times throughout my travels, I am stunned and amazed that such superlative architectural examples were left to rot.

From the auditorium, we made our way through the huge kitchen to the Olander Cafeteria. This feature was also an addition and was pretty bland with the exception of oval windows and a balcony at one end. The balcony was likely placed in such a way that guards could have an overview of the patients while they dined. I could imagine the clamor of days past as hundreds of patients ate their institutional meals in this expansive space. The only sound that day was our footsteps wetly echoing as we crossed the damp floor and the occasional flutter of a pigeon roosting high in the rafters.

Directly off the cafeteria was a door leading to the basement and tunnels. We went down into the cave-like blackness in search of the morgue, which we knew was directly under the cafeteria. I know that the Olander was built long after the basement containing the morgue, but it's a bizarre placement to say the least. There are levels and sublevels to the tunnels under Northampton and they snake not only under that main building, but to other buildings too. It was very easy to get turned around and lost and in a short time we found ourselves in the basement of a food storage building some distance from the main building. As we backtracked, we found completely flooded tunnels that lead even deeper underground.

We finally found our way back to the main basement and stumbled upon the pathology laboratory and morgue which was right by the stair leading to up to the cafeteria. The examination table sat in the middle of the small room as if waiting for the next autopsy to be performed. The morgue freezer was double-sided and passed though from the autopsy room to an area that may have housed a crematorium at one time. The lab was around the other side of the autopsy room and still contained unknown substances in jars, blood samples with patient's names and what appeared to be brain sections mounted on glass slides. The freezer trays that once held the unfortunates on their final way out of the asylum were brimming with dark rusty water. In fact, the whole basement and tunnel structure was infused with an artificial fog and the constant sound of dripping water. The effect is nerve wracking because every sound echoes in the endless tunnels. All senses are on high alert anyway and between the total darkness and the myriad sounds of the building, the underground portion of this trip was particularly grueling.

After a thorough examination of the morgue, we headed back up and spent some time in the upper floors and wards. Soon, it was time for me to leave to catch a plane home. Xavier decided to stay behind and look around by himself. The thought of being alone in that creaking, dripping building with its collapsed floors and the memories of the insane was chilling. I was actually glad to be leaving and the sunshine on my face as I walked out of the woods was like a drink of fresh, clear water.

A Decaying Masterpiece

It was difficult to get Northampton out of my mind. I even walked the silent corridors and dark tunnels in my dreams. I knew I had to go back because there was so much I hadn't seen on the first trip. The next time I went I decided to stay the entire night there and see as much as possible. A good friend, Bobio, and I were in New York City for an art exhibition and decided to use some free time to drive up and visit the old asylum. We left New York City at 11pm and headed up to Northampton. It was cold that night and as we made the drive, the temperature dropped even more. When we finally arrived the thermometer was reading a grim 9 degrees F. We bundled up and headed into the woods. Being outside for just a few minutes we realized exactly what 9 degrees F felt like and, if you haven't experienced it, I can tell you it's painfully cold. There was no moon that night and it was pitch black in the woods. We were hesitant to use flashlights for fear of being seen and we strained to see our way, all the while tripping over frozen ruts in the path. This was my first trip to an asylum at night and it was so dark that it was difficult to find even the massive building in the woods. When we finally caught a glimpse of it through the trees, a chill went up my spine and it had nothing to with the temperature. There's nothing quite as frightening as an abandoned lunatic asylum crouching in the dark, cold woods. I briefly wondered how crazy I must be to being doing this.

We crossed the courtyard and entered the same open door as before, but this time went down to the tunnels first. I didn't want to waste any time wandering around lost, so I was more prepared than last time with a floor plan of the building. That is, until Bobio promptly lost it. We later found it on the way out, but we were on our own for directions. Luckily, I remembered most of the general layout.

There were several things I specifically wanted to see on this trip and we set out to find them. One was an antique operating table that was used to perform lobotomies. I knew from research that it was somewhere in the tunnels. We wandered underground for hours down there. I'm not sure how long because time has its way with you when you're in that Stygian blackness. After a while, the cold stone under our feet began to seep through the soles of our boots. It was so cold we actually became concerned about frostbite. We decided to take a short break on the first floor, which was only slightly warmer, and let the feeling return to our toes. After a brief respite, we headed back down and found the table about 50 yards from where we decided to break. I was surprised to find not only the table but also antique IV bottles and an old Pickering Fluoroscope nearby. I felt that the operating table was an important medical artifact and I wanted to remove it from the tunnel for preservation. Bobio and I pored over the logistics of doing this and simply couldn't find a way to accomplish the feat. The table was steel and iron and too heavy to move in one piece. It was rusted and locked into position, so it would have been nearly impossible to disassemble and remove in pieces. Even after heading back to the City, we pondered the problem without a viable solution. In the end, we left the table where we found it and the company responsible for the demolition of Northampton State Hospital either destroyed that table along with the other antique medical instruments in the tunnel or buried them under tons of debris. Either way, they're lost forever.

Even though I wanted see the areas of the asylum that I missed last time, it would have been unfair to my friend if I didn't show him some of the defining features of the building such as the auditorium and the morgue. We had no trouble finding either, but I was very disappointed to discover that some disrespectful vandal had scribbled all over the morgue freezer doors since my last visit. Graffiti is an inevitable component of most abandoned buildings. Sometimes it's intelligent and thought provoking, but mostly it's just vulgar. The most interesting kind is the vintage graffiti of the type I saw in the attic on my last trip here. It was done by one of the workers who built Northampton and was dated 1855. Despite the vandalism, we spent a fair amount of time photographing the morgue. We also discovered that the previously flooded tunnels were now frozen nearly solid three to four feet from the roof. We briefly considered sliding along the icy surface to see where the tunnel went and then thought better of it. It would mean certain death if the ice cracked and we plunged into that frigid water.

We left the basement and headed up into the Olander Cafeteria, where we heard a noise that sounded like footsteps. We froze on the spot and extinguished our flashlights. We walked along a bit further then heard it again. It sounded like someone else was lurking in the cavernous space with us. After ten minutes of intent listening we came to the conclusion that the noise was just pieces of the building creaking and moving in the wind.

By now, the sun was beginning to rise and we went upstairs to find the other items on my list of things to see. One was a wall with a quote painted on it from when Northampton was used a set for the movie "In Dreams" starring Annette Benning. We didn't find that exact room, but we did find the same saying scratched into the plaster of a wall. The quote read:

My Daddy was a dollar
I wrote it on a fence
My Daddy was a dollar
Not worth a hundred cents

This rendering of the quote looked old and I have no idea if it was from the movie or if it was already there, and so patently insane that they decided to include it in the movie. It seemed that Northampton was quite an example of literary graffiti. There was this quote, the A.C. Swinburne poem, another piece that read "Poets, but not so much poetry" and a quote from an old U2 song "Where the Streets Have No Name".

From there we stumbled onto the last item on my list. This was a room containing an old porcelain slab tub used for bathing patients. The room also contained an interesting plumbing feature consisting of numerous pipes snaking around the walls. The pipes were connected a light system that may have been used as a warning system for water temperature. The walls in this room were a deep crimson and I can't see how that blood red color could have possibly been soothing to a patient.

The sun was beginning to suffuse the interior with a radiant glow displacing the gloom and shadows. In the new light, the true beauty of this decaying masterpiece began to unfold. Northampton was a most unusual asylum in that every ward had a different architectural treatment and color scheme. One ward was a soft, robin's egg blue, another a deep mahogany brown. Another was once a bright, cheerful yellow. All were now water stained, moldy and peeling in a multi color profusion showing bits of all the colors the place was painted over the exactly 150 years it stood. The architecture was as diverse as the colors, here the room doors were wood with square windows, there they were metal with diamond shaped windows and yet others had little round windows.

The morning was growing late and we had had a long, cold night in the asylum. There was still the matter of a long drive back to New York and the hike out with its risk of discovery. We decided to end what would be my last trip inside Northampton and made our way out. As we left, we found the map right by the door we came in. We left it for the next intrepid explorer.

Death of an Asylum

It turns out I was the next intrepid explorer. I was also likely the last. When my new friend, Billamack, and I arrived at Northampton on humid summer night and made the trek through the woods, we observed an ominous sight. Rising up over Old Main was the boom of not one, but two cranes. This did not bode well for our expedition. Needless to say it didn't bode well for the building either. We slipped from the real world into the timeless overgrown courtyard and headed towards our familiar open door. This time it was not so welcoming. Some dedicated construction worker had sealed it with 16d nails. If you're familiar with nail sizes, then you know that 16d's are about three and half inches long, very stout, and don't come once they are hammered in. No amount of sweat, foul language or wishing and pleading would open it. With a feeling of dread, we moved on to the next door. I don't know how many doors were in that building, but I'm pretty sure we tried every one of them that night. I think you may be getting a sense of where this is going. The next door was locked from the inside. And the next, and the next. We tried the windows. No luck there either. The one good thing about this frustrating development was that I was slowly getting a tour of the entire perimeter of the building. In excruciating detail, I might add. Every possible entrance along with some impossible ones were scrutinized, to no avail.

We started to backtrack, past our no longer friendly entrance, and turned the corner to discover a huge glaring spotlight installed in another courtyard. To enter that brightly lit area would have negated the need for flashlights, but also would have been incredibly foolish. Anything moving in that area would be visible from a quarter mile away. We headed back around the other side of the building trying doors along the way. We rounded the front corner of the building and finally saw the sight that I have dreaded since I discovered Northampton: two huge cranes, a front end loader and bulldozer sitting in a pile of bricks.

Determined to get into the building for what looked like the last time, we crept towards what was now a construction site. Or rather, a destruction site. We were shocked and saddened to see that the entire front part of the Administration Wing was gone along with the remains of the old portico. The building was sheared off as neatly as if some angry god of redevelopment had cut it with a giant sword. The bizarre and ultimately frustrating thing was that the gaping hole that should have given us easy access didn't exist. The marauding demolition hoards in charge of this structural pogrom threw salt in our wounds by building huge plywood walls to seal off the part of the building flayed open by the demolition.

We approached this abomination and gaped in wonder. It seemed the only purpose of this wall was to keep us out and it did that very effectively. There may have been some other noble purpose for the wall, like creating a barrier so that the toxic substances like asbestos and lead didn't waft into the general population, but at the time we were sure it was a conspiracy against us.

We did see a promising hole where a careless equipment operator had gouged the three quarter inch thick sheets of plywood. The problem was that it was on the second floor. Not to be denied, Billamack painstakingly climbed a teetering pile of bricks and crawled through the hole. At one point he grabbed a loose board and almost plunged in to the treacherous pile of debris below. His efforts were rewarded with a dead end room. The doorway that would have lead out of that particular room was resting below him in the pile.

He climbed back down and by now I had navigated the pit of bricks and wood fragments that were once the asylums grand entrance. I realized that the pit was actually the remnants of the tunnel system. This portion of the tunnel would have been the exact area that held the old lobotomy operation table. The tunnel was completely clogged with bricks. We examined the area in detail and found no sign of the table. It was either buried forever or gouged out along with the rest of the priceless vintage medical equipment in the tunnel.

There was another item of priceless historical value that I knew was buried somewhere in this vicinity. Back in 1855, when the construction of the hospital began, a time capsule was placed under the cornerstone. There are two accounts that I have found of the contents. One described various papers pertaining to the asylum, medical books, tourist paraphernalia from the Town of Northampton and five gold, double eagle twenty dollar gold coins. The other account was the same minus the gold coins. We of course looked for the time capsule but did not find it. When I got home, I read a newspaper article that said the capsule had been found early the next day sitting exposed in its hollowed out cornerstone. Right in the area of the demolished Administration Wing. We probably stepped on the thing and didn't even know it.

By now we had been at the site for hours. We were tired, sweaty and depressed. We concluded that The Northampton State Hospital, aka Northampton Lunatic Asylum, was finally and irrevocably closed.

The Next Afternoon

I went back alone. I don't know why, but then again it was never fully within my grasp as to why I was so compelled to visit this place time and time again. I watched with detached interest for a while as the huge construction machinery brainlessly munched away at an irreplaceable piece of history. After having my fill of that morbid sight, I started to wander the perimeter of the fence and take some final pictures and video. What I saw through my lens was like a kick in the groin. In the floodlit courtyard that we failed to examine for fear of being seen, was a wide-open window at ground level. If we had just walked a few yards in that general direction last night we would have certainly seen it and been inside the building. I tried to kicking myself, but my anatomy wouldn't allow it so I settled for a few moments of quiet mental flagellation.

When I got over how close we were last night to getting in, but yet so far, it dawned on me. I could still get in. Tonight. The window would be there later and it would likely still be open. Even if it wasn't, I discovered what looked like a tunnel entrance in the form of a manhole hidden near the fence. So, I had two possible means of entry. The spring returned to my step as I opened my phone to call Billamack and tell him the good news. He was glad to hear of my discoveries but politely declined another three-hour drive to Northampton later that night. Seems he had life, which included a girlfriend that he needed to attend to.

Not to be deterred, I knew I still had other traveling partners. Two family members were on their way to these parts with the specific intention of meeting up and visiting this very asylum with me. They were due to arrive at nine that night, which would be perfect timing. A quick refreshment and I would bundle them into the rental car and head back here. I would conquer Northampton one final time!

Nine o'clock came and went, as did ten and eleven. I sat staring at the television in my room. If I watched one more inane television program about unreal reality I would likely need to check into Northampton's contemporary equivalent for treatment. I left my room for food and discovered that every establishment within five miles of my hotel had a pathological aversion to serving the late night hungry. I found nothing open. Not even a 7-11, which until now I foolishly assumed were all open to at least 11pm.

Hungry and frustrated I headed back to the hotel for some vending cuisine when I saw my family members unloading their bags. A rush of anticipation filled me and I almost ran up to them, eagerly helping with backpacks and luggage. We got into the room and they dropped a boulder on my spirits. The four-hour drive to meet me had turned to six, due to traffic, and they were too tired to travel any further that night. "Fine," I said. "We still have small window of time to climb through that small window. We'll go tomorrow."

Tomorrow came and we went to a different abandoned hospital instead because our guide, Billamack, was only available during the day and we didn't want to risk Northampton in the daylight. No matter, I thought to myself, we can still go that night.

That night I was called home early for personal reasons. As I made my arrangements to take the next flight out, I knew that I would never see Northampton again. The soonest I could get back here would be too late and the only thing left would be a rubble strewn field where Dr. Thomas Kirkbride gallantly tried to fix broken minds one hundred and fifty years ago.

As my plane tried to outrun its white contrail six miles above the planet, I wondered how Kirkbride would diagnose my obsession with his creation. In the cramped seat I slipped into a fitful sleep and dreamt of Northampton.

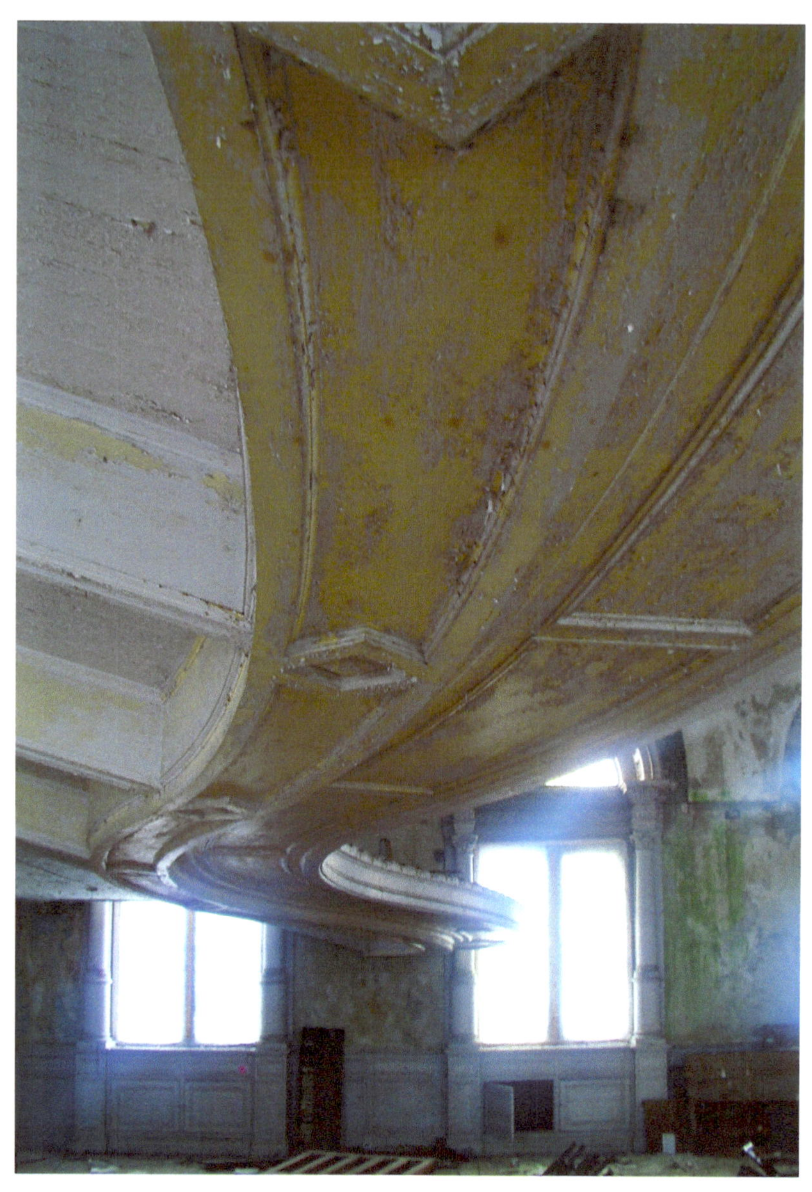

A Brief History of Northampton State Hospital

Originally named The Lunatic Hospital at Northampton, this was a massive example of Late Victorian architecture. The main building was over 400,000 square feet and the entire grounds once encompassed 172 acres on the Connecticut River. It opened in 1856 and the name was soon permanently changed to Northampton State Hospital. The floor plan was of staggered patient wings, which emanated from a central administration area. Consistent with the Kirkbride layout, the more dangerous and less treatable patients were located the farthest from the administration area. This asylum, at one point, was truly dedicated to patient comfort and recovery. The wards were painted in soft hues of blue, gray, brown and yellow to sooth and music therapy was considered an important part of patient daily life. In fact, an opulent auditorium was built for musical performances. Other additions over the years included a beauty parlor, additional wards and a cafeteria named the Olander.

For all the strides taken concerning the patients, the hospital could not prevent the escalating population and the inherent decline in treatment. At its peak, Northampton housed over 2700 patients and 500 staff; all in a setting designed for approximately 200 patients. Hydrotherapy, lobotomies, insulin, drug and electro shock therapy soon overtook music, art and beauty as the main forms of controlling and treating the mentally ill.

The hospital, like many others in the Northeast fell victim to federal deinstituitonalization and in 1978 it was ordered closed. It took until 1993 for the final patients to leave and when they did, the grounds were left empty and desolate only to be slowly reclaimed by the surrounding forest.

In 1999 the buildings were slated for demolition. In 2000 artist Anna Shuleit performed "Habeas Corpus: A Musical Installation for Northampton State Hospital," in an effort to save the structure and raise public awareness of the history of the hospital and the suffering of the patients. The performance consisted of Bach's "Magnificat" played through a sound system installed inside the primary hospital building, which was known as "Old Main". It was a dramatic and moving experience witnessed by over 1000 people and it resulted in the building being temporarily saved from the wrecking ball.

The entire grounds and buildings of Northampton State Hospital, like all other decommissioned sites owned by the State of Massachusetts, were once available, free of charge, to moviemakers as filming locations. In retrospect, this offering was likely a ploy to draw attention to the shamelessly neglected structures thus making them more attractive to developers. "Cider House Rules" and "In Dreams" were both filmed there. Despite the strenuous efforts of preservationists "Old Main", as the main Kirkbride building was known, along with most of the other buildings on the property, was demolished in 2006, exactly 150 years after it opened. A few of the minor buildings were redeveloped into condominiums. Strangely, these were completed and occupied before the rest of the demolition and the residents had the crumbling "Old Main" as a grim, creaking, smelly old neighbor for some time.

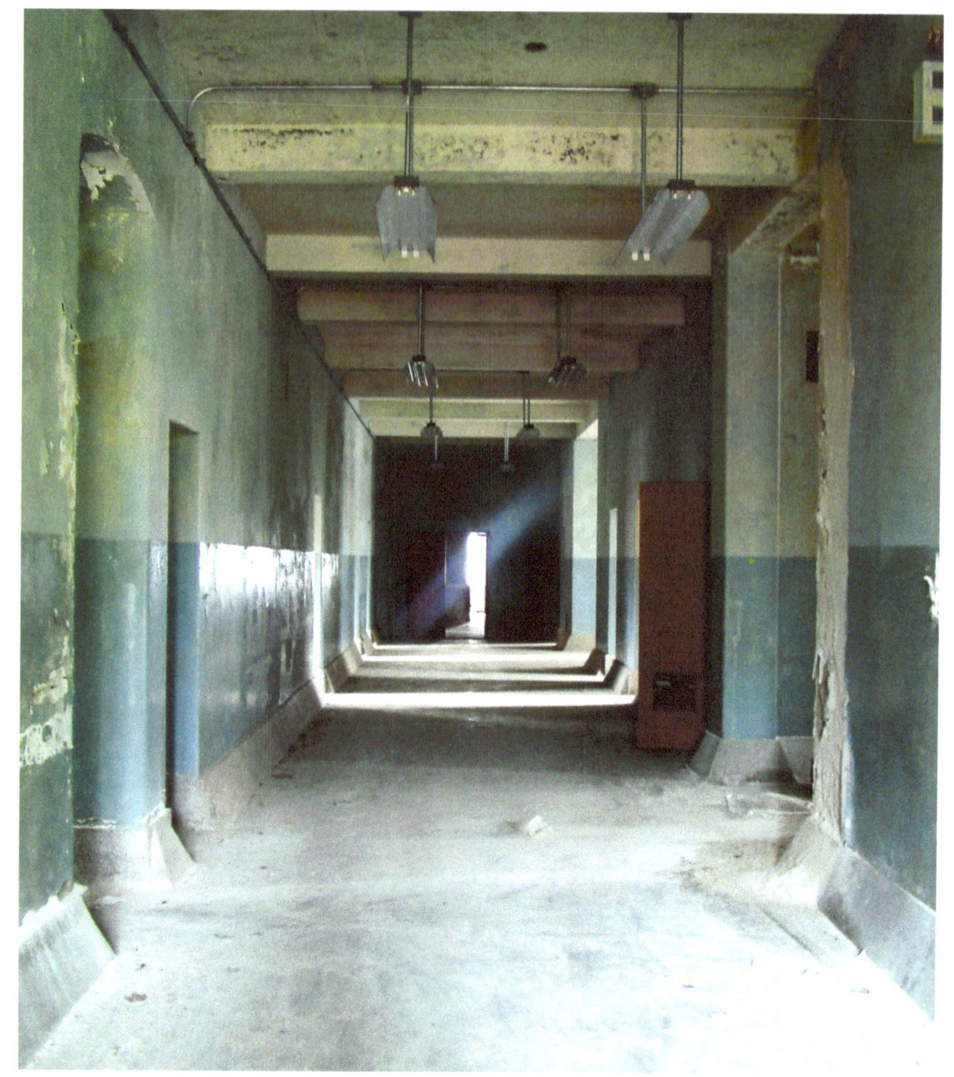

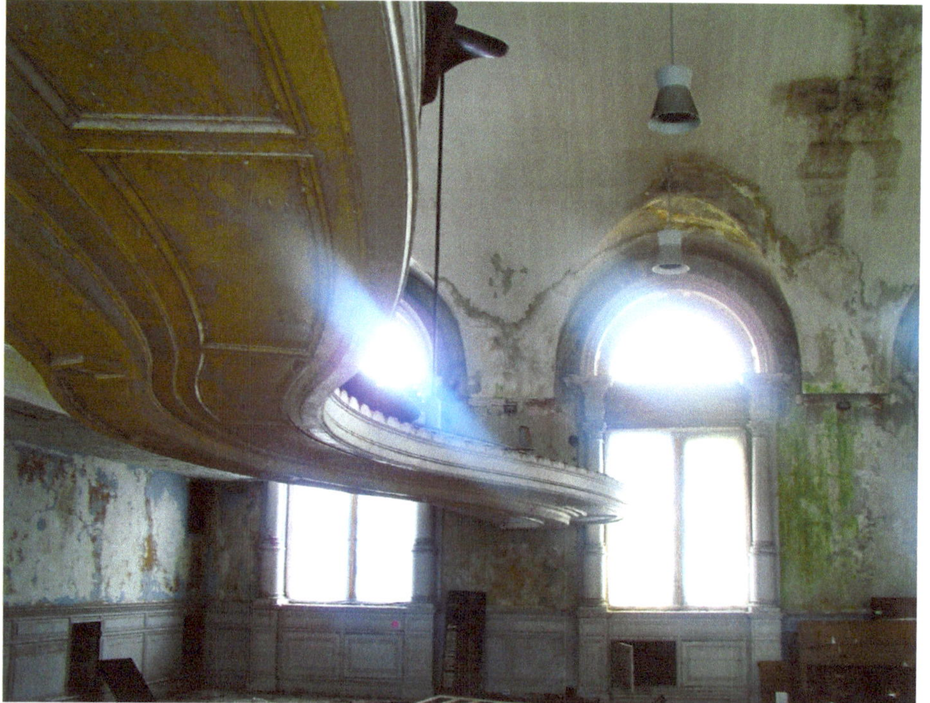

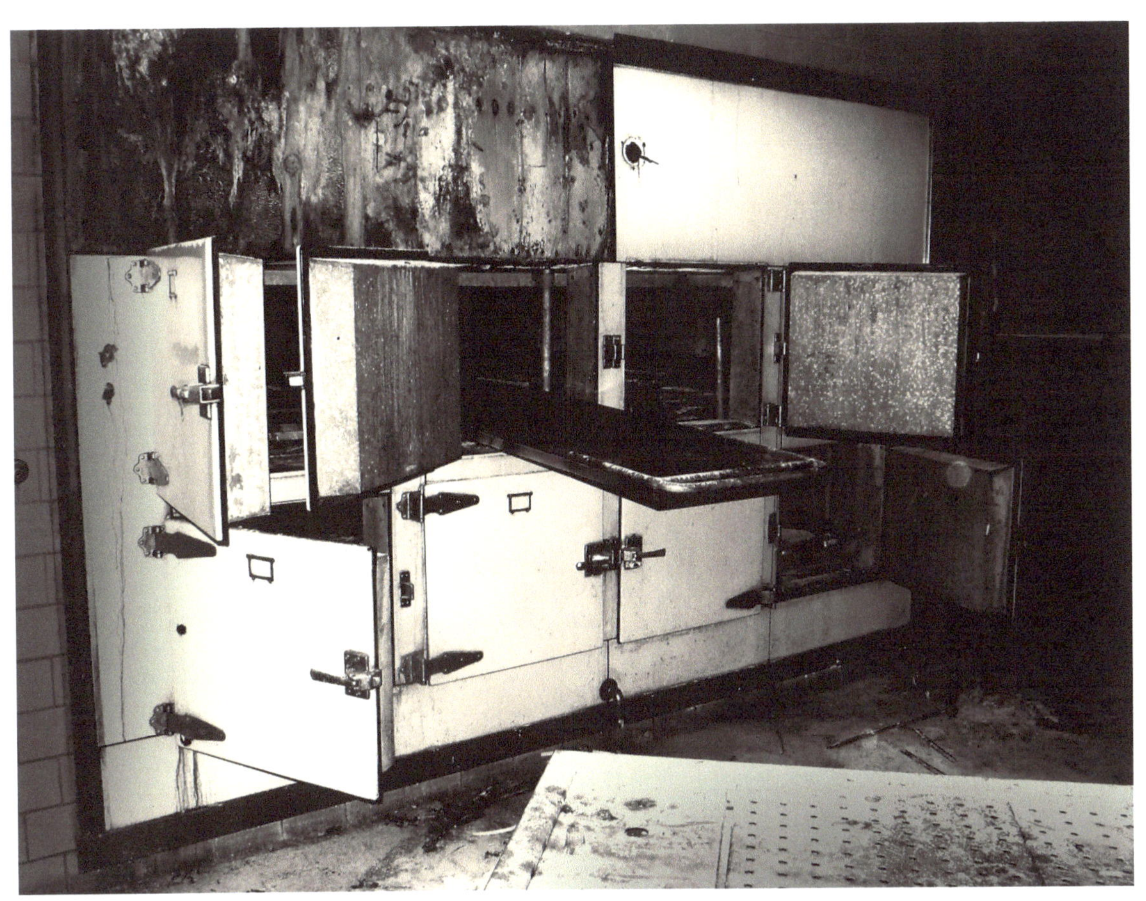

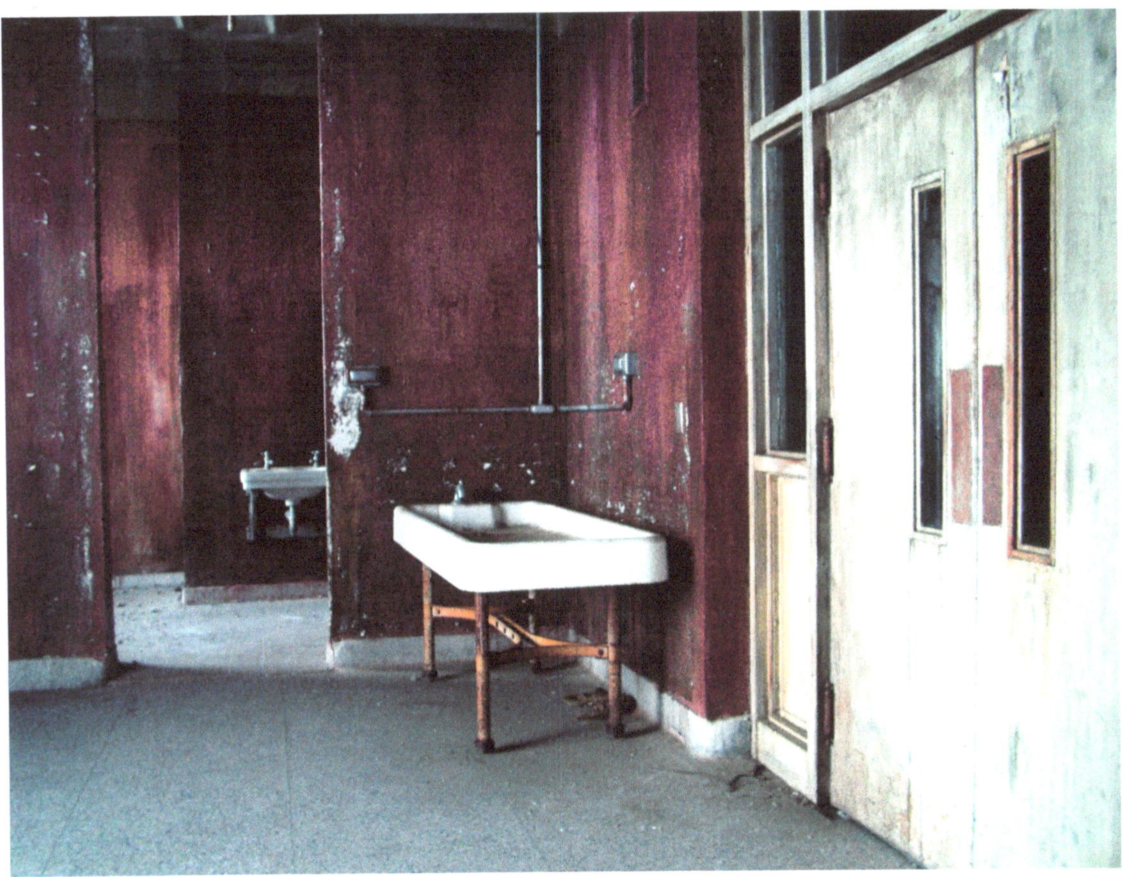

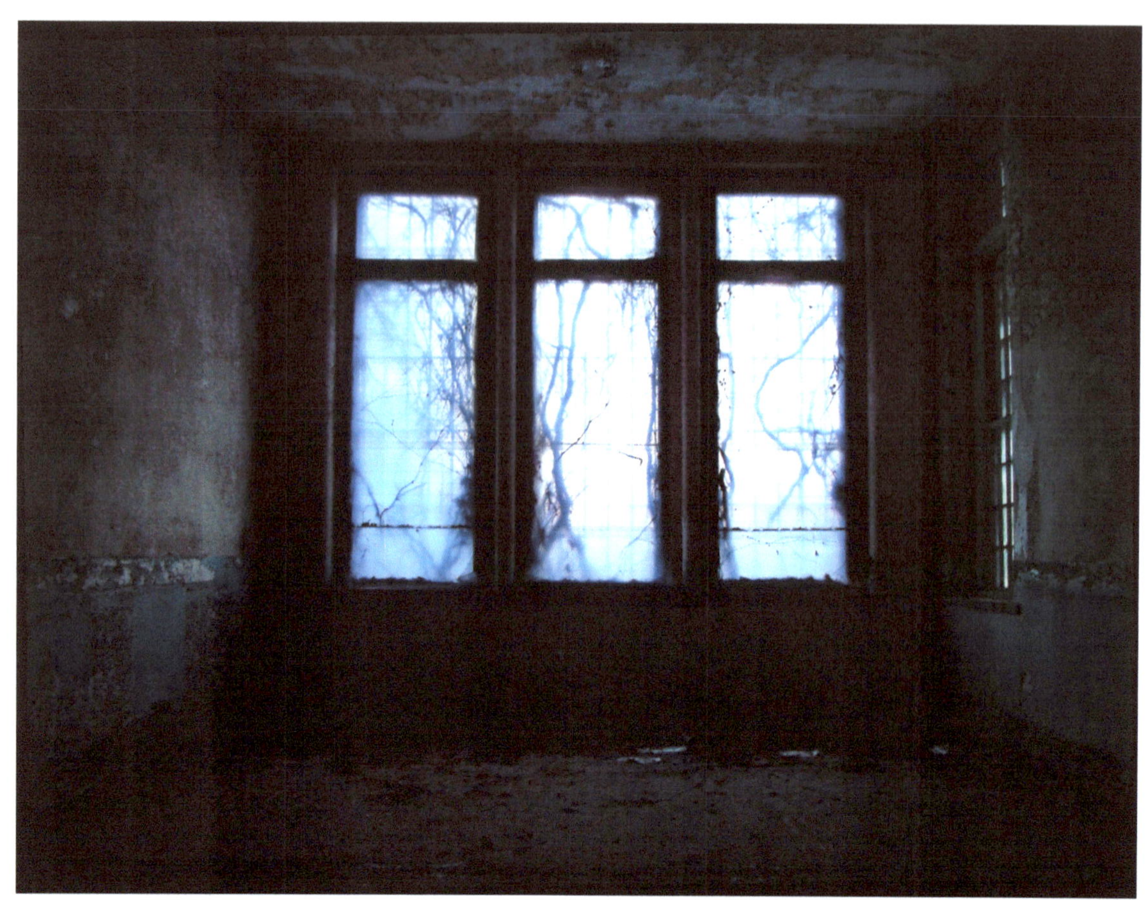

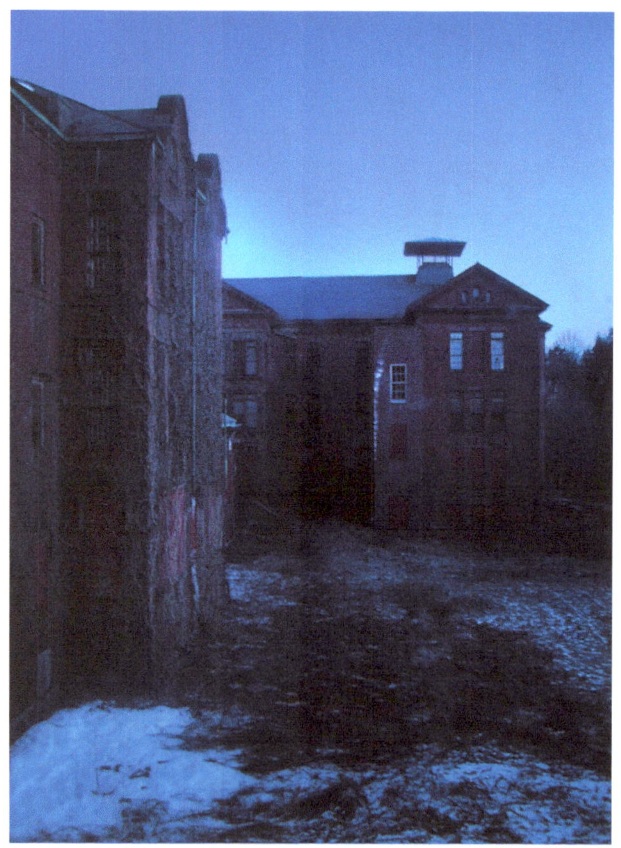

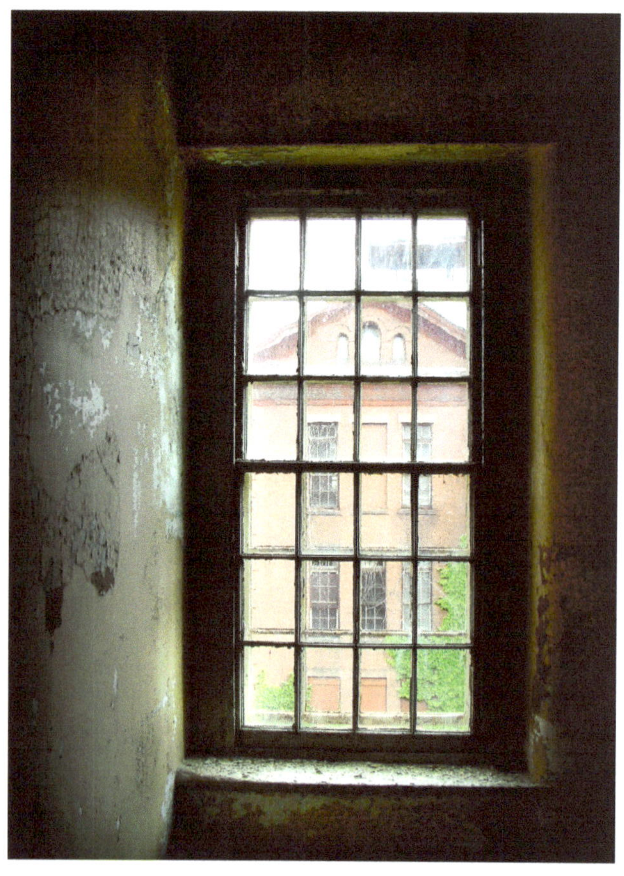

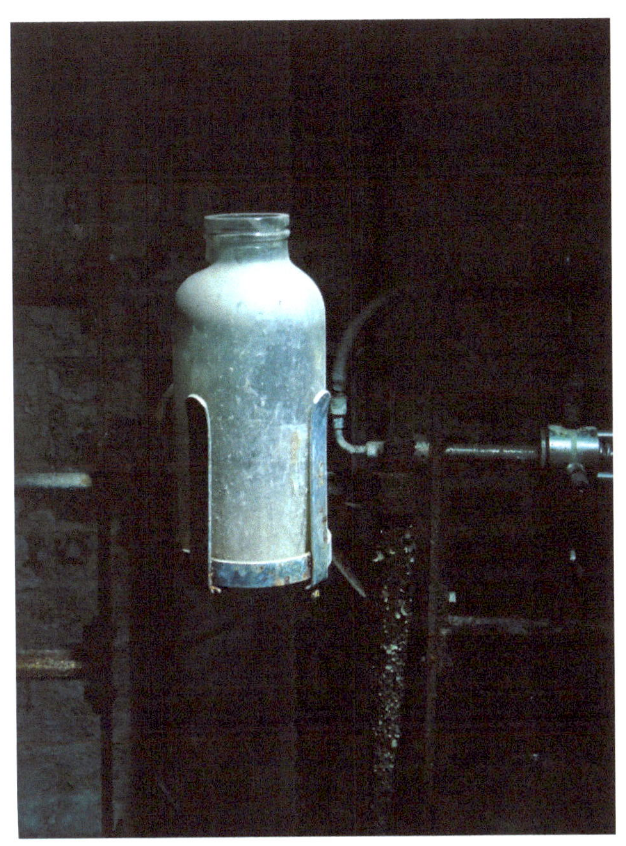

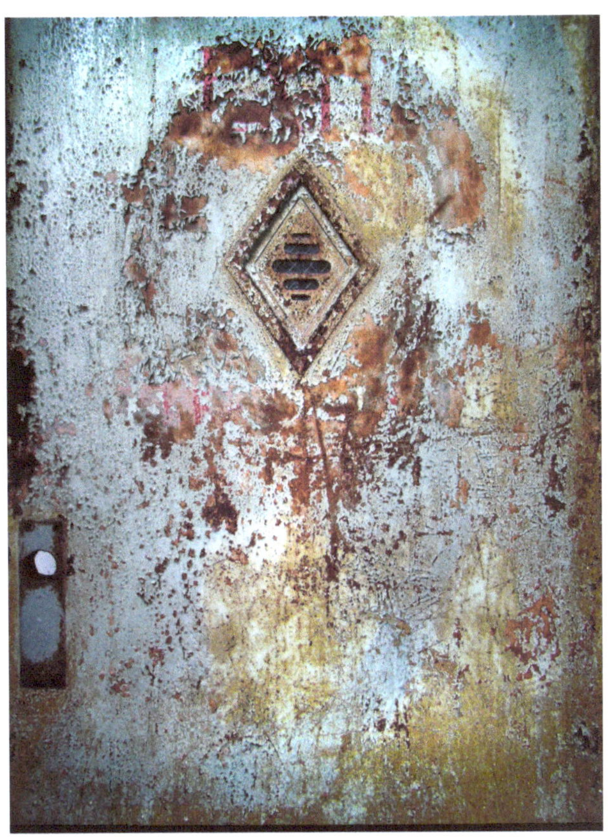

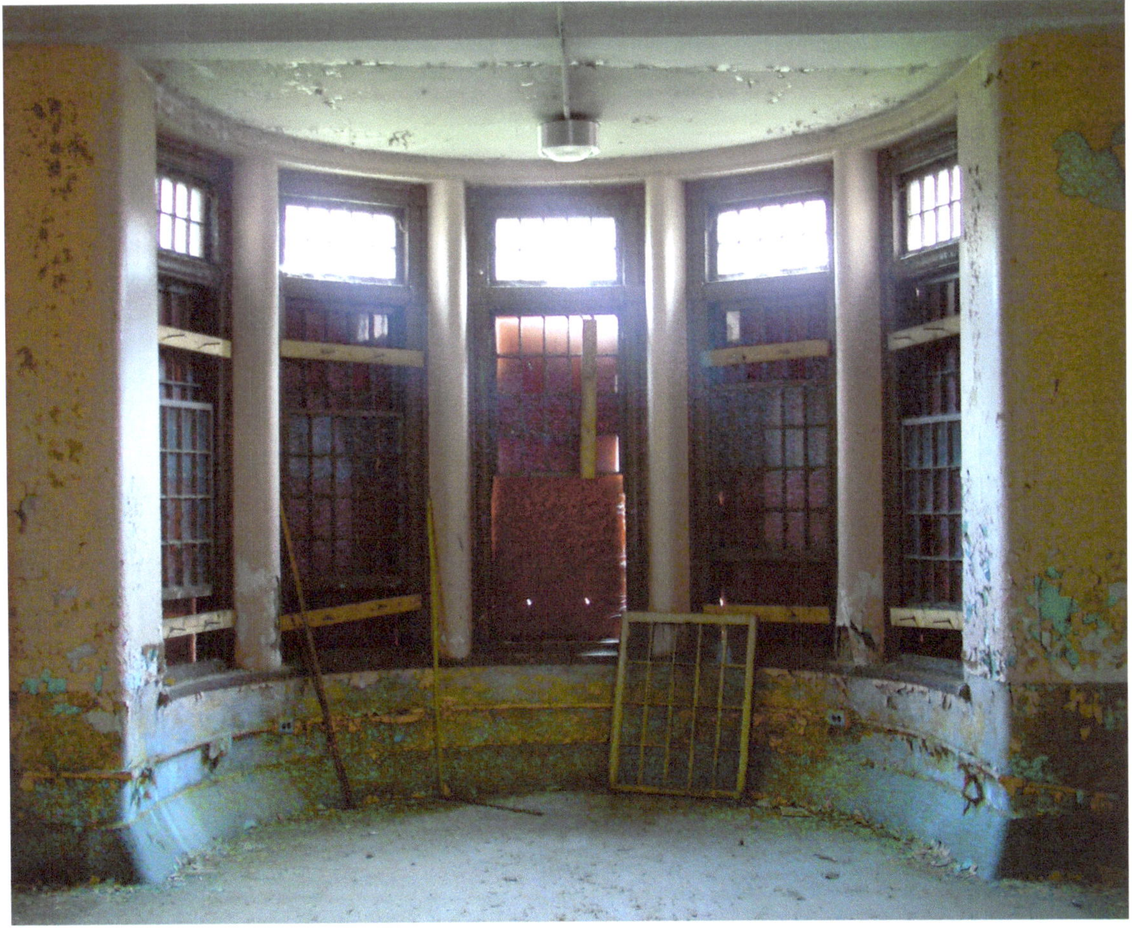

CHAPTER THREE

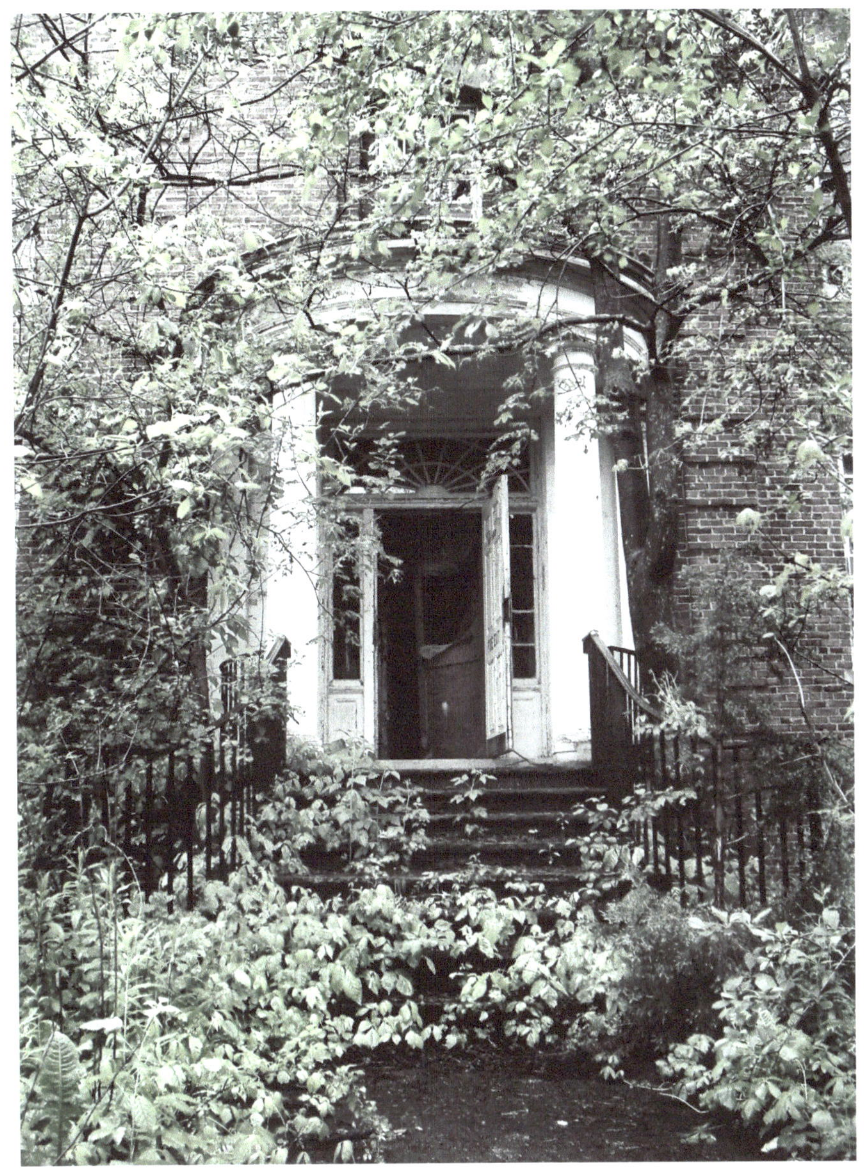

METROPOLITAN STATE HOSPITAL

Massachusetts

Metropolitan State Hospital

The Lost Morgue

It was a rainy summer day when I went to Met State for the first time. I was alone and at first I had trouble finding the place. For this trip, I only had a building legend and a street map and no aerial photographs. The sprawling grounds were tucked in the woods straddling three counties and the way in was not very easy to find. I went to the address that I had for the hospital and found the telltale cracked and overgrown drive, but there was a guard trailer so I continued driving. I found another promising entrance road to the north of the property. A steel gate blocked the road, so I parked the car and started up on foot. It was drizzling when I got out of the car and the walk through along the curving road through the woods was punctuated by rain dripping from the thick canopy of trees. When I came around the end of the curve, I saw the first of this hospitals many buildings: the power plant and the incinerator. On a gloomy day such as this, it was easy to imagine the huge smokestack and adjoining incinerator building serving as a crematorium for human remains rather than garbage. For all I knew, it did serve that purpose. My information on this place was sketchy at best even though I had a building legend. This particular psychiatric center was laid out in the "Cottage Plan", with many large buildings of varying purpose rather than one main building surrounded by lesser satellite buildings. They had cryptic names like Furcolo Building and CTG Unit and Kline Hall, so I had little idea of the purpose of the different structures.

I passed the incinerator and approached another utilitarian looking building with a loading dock that was labeled Maintenance. Beyond this was the main plaza with several other buildings that also had sensible names. The Medical Center. The St. Nicholas and Interfaith Chapels and the Laundry Building. The Medical Center was the most interesting of these, almost resembling a school or church. It was red brick topped by a huge, square, white clock tower. I wandered around the plaza snapping pictures and trying to keep my camera dry in the drizzle.

Finally it started raining in earnest, so I decided to call it a day. I hadn't looked around as much I would have liked, but the weather was miserable and it seemed that the buildings were locked up fairly tight with steel doors and boarded windows. I found out on a later trip that this wasn't the case at all. I simply tried to gain entrance on the more secure buildings. The CTG Unit was wide open. I had also left my building legend in the car, and the size of the campus didn't lend itself to aimless wandering, so off I went back down the road.

When I got back to the car, it was pouring. I climbed in and headed down the street to the airport. I got about a half a mile away when I decided to go back and try to find the morgue. I thought I wouldn't be back this way again and I might as well try to see it while I was here. It was in a smaller building away from the main plaza and I when I looked at the legend I realized I had walked right past the path that led to it.

I parked back in the same spot and started up the road. By now, it was pouring rain and I began to wonder if I could make it to the morgue without getting thoroughly soaked. After walking about a hundred yards up the road, a security guard in a small pickup raced up to me. He cracked the window open and asked me if I had seen the no trespassing signs. I said that I did but that I thought it meant you couldn't drive up the road. He just shook his head and not too politely told me to immediately evacuate the property.

I said, "Sorry for the misunderstanding. Can I get a lift back down to the gate? I'm getting soaked"

He said, "No way" This truck is for official business only."

Having concluded his official business of evicting me from the grounds, he promptly made a u-turn and headed back up the road leaving me standing there drenched. I dejectedly walked back to my car and headed to the airport falsely assuming this would be my last visit to Metropolitan State Hospital.

The Hospital of the Seven Teeth

The second time I visited Met State was the first time I went to an abandoned building with a group of people. I finally met up with Billamack and two of his friends, after spending an hour following incorrect directions from an online map service. We all parked down the street on the south side of the hospital grounds. It turned out that Billamack was the only one in the group who had actually been inside Met and he claimed to know his way around fairly well, especially the tunnels which were now critical for moving about the campus. Apparently, the days of parking at the gate and walking in were over. The developers had moved in and started dismantling various buildings. The morgue was one of the first to go, most likely since it was the smallest. The mysterious Furcolo building was also gone. Furcolo I could do without, but I was disappointed at not being able to see the morgue.

I don't know what it is with these local guys, but they all seem to enjoy walking miles to get into their asylums. We walked what seemed forever down a busy road, right past the main guard shack. We then entered a residential neighborhood that bordered the hospital grounds. I'm pretty sure us four guys with our backpacks and hiking boots stuck out like a sore thumb and the residents probably knew where we were headed. It seems Met State was quite the destination for the local kids to party, vandalize and cause general mayhem. In fact, there was just a fire in one of the buildings the week before and we were concerned that security had been stepped up.

That fire, which was the second or third at Met State, was suspicious in that it wasn't the only fire at an abandoned asylum in recent months. The entire administration building at Taunton State burned down and a building at Foxboro State Hospital burned too. Fires and abandoned buildings seem to go together, especially in the winter when people light small ones to stay warm and then they inevitably get out of control. There were several fires at Danvers before the demo started and I'm fairly certain that the stage at Northampton burned at some time in the past. But this was different. It was summer and there was no need of a fire to keep warm. It seemed that there was a serial arsonist out there targeting asylums. In a way, it was appropriate that someone with the sociopathic habit of arson would burn the very type of place they would go if caught. There was some speculation that there was a more commercial motive at work. If the buildings were burned down, it could save millions of dollars in demolition costs. It was also suspicious that the areas of the buildings that burned contained patient records. But this was just speculation amongst laymen and never officially investigated.

We finally reached the fence that separated the mental institution grounds from the rest of the world. We quickly squeezed through the broken gate in the fence and started down an overgrown path through a field and into the woods. It was a mushy, humid walk because that summer saw torrential, flooding rains in the Northeast. We soon entered the woods, which cooled us down a bit. The woods also brought a genuine chill because someone mentioned The Hospital of the Seven Teeth. In 1978 a violent patient kidnapped, killed and dismembered a nurse and buried her remains in several shallow graves throughout the woods. The murder was only brought to light when the patient was discovered with seven human teeth in his possession. Apparently, the two had been meeting illicitly in a hut he constructed in the woods for some time. Even though the hut had been discovered, along with a bloody axe and clothing, it took hospital staff two months to investigate the nurse's disappearance. Administration just assumed she quit one day and never returned. When questioned, the male patient led investigators to some of the graves, but was unable to remember where he buried all of the body parts. They're still scattered about these woods to this day. The sloppy investigation was indicative of the shocking ineptitude of the Massachusetts Department of Mental Health at the time. To top it all off, the state then lost the most critical evidence related to the case such as the hatchet and the seven teeth. For all I know, the teeth and the hatchet are hidden in a building on the campus somewhere. It sounds very much like an urban legend or typical haunted asylum story to scare the uninitiated, but I assure you it's true.

We finally breached the woods and found ourselves standing next to the CTG Unit. I'm not sure what the acronym means, but I have read that the criminally insane were once housed in this building. Once again, I started my asylum journey in the violent ward. My first impression of the interior was that is was a complete wreck. Totally collapsed floors, light fixtures dangling from their wires and copious amounts of water all helped to make this structure a dangerous challenge to navigate. The sense of chaotic disarray also contributed to a feeling malevolent insanity. It's ironic that developers decided to reuse many of the decrepit buildings here rather than tear them down like they did the much more substantial and important buildings at Danvers and Northampton. I personally would have gone to great lengths to save the latter and bulldoze this mess instead. I guess that's why I'm an artist and not a developer. We continued to wander the CTG, which is a huge building surrounding a large courtyard. Outside, we found the courtyard completely overgrown and nearly impassable. A basketball hoop on a pole stood mired in vines and the desolation of that sight has stayed with me as an example of the general hopeless feeling of this place.

We went back into the CTG through a relatively ornate portico. This was surprising feature because Metropolitan State is a rather bland, utilitarian campus. It opened in 1930 and the institutional trend had moved far from the decorative Victorian and Gothic turn of the century examples of mental healing. Underground tunnels connected the CTG and all buildings at Met State, and that's where we headed. Our ultimate goal was the Medical Center and its clock tower. Along the way, we stopped at the Male Ward and then Kline Hall, which was the auditorium building. This structure was not nearly as opulent as others I have seen, but it did still have the old movie projectors and a complete stage. There was also various medical equipment strewn about the auditorium, which was a weird juxtaposition. Another bizarre feature was a bowling alley in the basement of one of the buildings. Fortunately, these tunnels at least had some labels and directions on the walls, but I'm still not sure which building sat atop the bowling alley. Tunnel travel, even with signs, can be very confusing until you become familiar with them.

Down in the basement of most buildings we found a dizzying array of discarded and decaying equipment. The massive amount of rotting surplus and the buildings crumbling around them produced a moist, putrid stench. Beds, chairs, office and medical equipment clogged just about every underground room and even some of the passageways. One room contained lockers with what looked like patient belongings. I discovered a vintage children's shoe in one and wondered why it was there. As far as I knew, no children were treated here. There was another complex on the same property, but across the vast woods, for that purpose. I considered that maybe a confused and lonely patient brought it as a reminder of a loved one back home. I didn't ponder the question too long because any reason for a child's shoe to be here just seemed too painful to think about.

After wending our way through tunnels, we finally reached the Medical Center and found it heavily vandalized with graffiti, smashed windows and general destruction. Even though it was fairly bland architecturally inside, there were still some interesting things to see. In one area there were clear acrylic blocks mounted in the floor designed to allow light to filter down through to the next level. Another intriguing feature was the dichotomy of the buildings decay. In some areas the paint was peeling off the walls in sheets and other areas looked almost pristine. It was weird and a little disconcerting.

We climbed to the top floor and started the perilous journey up and into the clock tower. The route to the clock itself is a convoluted climb over huge ventilation systems, up slippery wet metal ladders and still more ladders. It was so tight in some areas that we had to leave our backpacks behind. It was not a place for the claustrophobic. Luckily, it was daytime so we didn't need flashlights. Without a headlamp, it would require a fumbling, one-handed climb, which would be risky. When we finally got into the tower, another story and a half climb was necessary to reach the clock faces. Around the inside of the clock face was an elevated walkway made of only a two inch by six-inch wooden board, much like a scaffold with narrow planks, that was barely wide enough for one person. The once impressive milk glass clock faces had been smashed out and the only thing separating us from a five-story drop were the thin metal clock mechanisms. The view was certainly worth the climb with entire campus was spread out before us. My fellow travelers were all squeezing past each other, including me, in an effort to see the view out each of the four clock faces. Impressive view or not, we snapped our pictures and climbed down. The stiff breeze and wide-open clock faces made for a heart wrenching perch.

Back in the Medical Center tunnel we made for the Administration Building. Our underground route was cut short by a completely flooded tunnel and we had no choice but to head there topside. At first the Administration seemed tightly secured until we found a door that craftily pretended to be locked. The building was as interesting as any in the compound, which is to say not very. From there went into a building that suffered one of the fires. The suspicious thing about the area that burned was that it was a records storage area. The bulk of the records had turned to an oatmeal-like mush from the all the rain and it was amazing they burned at all. Some records were still readable, along with patient names, diagnosis, and treatment programs. Most of the treatments seemed to consist of large and regular amounts of psychotropic medication. If anyone was actually cured there, I don't think it was the poor souls gobbling Thorazine all day.

We peeked into the female ward, scene of the most recent fire. It still had yellow crime scene tape fluttering in the breeze and the stench of burned wood in the air. We had spent the day wandering a place that was generally unpleasant and foul smelling and this area proved unbearable so we called our tour a success and headed out the grounds.

Whispers in the Dark

Two family members, John and Johnny, met me in Massachusetts to tour several asylums. Met State was not on the list, but since Northampton was inaccessible and our hotel was nearby we made a spur of the moment decision to make a night visit. Even though I had not planned to go there this trip, I still had my aerial photos and maps so I felt I could find my way around fairly well even at night. That was until J failed to bring the package of maps from the hotel like I asked him. I decided from that point on to carry my own maps.

We got to the general vicinity of the hospital and parked much closer than last time. I personally am not one to walk any farther than stealth requires. We hit the path through the field and realized it was hopelessly overgrown since last time and completely impassable. We decided to forge ahead through the woods along the fence line correctly assuming that we wouldn't get lost that way. Along the bramble and root strewn way I told them the story of the Seven Teeth. The dark woods and treacherous hike lent itself especially well to the story.

The woods ejected us right next to the CTG and we wandered around in the dark for a bit looking for a way in. We finally found an open door and headed straight to the basement in search of the tunnels. We examined the selection of discarded beds, furniture and every other type of thing a huge hospital needs to operate. We even found one entire room full of just chairs. What we didn't find was the tunnel. I thought that maybe I was wrong and the CTG didn't have a tunnel so we left and headed to the Male Ward.

Right inside the doorway of the Male Ward we found a stairwell leading to the tunnel. After the hospital closed, some tunnel entrances were bricked over in an attempt to keep people out. Some ambitious soul or souls defeated this blockage with sledgehammers and as a result some tunnel entrance were no more than two to three foot holes. We were presented with one of these holes and painstakingly climbed through. Our efforts were rewarded with a downward sloping tunnel that became more and more flooded until it was over ankle deep. It was unanimously decided to abandon the flooded tunnel and try the CTG again.

Back in the CTG Building, we wandered the basement in search of a tunnel. The whole time we tried to keep our flashlights off as much as possible for fear of being seen since there were windows down there level with the ground outside. Every time we stopped to get our bearings, the incessant drip of water permeated the silence. Then we heard a sound that didn't fit. I whispered to John and Johnny to stop goofing off and they assured me that they did not make the sound. It almost sounded like someone breathing. Then there was a sound that resembled a boot scraping on the wet ground. I knew that there was recently a guard employed on the site who actually went into the buildings and tunnels after the curious. The security guards and even the police were typically prohibited from entering the buildings due to safety concerns. This rule usually meant that once you were in, you were safe from discovery. At least until you left. Not so with this enthusiastic guard. He hunted people down in the buildings and was even rumored to lurk in the tunnels, not just catching his prey, but also scaring them half to death in the process. I heard that he had been recently fired, but I thought if this guy was twisted enough to lurk in the tunnels he might be twisted enough to come back on his own. We strained with the effort of listening as the minutes stretched out but we couldn't make sense of the noise. In the end, we decided it must have been an inanimate object freakishly creating the sound of something alive. Regardless, by now our nerves were frazzled and we decided to call it a night.

After a frustrating and truncated trip, we didn't have the energy to trek back through the dark woods, so we just scaled the ten-foot fence. I caught my watch on the fence going over and broke it. Then, for a moment, we thought that Johnny was going to get stuck halfway over. It seemed a fitting end to a foul trip and I was glad to get back to the car and away from Metropolitan State Hospital for the last time.

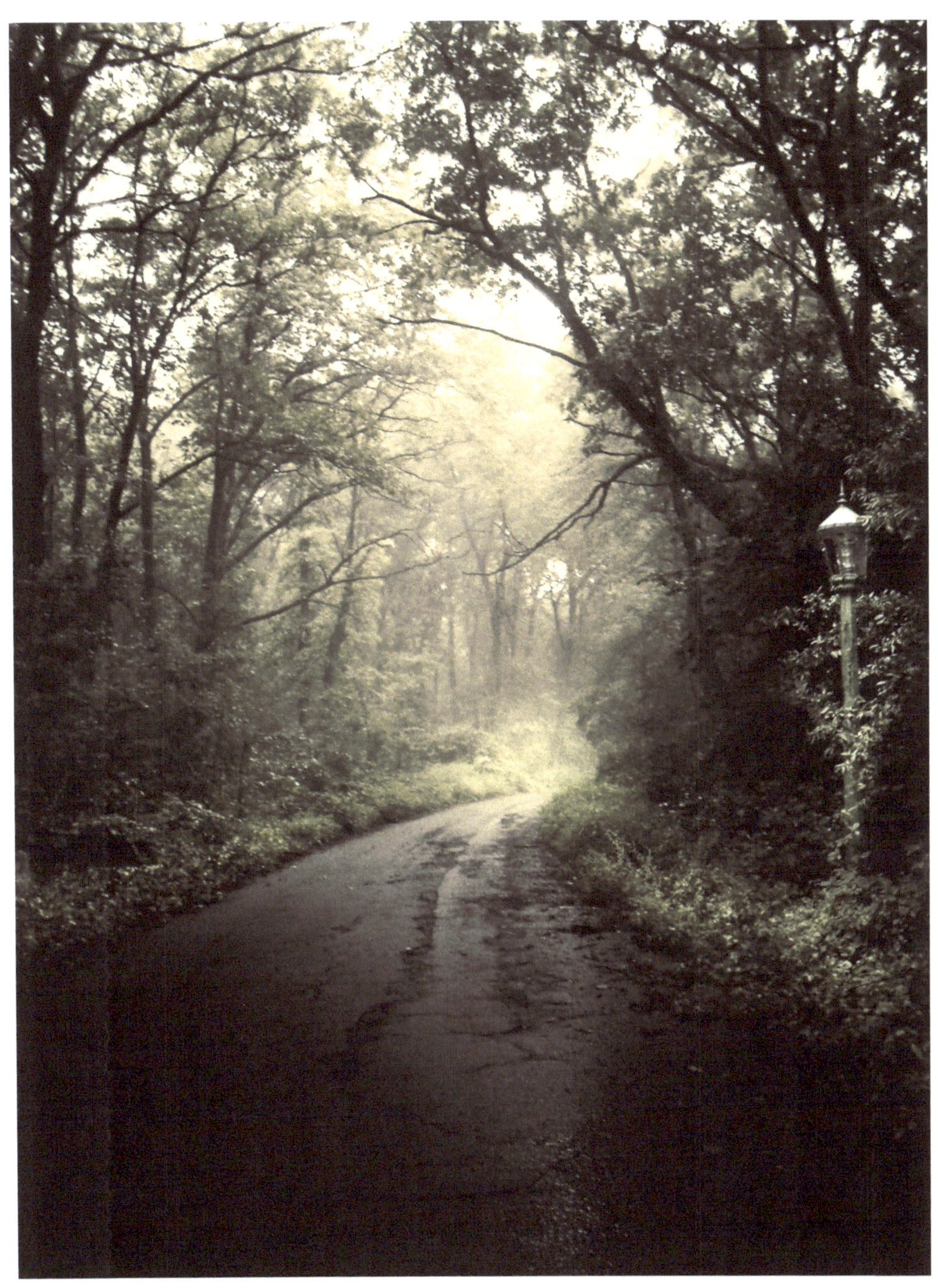

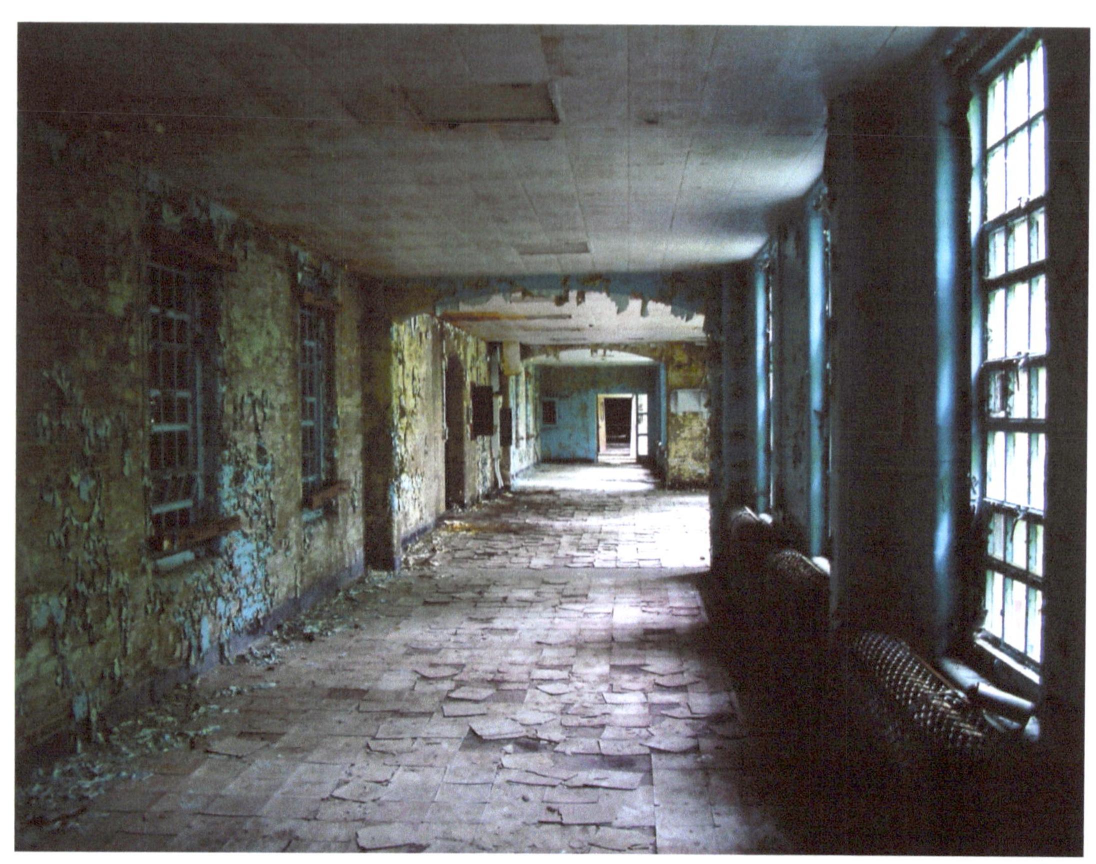

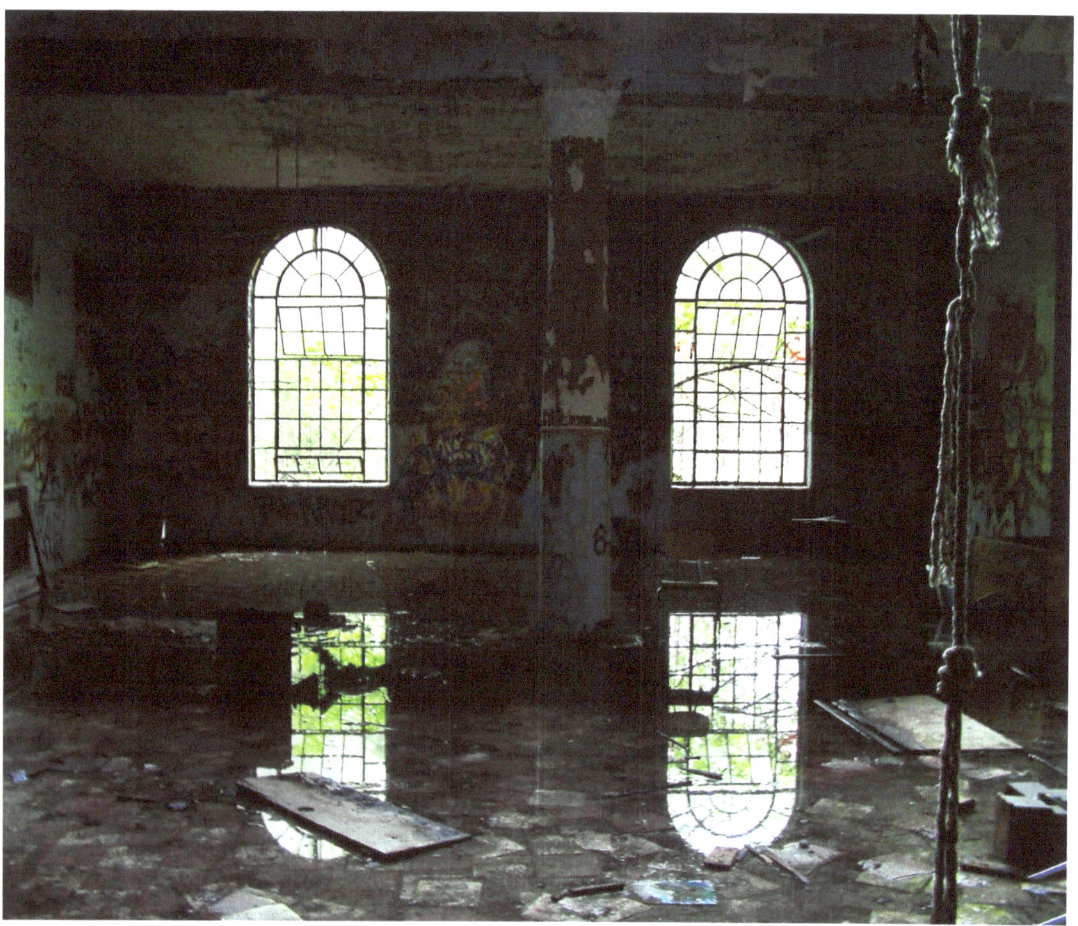

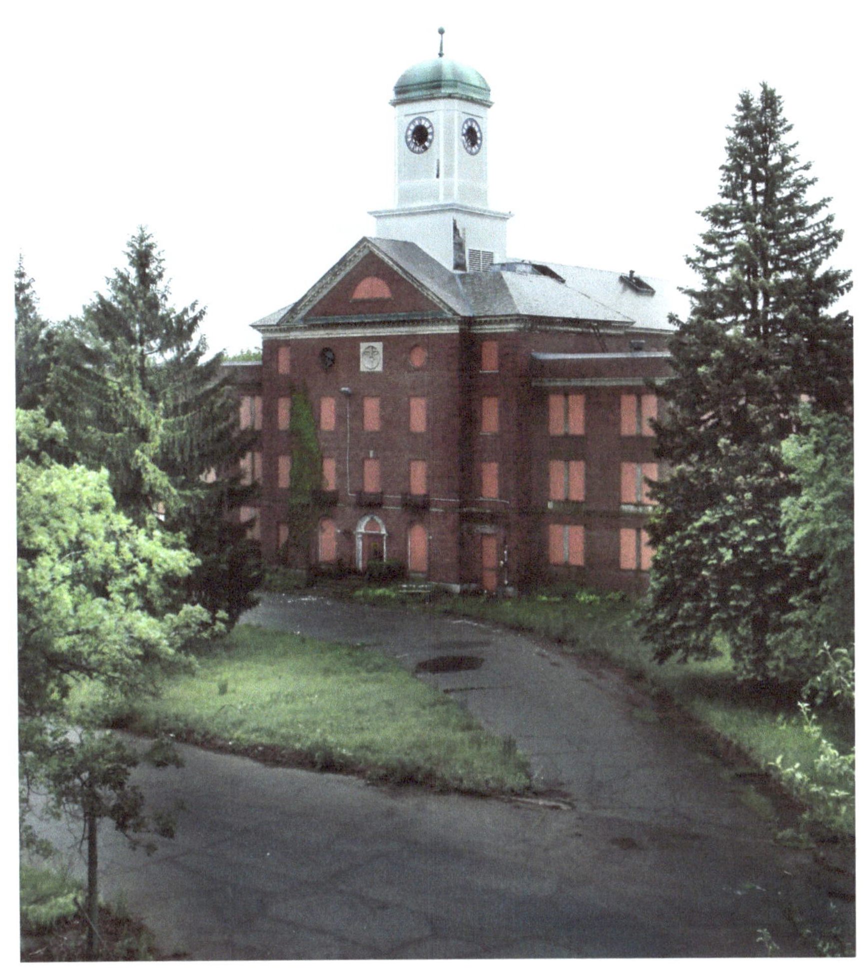

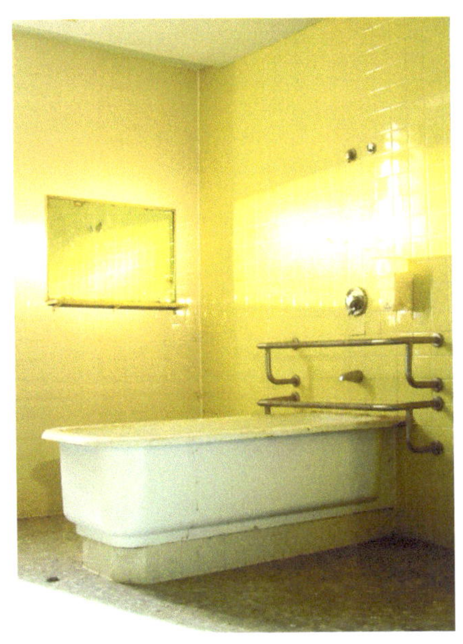

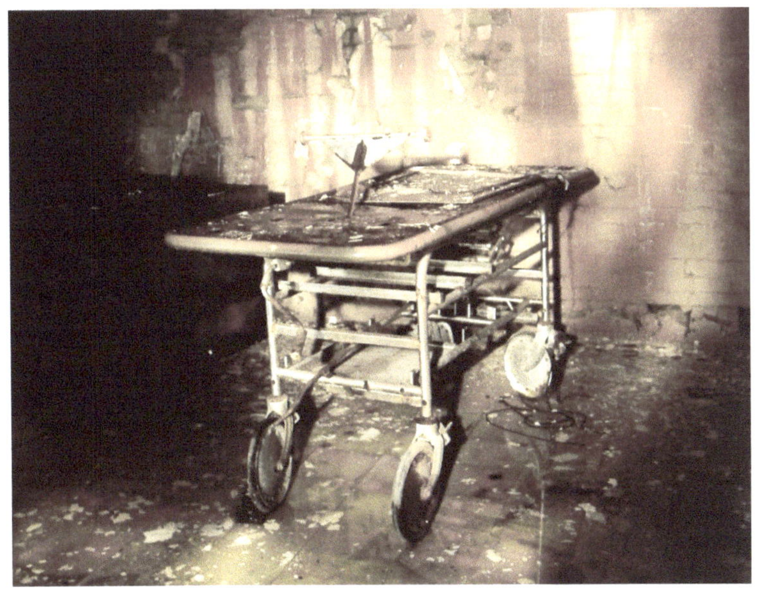

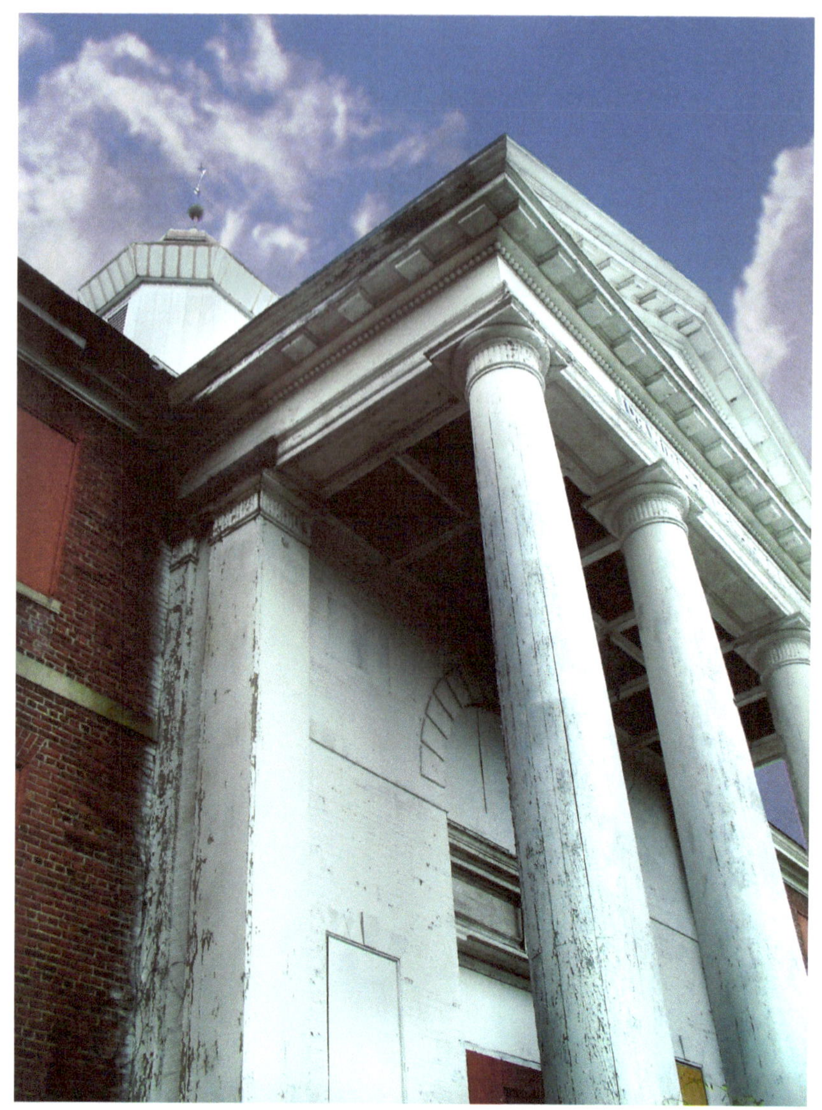

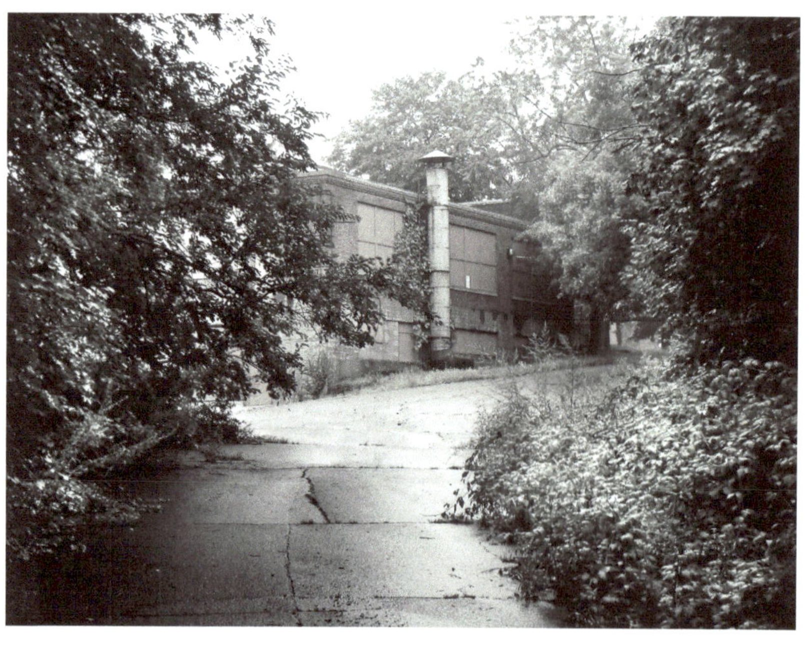

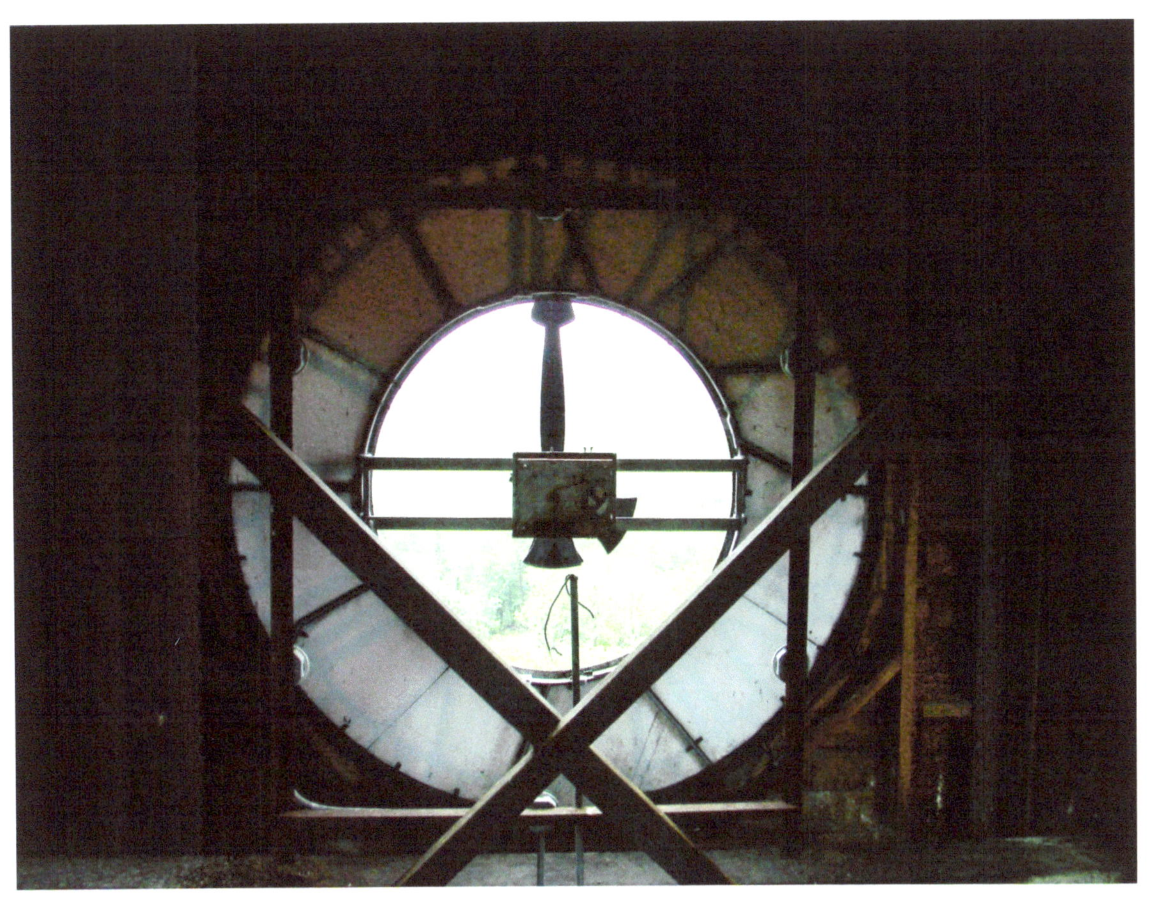

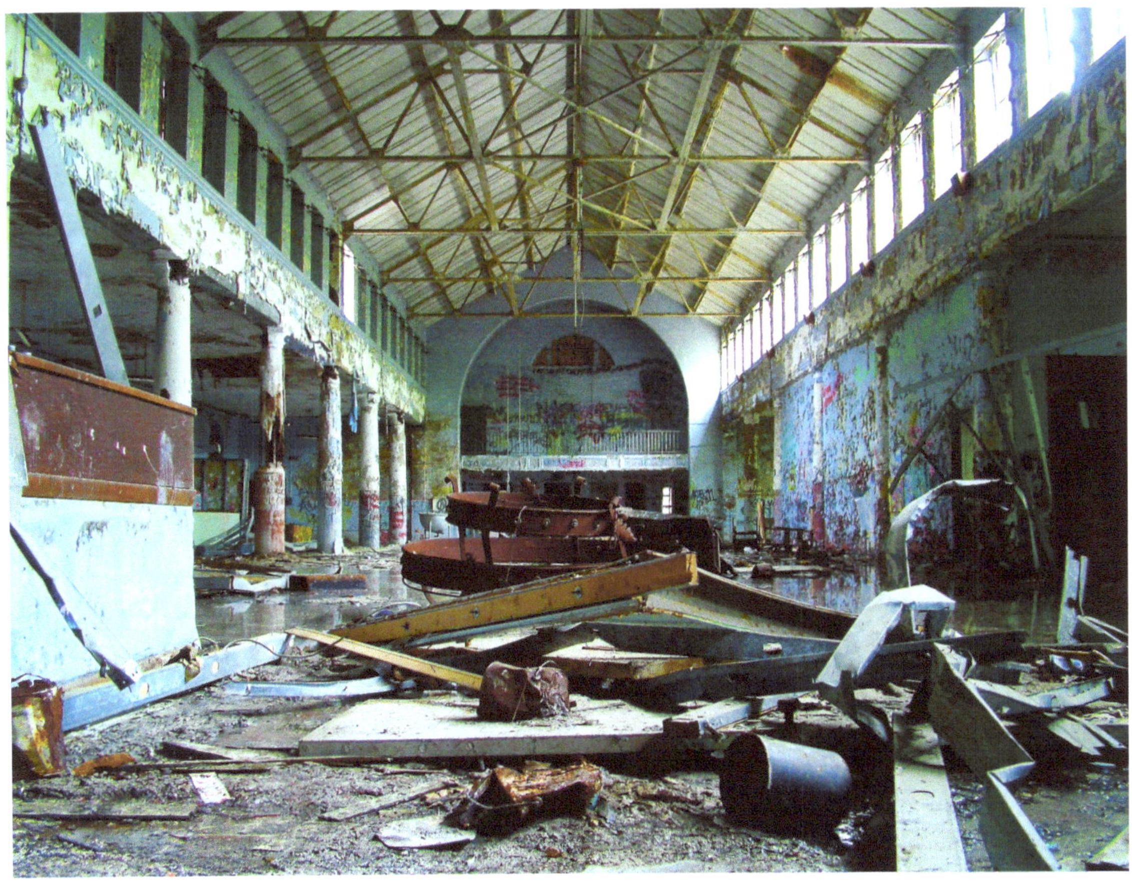

CHAPTER FOUR

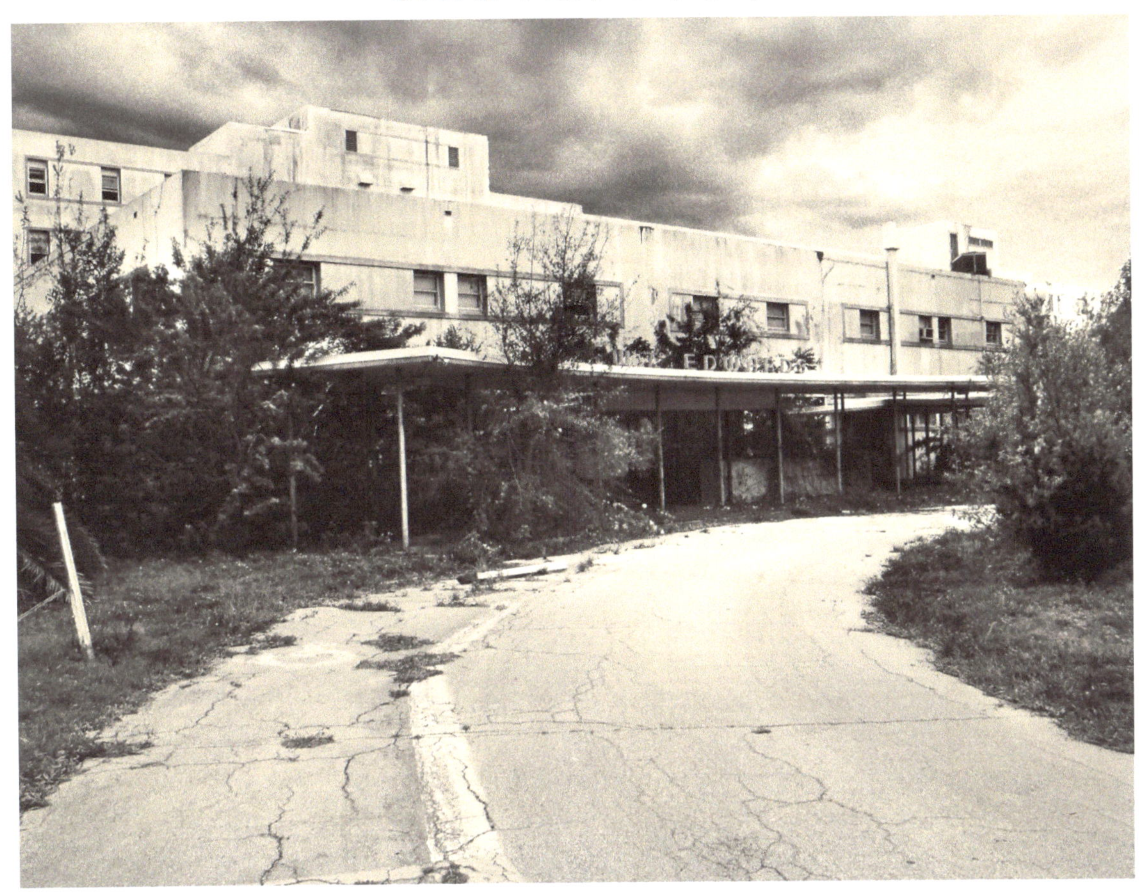

W.T. Edwards Tuberculosis Hospital

Florida

W.T. Edwards Tuberculosis Hospital

Blood Stains in the Lab

W.T. Edwards Hospital was wedged between an open college, a law enforcement agency building and a juvenile detention center. You would think this proximity to so many active institutions would make it a pretty risky trip. Not so. In fact, it was one of the easier abandoned structures I've visited. Most of the doors were welded shut, but near the old front entrance was a battered and open door into the laboratory building. I first time I went with another artist friend named Steele and we walked right in.

W.T. Edwards was built in the 1940's. It was a relatively undecorated, post-war, minimalist, concrete box with little architectural charm. The rooms were bland, the halls were bland and the outside was bland, albeit slightly better with a tinge of Art Deco styling. But, it was a hospital and it was abandoned and it was close to where I live so I went. A lot. Probably more that I should have, but it was a good fix for those in between times when I couldn't visit a more interesting location.

I heard from a fairly unreliable source that there was a morgue in the basement. It was a nervous source, too, because he said he was scared to go down there and look. I believed the part about the morgue because, after all, it was a tuberculosis hospital and the recovery rate when this place was built was not good. The basement was a different story. Basements in Florida tend to become underground swimming pools because of all the rain and the poor soil constitution. There are buildings here with basements, but they're rare. In any case, the basement was the first thing we attempted to find.

We entered through the laboratory and found all sorts of sinister sounding rooms such as "Animal Testing, Nuclear Science and Gen. (genetic? general?) Bacteriology, but no basement. We did find a walk-in freezer, but it didn't look like a morgue so we headed into the main building. The route to the main building was from an elevated walkway connected to the second floor of the lab. This was probably the singular most interesting architectural feature of the place. It also made for a completely exposed walk. Luckily security was non-existent so we were exposed to nothing but the lizards scampering out of our way. The walkway placed us on the second floor and from there we headed straight down to the ground floor in search of the mythical basement.

The ground floor was dark due to the boarded windows and in a state of disrepair. Ceiling tiles and broken light fixtures littered the floor. We gave some rooms a cursory glance, but examined each stairwell carefully in search of a way down. After traversing the entire first floor it became obvious that the basement was indeed mythical because it didn't exist. There was one promising stairwell that appeared to go down further than the first floor, but it dead-ended into a small closet under the stairs. I assumed this was the "scary basement" entrance that our nervous source mentioned. It was dark there, and I can imagine the inexperienced being too scared to enter, but a simple glance around the corner would have shown that it was a place of retired brooms not restless spirits.

A bit disappointed at the lack of basement and consequently no morgue, we headed off in search of something dramatic to see on the first floor. We soon found it. A sign taped to the wall of an office indicated that there was an animal head in the walk-in freezer. The walk-in freezer in the lab didn't contain a head, but we had walked past another one on our quick sweep of the first floor. On the way to the other freezer, we found another lab. This one was with filled with medical potions such as jars of blood stain and rotting bags of plasma.

We left the phlebotomy lab and headed towards the walk-in freezer. There was sign on the door warning of hazardous waste so we opened the door with trepidation. The freezer had more than one chamber and the first was littered with empty biohazard bags. We gave each other a knowing look and steeled ourselves for the horror of a mummified animal head in the next chamber. A quick peek showed that there was no head in the second chamber. A closer look showed us something much more sinister.

Scattered on the floor were hundreds of small glass vials. Some were shattered and those that were intact were labeled as tuberculosis samples. The labels indicated not only the date and time of the sample but also whether the patient was positive for the disease. The patient's name, address and phone number were also clearly marked. It was a grim discovery, to say the least, and we wondered aloud about the longevity of tuberculosis in a vial exposed to the sweltering Florida heat.

Not being inclined to test the virility of the White Plague, as tuberculosis was once known, we evacuated the freezer and continued our examination of the first floor. Our next find was what appeared to be an intact x-ray lab. It contained a large examination table with a ceiling mounted x-ray gun on a mobile dolly above it. There was also a massive shield room with thick glass and large amount of x-ray films littering the floor. I suppose if we had the inclination, we could have matched some of those films to the samples in the freezer. We weren't so inclined, so we moved on to the x-ray developing lab. The lab contained all manner of developing chemicals slowly leaching from their containers and pooling on the floor in a noxious mess. On the other side there was a light safe fully stocked with undeveloped film. I'm sure some teaching school or even underprivileged hospital somewhere could have made good use of those supplies had they been donated in a timely manner instead of being left to rot. Waste on a mind-boggling industrial scale such as this is something I've witnessed at a lot of abandoned locations. You could probably outfit an entire small city in the third world for a year with what I've seen discarded in abandoned institutions.

We wandered the first floor for a while more and located the old admissions desk, a childcare ward, an autoclave and sterilization room festooned with pipes and gauges and, strangely enough for a tuberculosis hospital, a smoking area that was in a hidden and overgrown outdoor courtyard. There wasn't much else of interest except a few defunct elevators so we headed up to the next floor. The second through fourth floors were virtually identical with the exception of a computer room on three that had a unique raised floor used for snaking network cables about. The operating theaters and patient rooms had been stripped of their contents long ago making for one empty room after another. The only other high point was room 420 that looked like it was regularly used a party spot for locals. It was heavily vandalized with drug graffiti and contained a smelly old stained couch.

The thick atmosphere inside the musty old hospital became oppressive and we decided to leave W.T. Edwards alone to continue it's inexorable decay.

The Headless Doll

I visited W.T. Edwards again on numerous occasions with different people, mostly as a tour guide. One notable trip was taken late at night after a U2 concert with Webb and Greywolf. The entire building had been fenced off and it looked like we wouldn't be able to get in. Webb was the victim of various joint replacements and back surgeries and was unable to scale a fence. Luckily, while walking the perimeter we found an open gate. Greywolf had been in before but never at night and Webb had never been inside and abandoned building. It was satisfying to share this dilapidated wreck and give Webb a taste of my world.

There were a few new discoveries, such as an incinerator that may or may have been used for human remains. It still had a large quantity of ash inside and I shiver to think that it might have been biological. The view from the roof of the main building was impressive at night, providing a spectacular view of a nearby NFL stadium. There were several outbuildings on the property, a warehouse, a dormitory and few other buildings of unknown purpose. They were all unremarkable with the exception of the dorm which had a headless doll perched on a chair guarding the entrance along with some satanic symbols spray painted on the walls.

My final trip there brought an unpleasant surprise. The entire main building was stripped of doors, windows and pretty much everything but the concrete walls and floors. It looked like W.T. Edwards would soon fall under the developers axe. It wouldn't be a huge architectural loss, but it was an incredibly stout building, being constructed as it was of mostly solid poured concrete. You would think that someone would see the value in a structure built so massively. After all, this hospital did survive sixty plus years of searing heat and torrential rains not to mention hurricanes and tropical storms. At the time of publication, it's since been demolished and converted to a parking lot. What a waste.

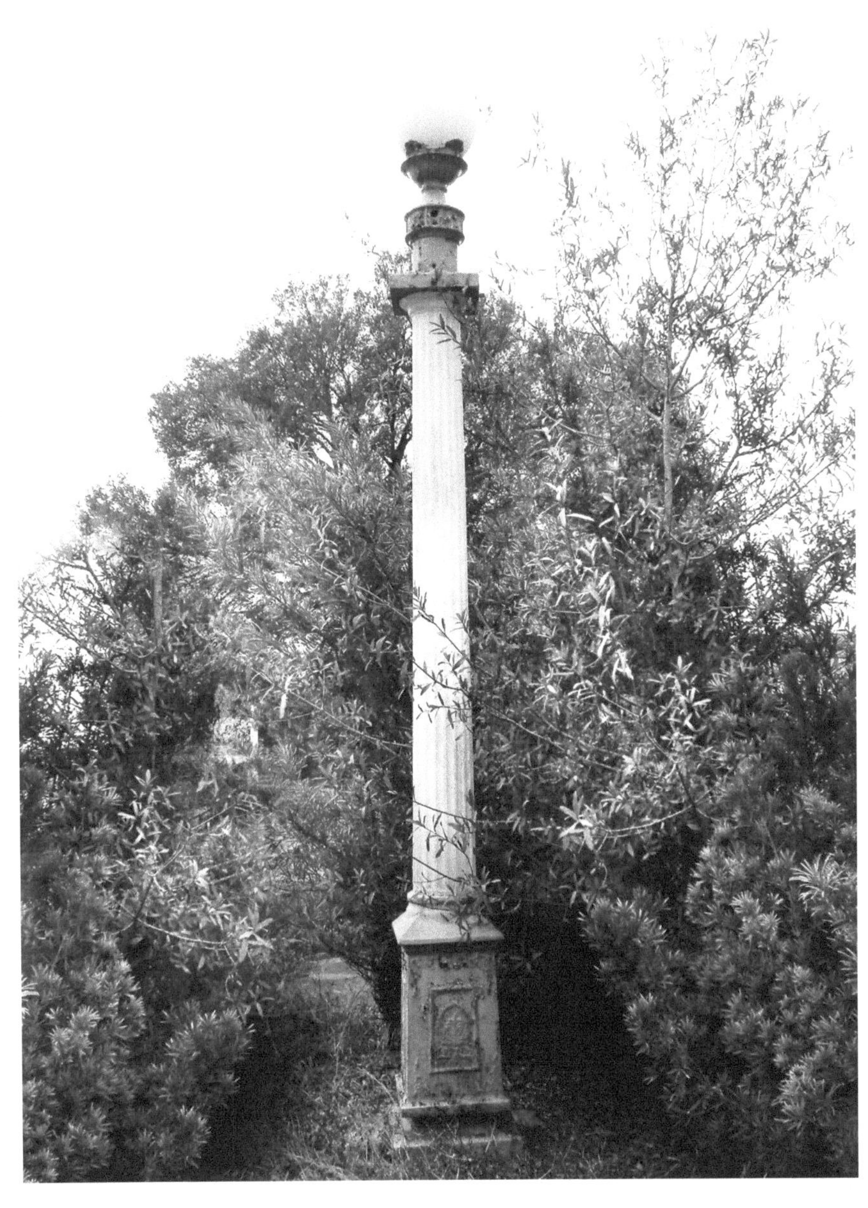

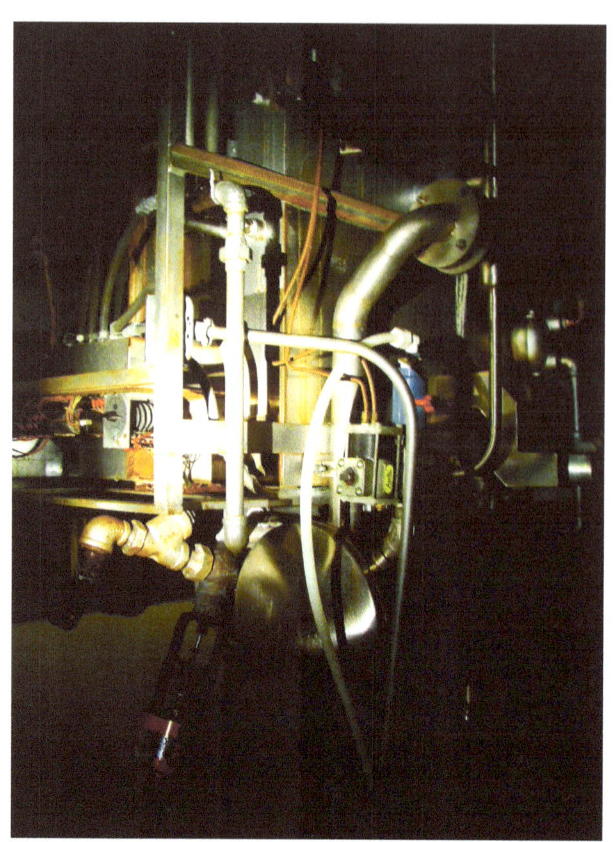

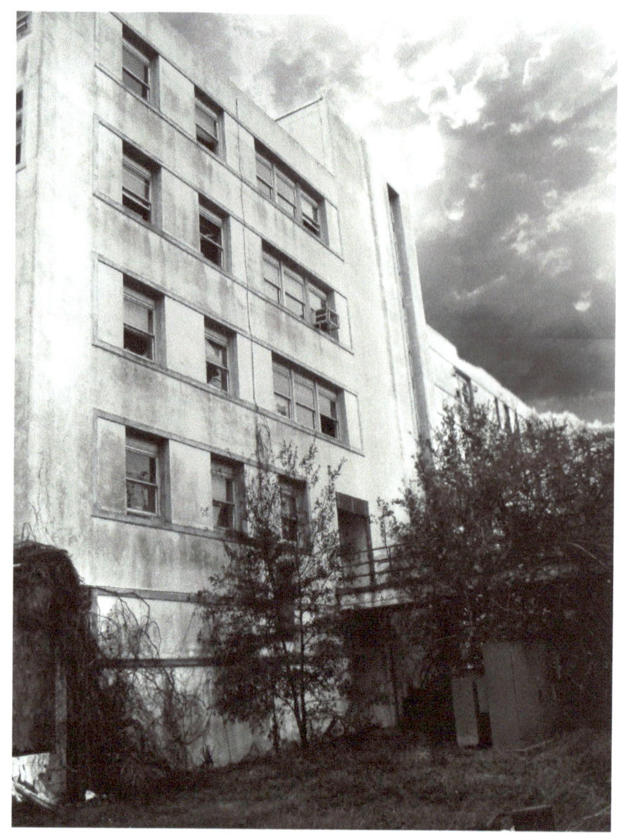

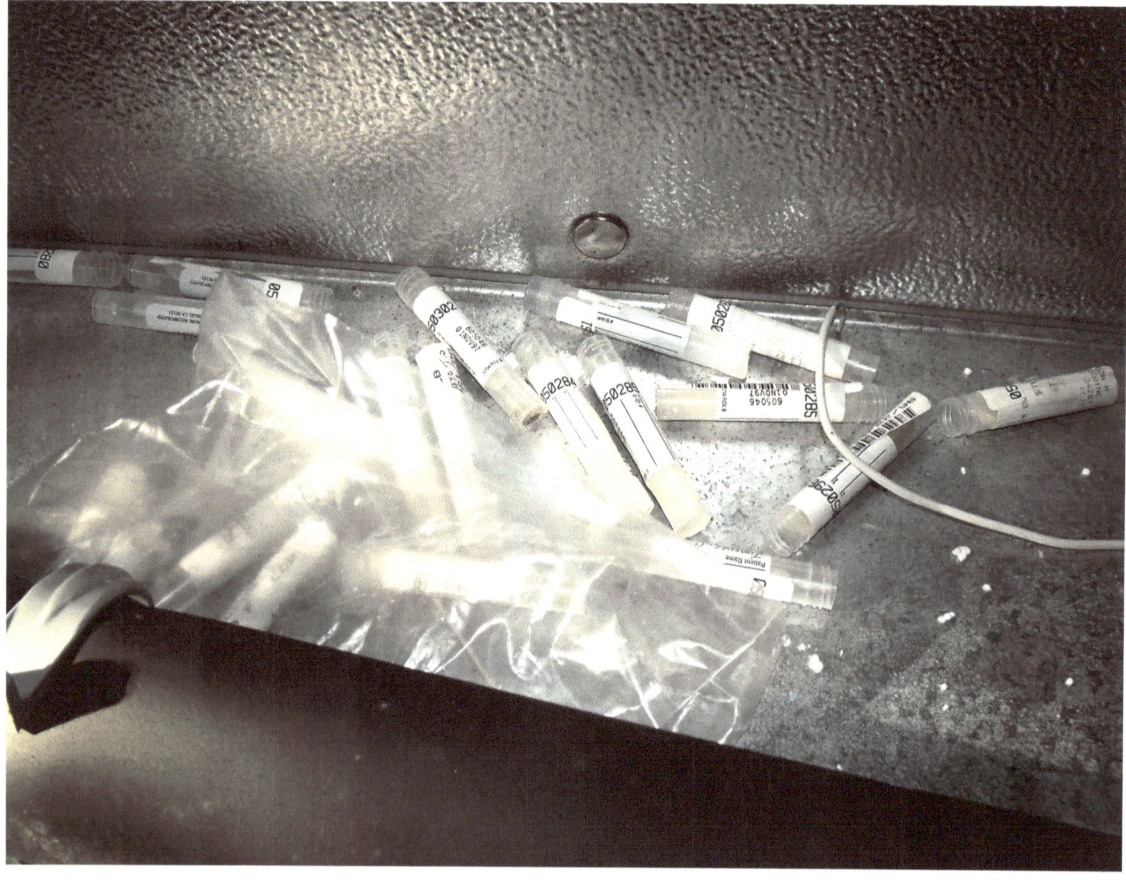

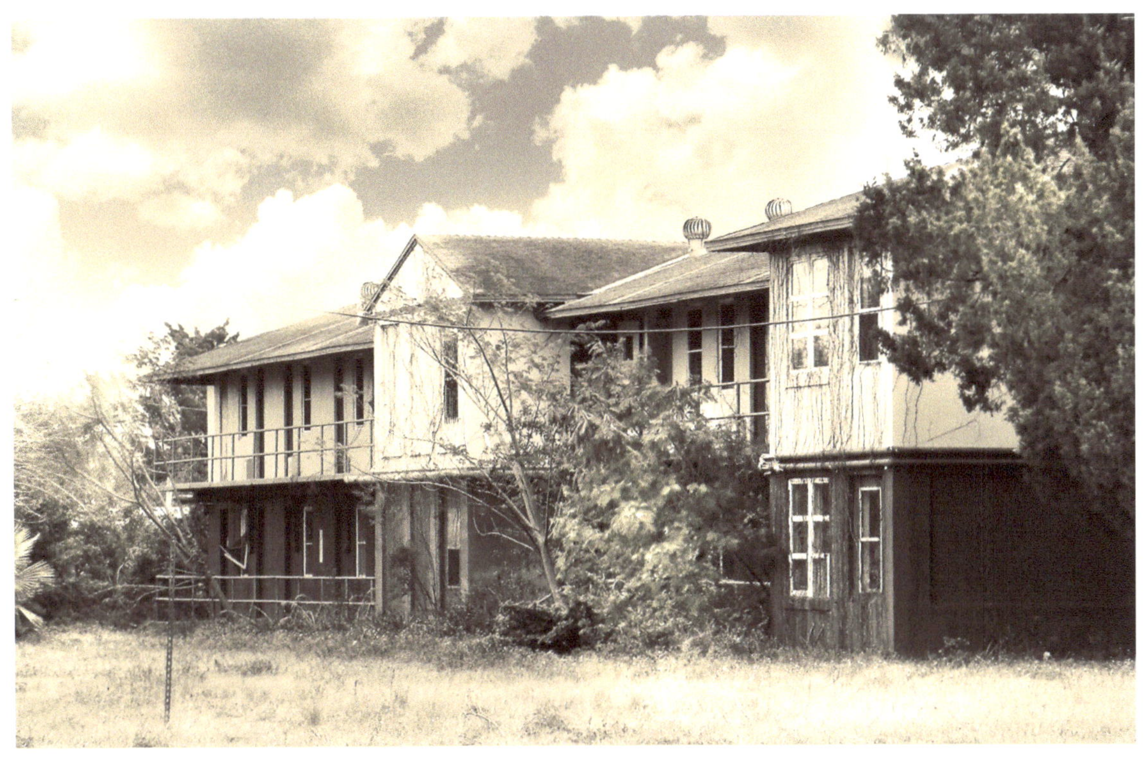

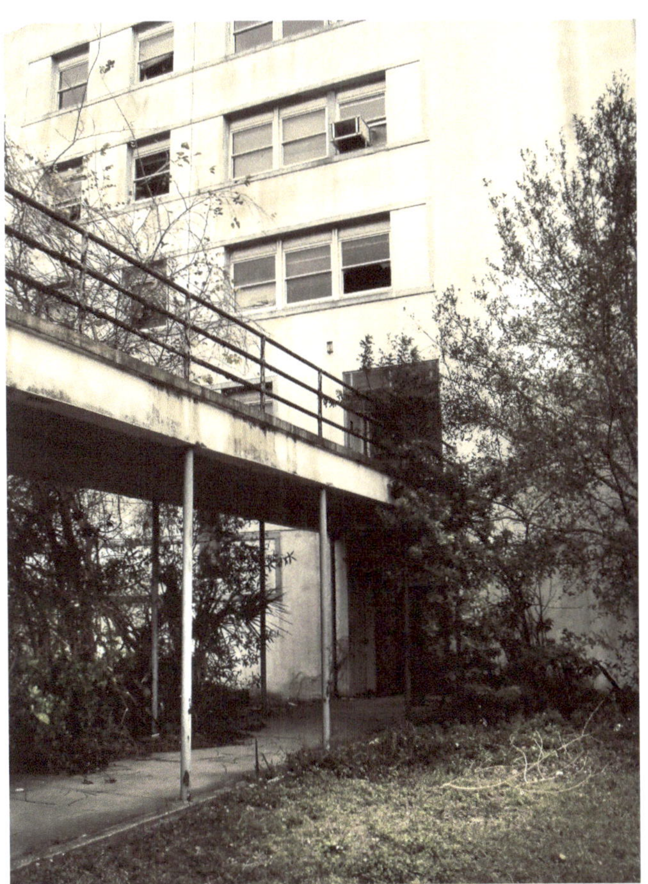

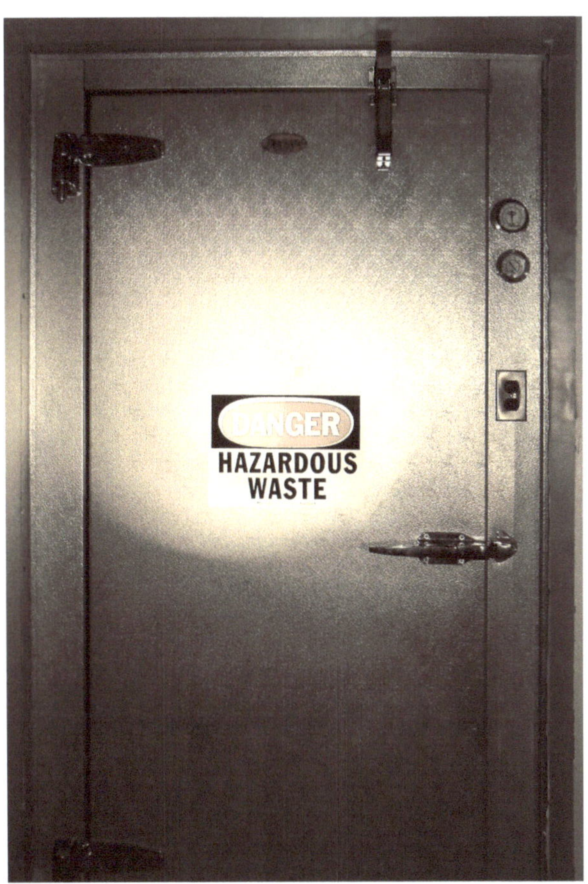
DANGER
HAZARDOUS
WASTE

Day Trips

Places that were only visited once. Some may yet become Journeys.
All are still standing. For now.

CHAPTER FIVE

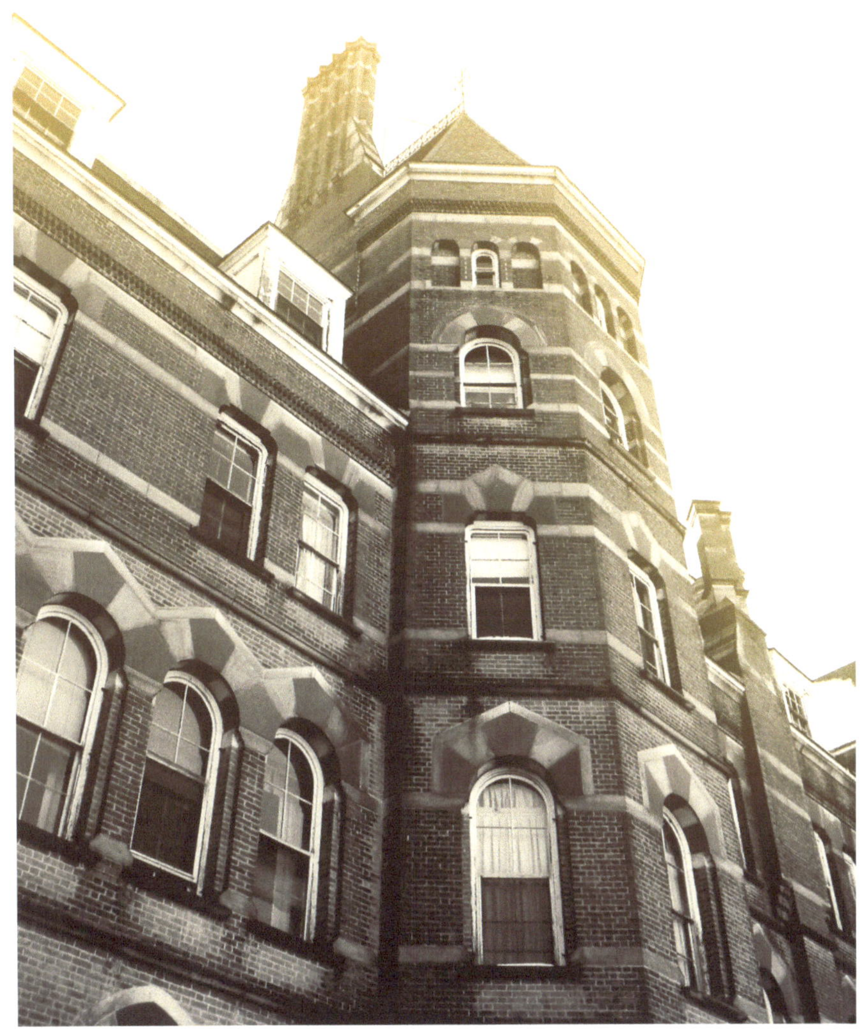

Riverside Psychiatric Center
New York

Riverside Psychiatric Center

The Screams of the Mad

This was another trip originating out of New York City and Bobio's first asylum experience. We left the city at some unholy hour of the early morning and took the long ride upstate. It was nice drive along the Hudson River Valley, which is brimming with history and abandoned buildings. One that I know of is actually on an island in the middle of the river. It's a huge castle, accessible only by boat, and I plan to visit it one day soon. But, that's a journey for another time. For this venture we were to meet up with our guide, Sam, at a predetermined location near the site at six am sharp. We arrived at the meeting point and waited for our guide with the temperature the low twenties. It was an unpleasant wait and made even more so when, after an hour, he failed to show. I think he may have been one of the last people in North America without a cell phone so we couldn't even call him. We didn't want to wait any longer so we decided to attempt entry on our own.

Riverside Psychiatric Center is comprised of the older campus, with its Kirkbride and other buildings and a newer contemporary nine story medical center; all abandoned. The newer medical center is visible from the road and gives you a good point of reference for locating the older part. Since we were relying on a guide, I had no maps or building layouts with me. I remembered that we were supposed to walk along some railroad tracks that border the property and start at the medical center. From there, we would traverse the tunnels that led straight into the old Kirkbride building. I had little interest in the newer building and even less interest in walking a rail line in the bitter cold so we drove away from the meeting point, and using the towering medical center as a landmark, followed some residential streets that bordered the property to where they dead ended. There was a fence and woods so we thought we located an entrance to the property.

We parked the car got our gear together and began hiking up a steep hill in about two and a half feet of virgin snow. It was a grueling trek and we had to stop several times to catch our breath and get our bearings. Finally, we reached a paved road that we assumed led into the campus. After short walk we began to see buildings. The first was a barn and we began to wonder if we had mistakenly wandered onto a farm that bordered the hospital, but then we saw the ubiquitous power station that served the asylum. Then warehouses and other utilitarian buildings, all old, all boarded and locked.

As we continued down the road, we saw a more ornate four-story building that could only be the Kirkbride. We carefully scanned windows and doors for an obvious way in. There was none that we could see. The ground floor windows were solidly boarded and all the doors locked. Around the front of the structure we were two decorative arched porticos, both with massive locked mahogany doors. We started to wonder if this was going to be a long drive and a strenuous walk for only an outside view. Then, I noticed that the lock on one front door was not nearly as stout as the door itself and with a strong pull I was able to open the door. For all the planning, the perceived need of a guide with his expert way in, and the apparent secure nature of the building, we ended up walking right in the front door as if we had the key.

This part of the Kirkbride was obviously the Administration Wing and it was amazingly well preserved. I don't know exactly when this portion of the campus was evacuated, but I do know it was much later that the rest. It seemed to have been closed for a decade or more judging from the vintage of the various office equipment cluttering the rooms and halls. There were desks, typewriters, dial phones and all other manner of office supplies haphazardly stored all over the first floor. We looked around and found a bathroom complete with a shower curtain, soap on the sink and toilet paper thoughtfully stocked in the closet. There were untattered curtains on the wall and carpets on the floor that needed only to be vacuumed. The place gave me a creepy sense that it could still be in use. Or, more like a ghost ship found gently bobbing on the swells, devoid of human life, but with food cooling on the galley table and boots still sitting silently by empty bunks.

We went up a few floors and found more of the deserted, yet nearly pristine administration. There was paint peeling off the walls in some places and musty smell permeated the place but the state of preservation was consistent. We found a bookcase filled with medical volumes and even children's science books. I picked one of these up and was surprised to see Northampton State Hospital and its address written in pencil inside the cover. I hadn't been to Northampton yet and I took this an omen that I should visit there. Everywhere we looked there were architectural details of the type seen only in a building of this vintage. Marble fireplaces, a huge curved wooden stairwell, arched windows and even ornate metal heat registers. As interesting as all this was, we wanted to get into the tunnels, basement and patient wards, so we headed back down.

The first floor was dim, but there was some light coming in through the arched window tops that the boards didn't cover, so we had no trouble navigating the ground floor. We found a stairwell conveniently marked "tunnel". We went down and found an old black steel door with an old fashioned, impenetrable, skeleton type lock. Undaunted, we went back up and looked further. There was probably another tunnel entrance somewhere in the large building so we agreed to keep an eye for it while we searched for the entrance to the patient wings. They should have been clearly marked or at least obvious with a gated or barred entry. We moved in the general direction of one wing, but could find no entrance. We briefly considered the possibility that the wings were only accessible from the second floor. Then we found a wall of recent construction that looked obviously out of place. The wall was definitely odd because it was made of drywall while the other walls were made of plaster that was more consistent with the age of the building. There was a hole broken through the wall near the bottom and I peered in. There was a hallway and the condition was much worse than the area we were in. It looked like we had found a patient wing.

We crawled through the hole into a different world. This area was in a much more advanced state of decay. I remembered that the patient wings were closed long before the administration and this wall must have been built to separate the disused section from the active one. The area looked as though it had been used to store items that no one cared about. In the dim light we saw a confusing array of seemingly unrelated equipment, all in disrepair. There was a printing machine of some type standing next to a loom. The yarn on the loom was rotted and turned to dust at a touch. There was so much equipment blocking the hall that we turned and went down a different corridor.

The next room we found appeared to be a dayroom or some other large common area. I say room, but what I really mean is treasure trove. The huge space was filled from one end to the other with old medical equipment, beds, tools and furniture. We saw a large round operating theater light in perfect condition, IV stands lined up like soldiers at parade rest and dental chairs that looked like you could sit down and have a cavity filled on the spot. There was apparatus that would require a medical degree to identify along with everyday items. Wastebaskets, desks, stacked chairs by the hundreds and sundry medical supplies such as cases of bandages, gauze and swabs. Everything was in fairly good condition here but it was obvious this store of goods and equipment had been here for some time.

As we moved away from that area it became apparent that the patient wings were devastated by the elements. There were floors that had collapsed all the way from the top level down into the basement. We saw another dental examination chair that had crashed through four floors into the pit of rubble below. Looking up the hole through several floors we saw another one perched on the precipice ready to tumble in on its twin. The way the destroyed wood was broken and splintered it appeared that collapses were sudden and violent. We vowed to carefully watch our step for fear of ending up on a one-way ride into the basement.

We located a stairwell and headed up. The stairs were concrete and solid so we knew were safe from floor collapse in there. On the top floor we discovered the reason for the massive amount of destruction.

There were gaping holes in the roof that you could drive a small car through. Of course, if you had a small car, and could get the thing up there, it would just end up crashing down into the basement with a pile of shattered asylum debris on top of it. We started down the corridor and soon realized that this floor was not safe. The ominous creaking and groaning noises coming from the floor made up our minds for us and we headed down. The next level was only slightly better. The floor was soft in places but seemed strong enough to walk on. We tried to stay near the edge of the wall where we figured the floor would be the strongest. This level looked as if it had not seen a living person in decades. There were piles of paint chips and drifts of dust on the floor where they had lay undisturbed for years. The structural failure of the joist system was amazing. Massive beams had bent and warped with the weight of the collapsing building and were now curved and exposed through the old hardwood floorboards. In some places the warping was so violent the floorboards were scattered about as if they had been blown up in a spray of splinters.

The devastation in this area made for slow going. Most of the rooms we saw were empty with the exception of an odd piece of furniture or clothing here and there. I found an old nurse's uniform on the floor and it brought home the realization that this was not just an interesting ruin, but a place the severely mentally ill called home. As I gazed into a tiny cell-like room with barred windows I wondered about the nurse who wore that uniform and those in her care. Most mental institutions separate the sexes and I didn't know if we were in the male or female wing, but for some reason this felt like the female ward. There was nothing to indicate that this was true, but it was a feeling I couldn't shake and it just seemed right. After a few moments of reflection, we decided we had enough of this wing and headed back down the stairs.

We continued all the way down into the basement. There was some vintage trash strewn about down there and we found old beer cans with pop-tops in surprisingly good condition. We wondered if the contents had been imbibed long ago by a hospital worker taking a surreptitious break from the screams of the mad. We noticed a door that lead to what seemed like a dark promising tunnel with small rooms leading off on either side. There was a lone wheelchair down there and we wondered why it was there and what had happened to its rider. It was a strange place for wheelchair and in the dim tunnel it took on a sinister look. The tunnel itself was sinister in the near total darkness especially with the dark rooms gaping open on each side. We peered into a few and some contained old tools and various utility devices. The end of the tunnel wasn't visible and it seemed to go on forever. I wondered if this was the passage to the medical center which was likely a quarter mile or more away. Since we weren't interested in that building, and we weren't sure if this was even part of the tunnel system or simply a sub-basement, we decided to head out of the Kirkbride and examine some of the other buildings we saw on the way in.

Those other buildings included the morgue, which I knew from research, was very old and had a body freezer with rare wooden doors. It was likely connected to this one by the tunnel system, but we were not having luck navigating this underground netherworld. Rather than wander around lost or possibly encounter more of those locked black steel doors we decided to take the outside route.

We backtracked through the administration area to the front door. Opening the door just a crack, we peered out to see if the coast was clear. The windows were boarded and we didn't want to just barge out and find a security guard sitting by the side of the road. Just because security here seemed as casual as any other place I've visited I saw no reason to make their job any easier than it already was. I seriously doubted we would run into any problems, but better safe than sorry.

We got out with no problems and mugged for some shots in the front of the building then headed back the way we came in search of the morgue. Wow, was I wrong about the security. We soon heard a car approach from behind and when we turned to look it wasn't security like we expected, but a state trooper. He approached fast and braked hard in that patented cop driving technique designed to instill fear in the soon to be arrested. It worked and the fear sat like a hard greasy lump in my gut. I was already mentally counting the funds in my wallet to see if I had enough to bail both of us out. The trooper opened his window a crack

- it was still cold out - and politely asked what the hell we thought we were doing here. Quick thinking on my part varnished the truth from taking pictures to just looking at the buildings. I didn't want him to know I had a camera filled with incriminating interior pictures. He informed us in cop-speak that we were no longer looking at the buildings and that we were promptly and directly leaving the property. A perfect sprinkling of yes-sir and no-sir in all the right places, a healthy dollop of inclement weather and a dash of trooper on his way to someplace that was actually important was the perfect recipe for our escape

We took the not so subtle hint and fortuitous break in stride and walked out of the former Riverside State Hospital for the Insane the way we came in. The morgue would have to wait for another visit. Hopefully it and the Kirkbride are there when I make it back.

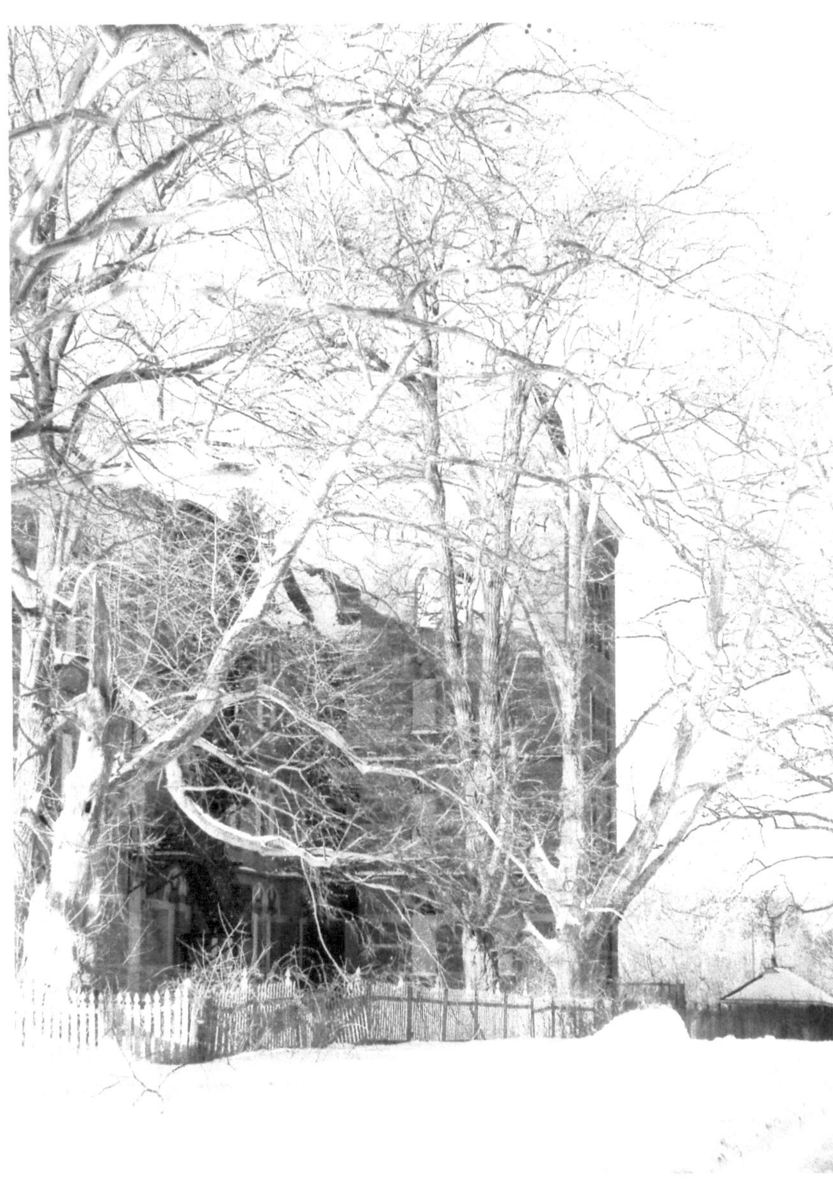

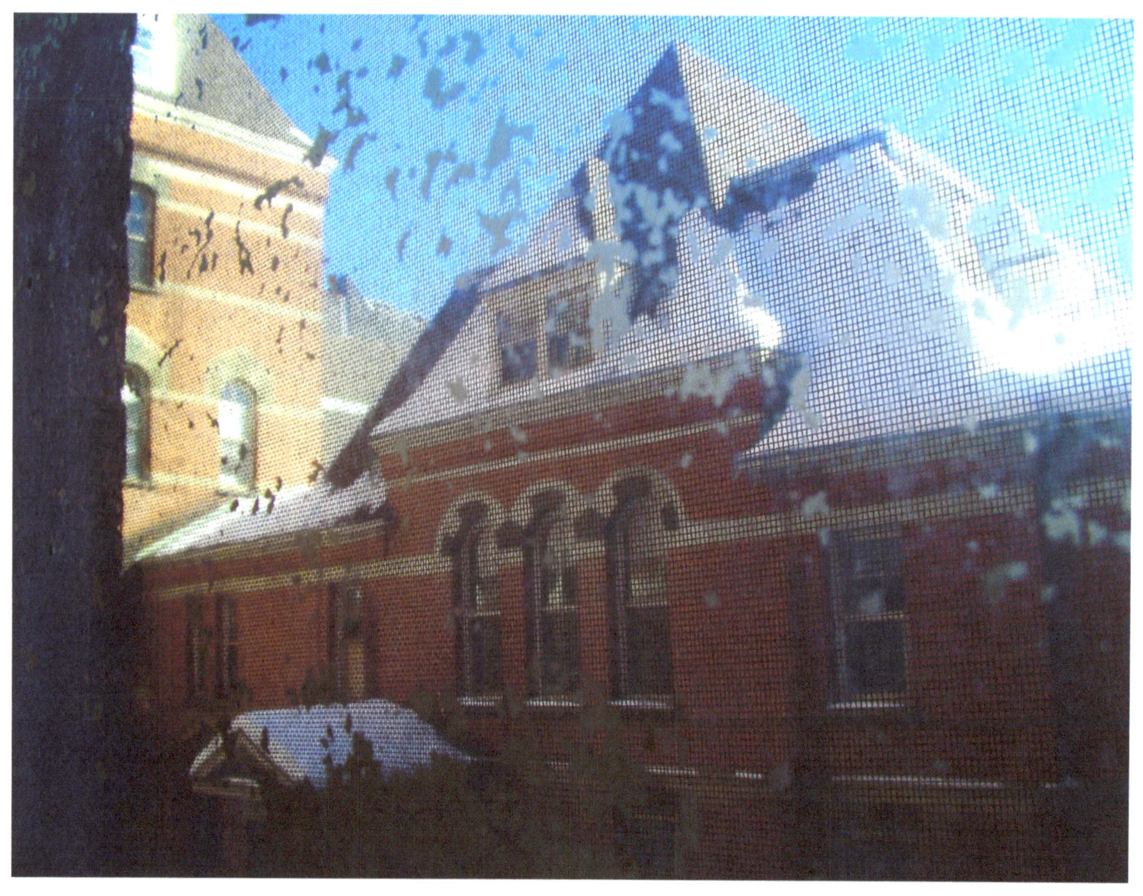

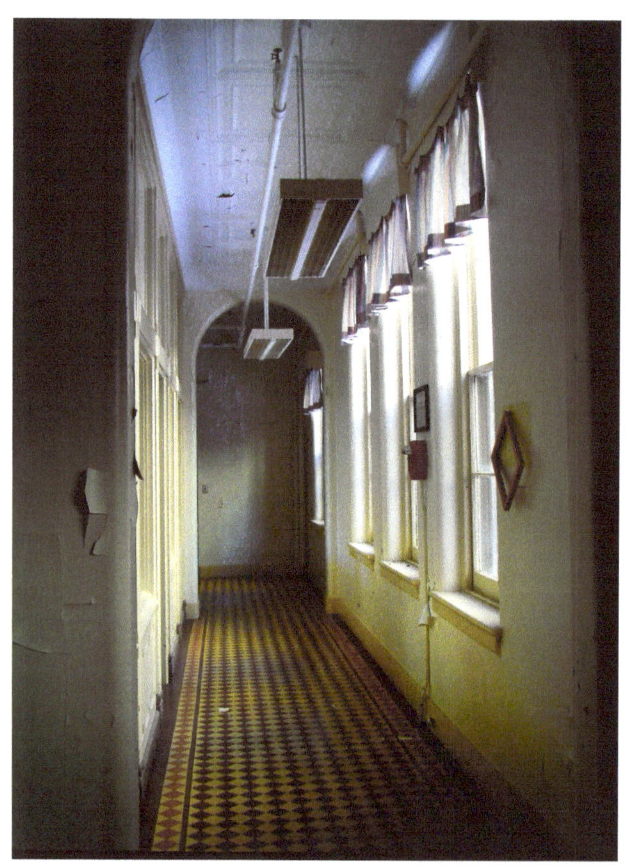

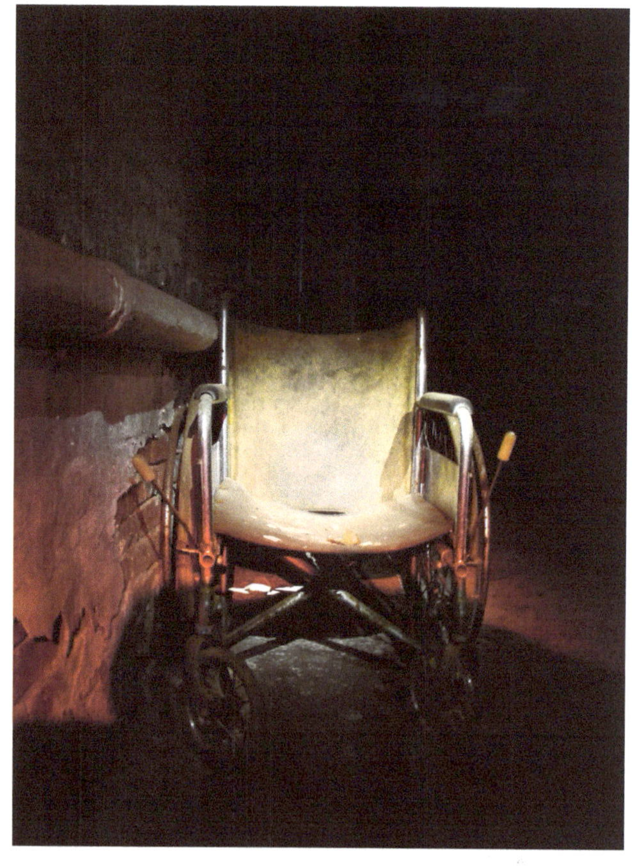

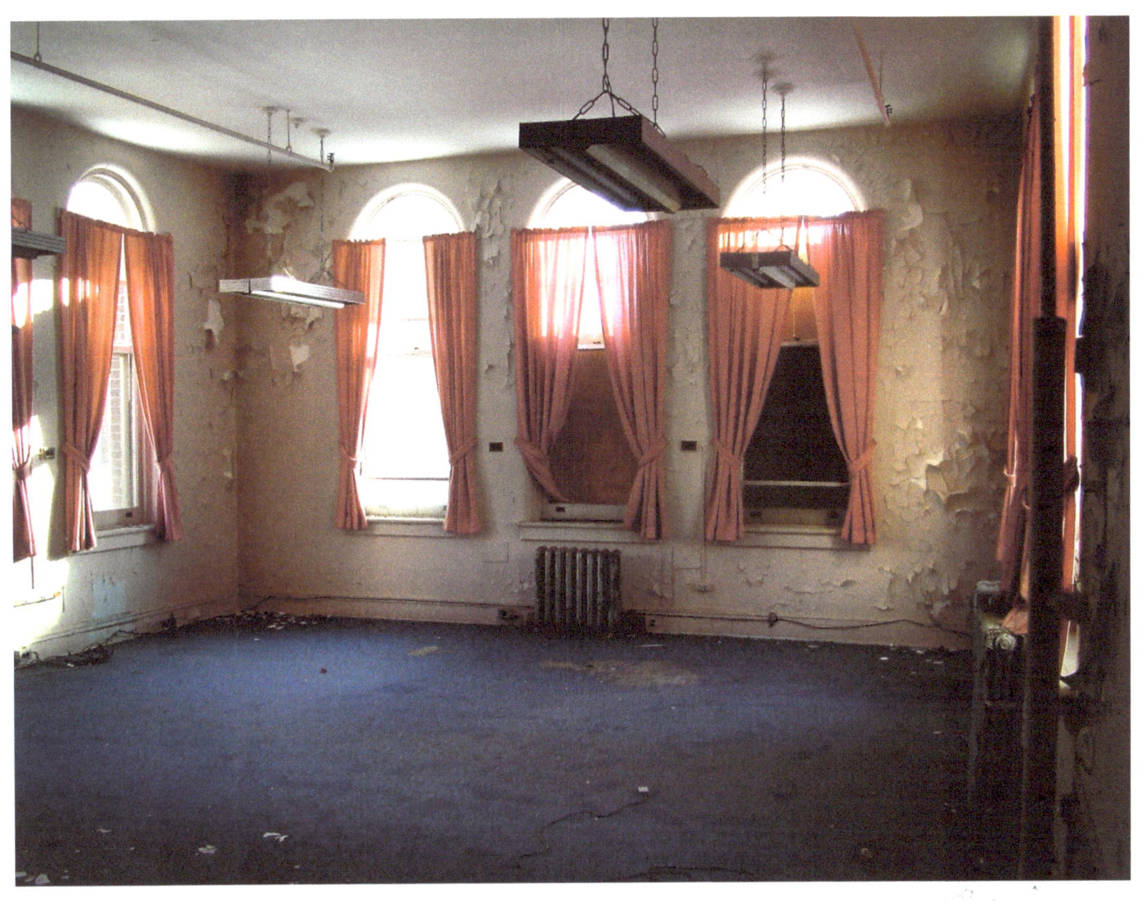

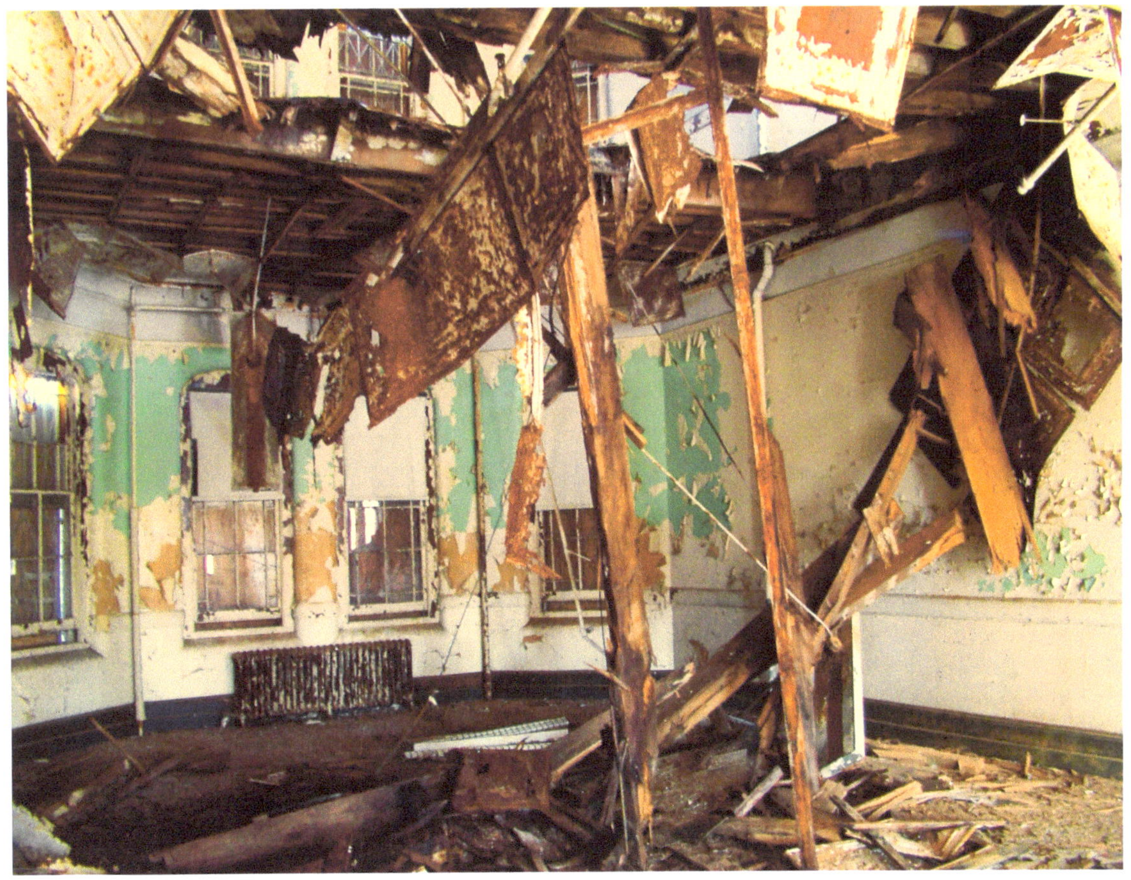

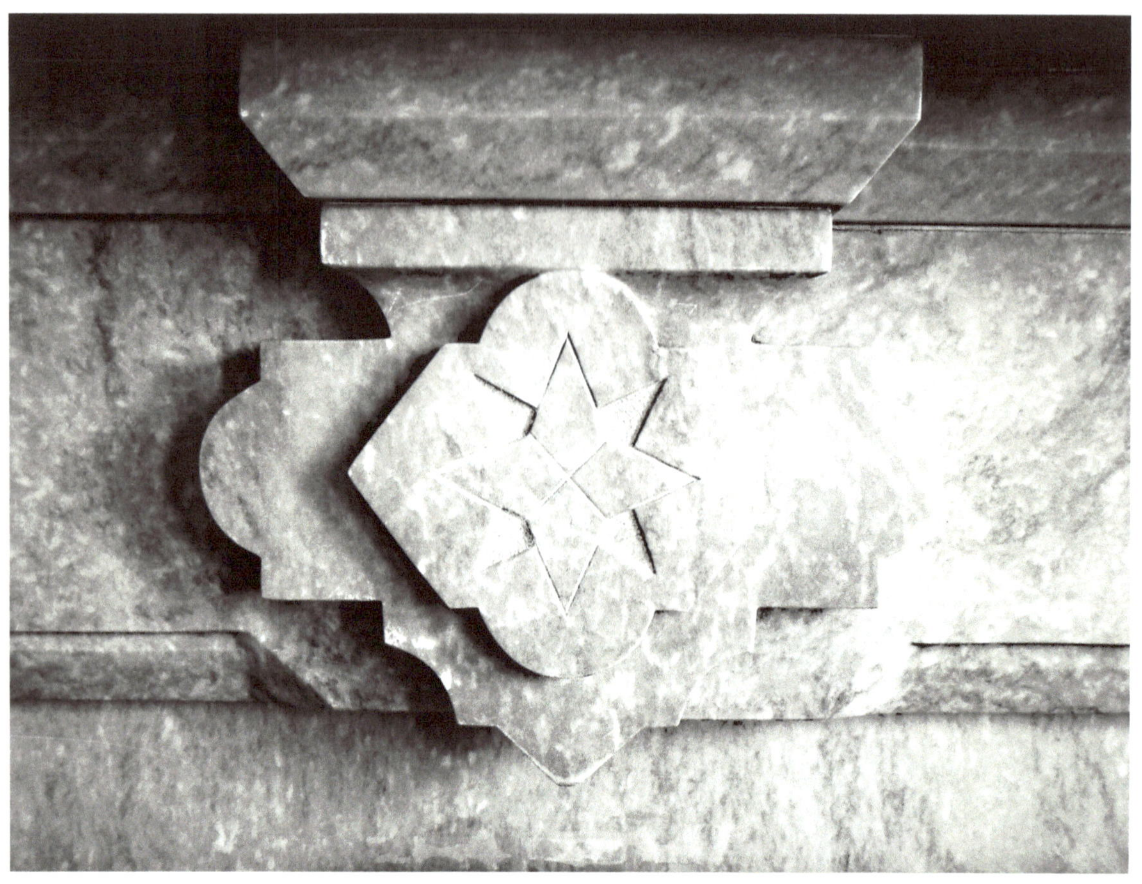

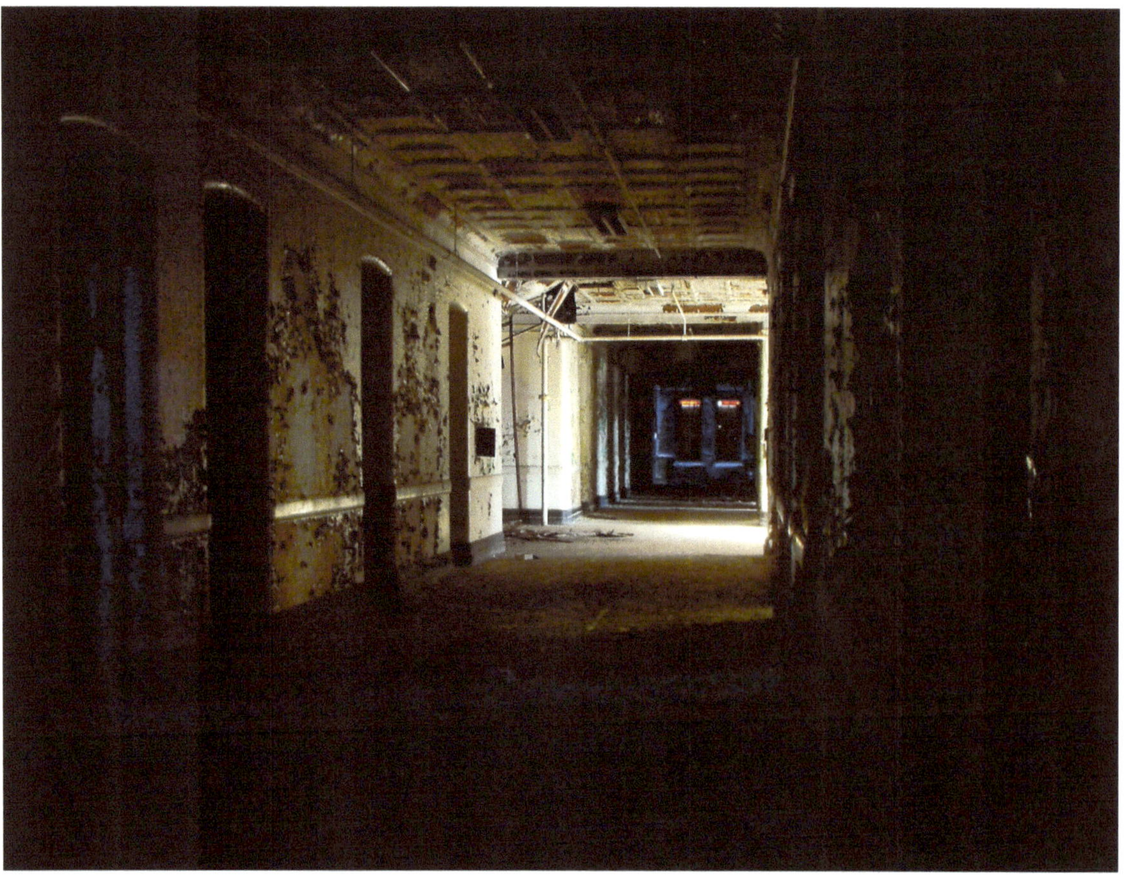

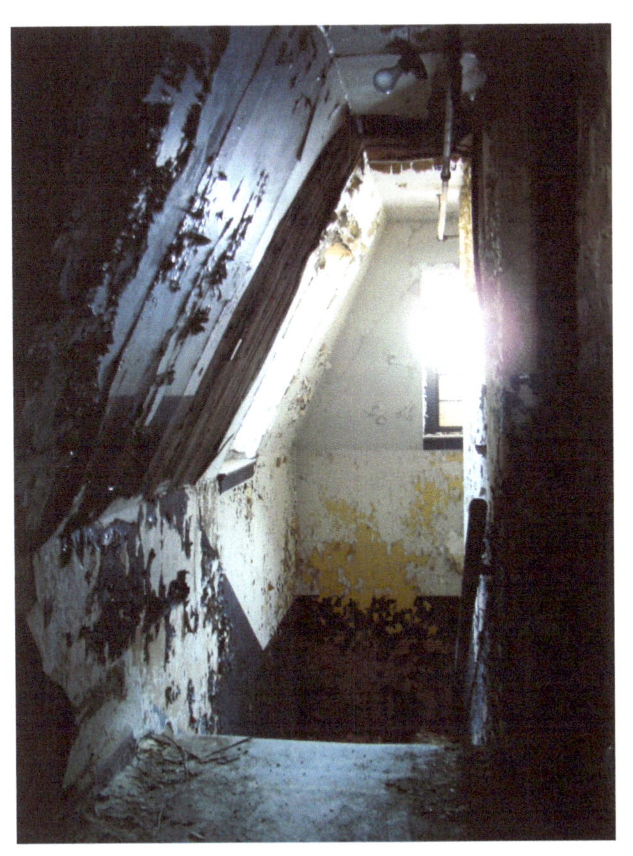

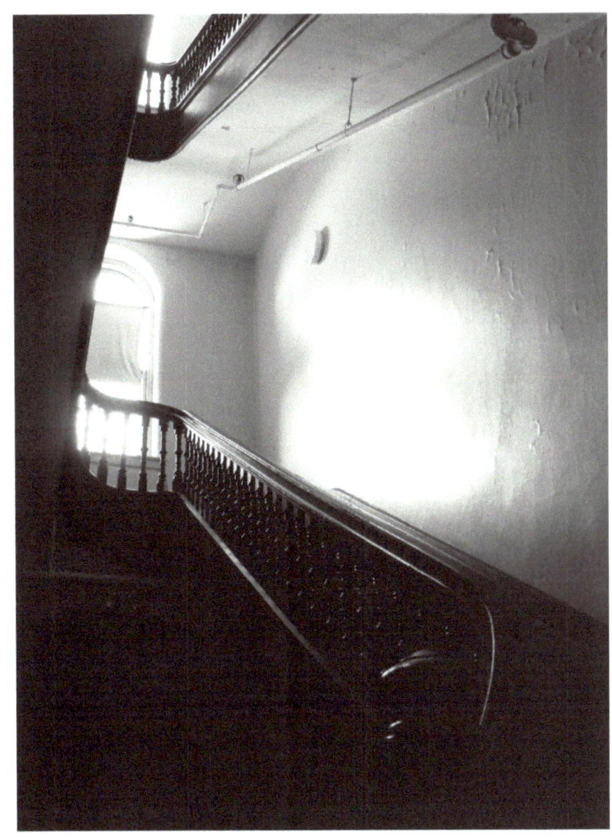

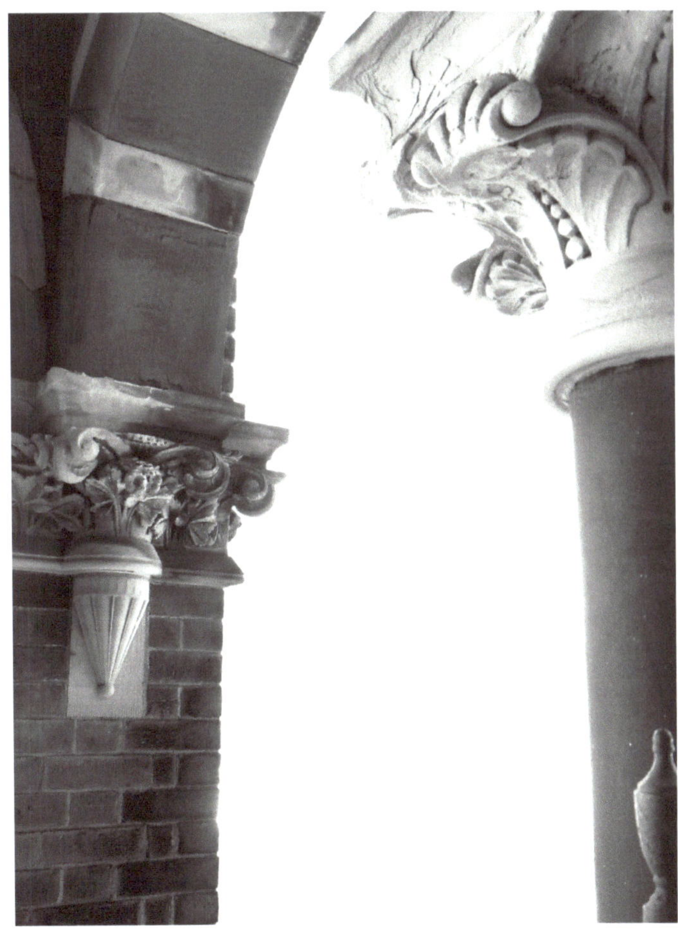

CHAPTER SIX

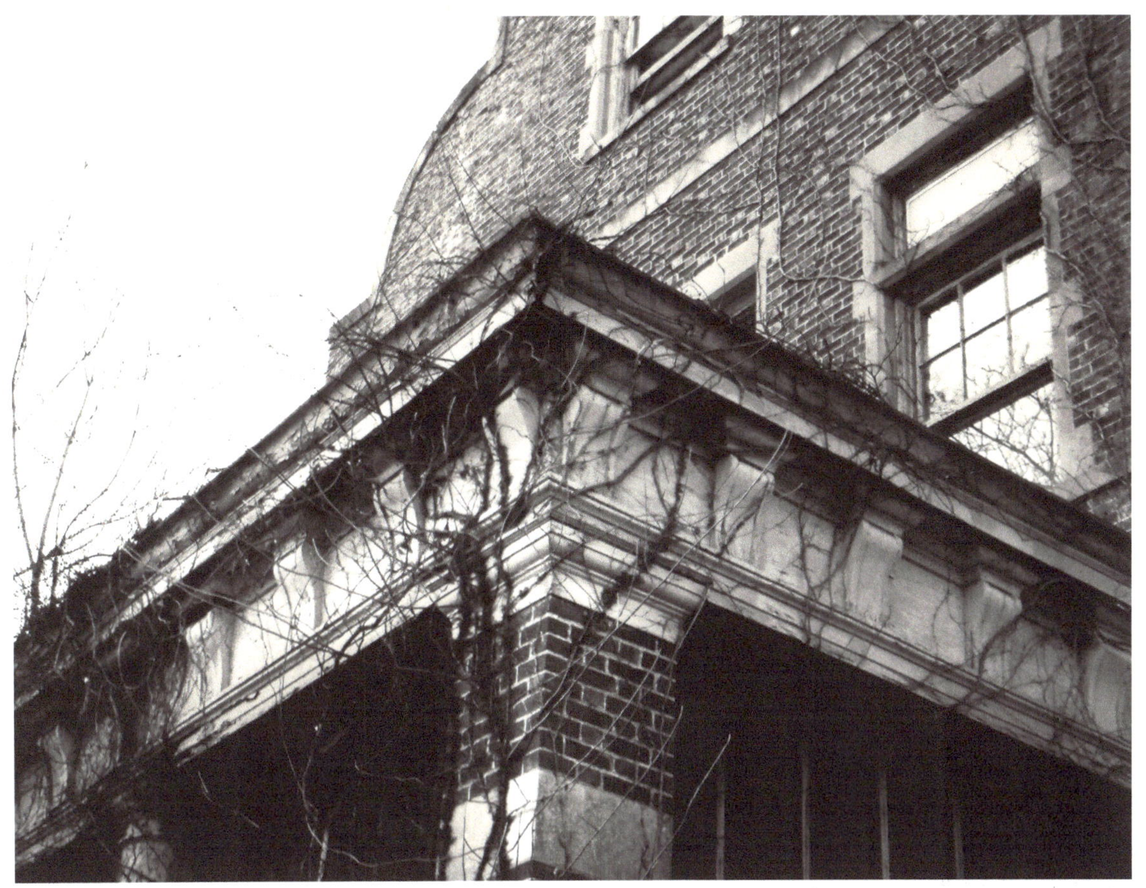

Pinehaven State School & Hospital

Pennsylvania

Pinehaven State School & Hospital

Echoes of Abuse

Pinehaven is a grim place. In the 1970's, it was the scene of horrific patient abuse, most of whom were children. That knowledge certainly weighs heavy, especially when you see a rusted metal crib sitting in a ruined ward. I believe the place would seem grim even if you didn't know the sinister history. It just has a bleak and depressing feel. I went in the dead of winter, which certainly didn't help. I'm not really sure if spring in full bloom could improve this desolate sprawl of early twentieth century brick buildings. The campus is situated deep in the woods with only a municipal depot and a military base for neighbors. It's laid out in the cottage plan, which is to say it's many buildings of specific purpose rather than one large one.

We met up with my friend, who I will just call MmT, who happened to be from the area but had never toured the campus. Bobio and I had instructions from an experienced traveler on where to park and how to approach this location. As is typical, these instructions called for parking miles away and hiking in. This time there was a nasty little twist. Not only did we have to walk an inordinate distance, but along the way it was necessary to walk across the narrow remains of wrecked train trestle that spanned a river. Under the best possible weather conditions, this may not have been too bad, but it was before dawn, about fifteen degrees F out and the trestle spanned a river covered in sheets of ice. I'm sure the steel trestle would have been iced too. One slip and we would be dealing with a nasty fall plus hypothermia. Preferring to spend the day in an abandoned hospital taking pictures rather than an active one recovering from frostbite or worse, we decided to drive by the place and look for a closer point of egress.

The road leading up to the grounds took us past the active municipal building and we quickly left civilization behind. A ruined power station on the left told us we were going the right way. Not that we really needed to see it to be sure. After a while, you begin to recognize the unique look and feel of the woods around abandoned asylums. It's the look of an area once groomed but now gone to seed. There are other subtle signs like antique light poles or overgrown fire hydrants. Then there are some not so subtle signs that usually say something like keep out. I was never really sure if whoever put up those signs meant it or not because it seemed that they never tried too hard too keep anyone out.

As we drove through the dark woods past the empty, staring buildings it became obvious that there was only two ways to approach this excursion. Either walk from two miles away or park right on the road next to the buildings in plain sight. We had been driving all night, and this place was a stop on the way to New York, so we didn't much feel like walking any more than necessary. We decided to take our chances and park right there.

Pinehaven was different from most of the other hospitals I have visited. There were no boards on the windows at all and every door seemed to be wide open. We took this as a good sign and invited ourselves into the building directly in front of us. The buildings here were all named and conveniently labeled on the outside with a bright red sign. This particular one was the Mayflower. From a distance the buildings, although obviously abandoned, seemed to be in decent condition from the outside. On closer inspection this proved false. They were not as bad as some that I've seen but they were in pretty poor condition. The Mayflower looked like it was a ward of some kind. There were rusted beds still made up with moldering sheets. The floor was littered with broken glass, plaster and trash. We saw signs of vandalism and graffiti here and there, and some areas were devoid of purposeful damage.

All the buildings on this campus were connected by a tunnel system and we made immediate use of it to gain access to the next building. It was more of a comfort issue than anything because the tunnels were slightly warmer than going outside. There was certainly no need for stealth with our car parked right out front. We went down into the dark tunnel and headed towards the next building. I guess we missed the stairs because we passed right under Administration and ended up in the Limerick Building. Limerick?

I have no idea what went on in this building but I have a feeling it wasn't creative writing. Despite its jaunty name, the Limerick was just another battered and vandalized space so we decided to head outside and find the Whitman Building, which was the site of the infirmary and the morgue.

Walking outside in the huge space between the buildings was harder than we expected. There were paved walkways, but they were overgrown. The whole area was a choked mass of dead trees, briars and tall weeds. This area may have been impassable in spring or summer with the underbrush in full bloom rather than dead and brittle as it was. I'm sure we made a huge racket crunching and snapping twigs and cursing the small branches whipping us at every step. We made it into a slightly clearer area and stood in front of Industry Hall. We went in and didn't really see anything that indicated that this building was used for anything more industrious than warehousing mentally ill children. The Whitman was across the way and on the other side of a small road so we went downstairs in hopes of a tunnel passage that would be easier than walking through the nasty briars outside.

Following the tunnel brought us right into the Whitman's basement. There we found a prosthetics lab complete with the bizarre discovery of an artificial leg. There were other mysterious medical devices and supplies down there along with recognizable items like bandages and splints. There were also beds. We found beds in just about very area that we had visited including the tunnels and basements. The disturbing thing was that the beds didn't seem to be in those areas for storage, they appeared to have been used there by patients. The fact that they were outfitted with sheets and pillows reinforced this opinion. If this was true, I can't imagine the feeling of desolation and despair a mental patient must have experienced while sleeping alone in a tunnel or basement.

We headed upstairs from there and almost missed the morgue. It was in a small room and didn't contain any other pathology equipment, like an autopsy table, identifying it as such. The body freezers faced away from the door inside a small alcove and if we hadn't looked in every room we would have missed it. The morgue was small and it sadly seemed scaled down to fit its main customer: children. Unkind visitors before us had removed the wooden doors from the freezer and scrawled obscenities around the room. It was the final indignity on the poor clients, as the patients were referred to, of this terrible place.

We had been up for over twenty-four hours and New York was still hours away. The cold was seeping into our bones and I imagined dreams of mad children reverberating through the empty wards. We got out of the Whitman and headed down the main road back to our vehicle. We walked passed the Administration Building on our way and I stopped to take a few outside shots. Curiosity got the best of me and I walked up to peek in the window. It looked much more ornate inside than the other buildings. Bobio grudgingly agreed to have a look inside with me. The main hall had huge soaring archways and large spacious offices paneled in dark wood. At least the keepers of this hellhole were comfortable while their wards suffered. We found a wide-open antique safe that would never again secure anything. I briefly wondered if some former director of this facility used it to keep evidence of abuse from prying eyes. A few more pictures inside and we headed out for good.

Back outside, morning was in full swing. A dedicated jogger was approaching and we wondered if he would cause us any problems. I told Bobio to look natural. As if there was anything natural about rummaging through the dead remnants of an abandoned children's asylum at dawn. As he got closer, it became obvious that this was no ordinary citizen jogger. This guy was athletic and ran with military precision. I started worrying that he wasn't jogging at all, but running towards us. There was that military base nearby. Maybe he saw us on the grounds and was rushing over here to hold us while the proper authorities were in transit. He passed with us with a nod and went on his way down the road.

We took our cue from the jogger and went on our way down the road leaving the bulk of this sad place unexplored. There's a possibility I may come back here some day to see the other thirty or so buildings we missed. If I happen to be nearby. But I seriously doubt I will.

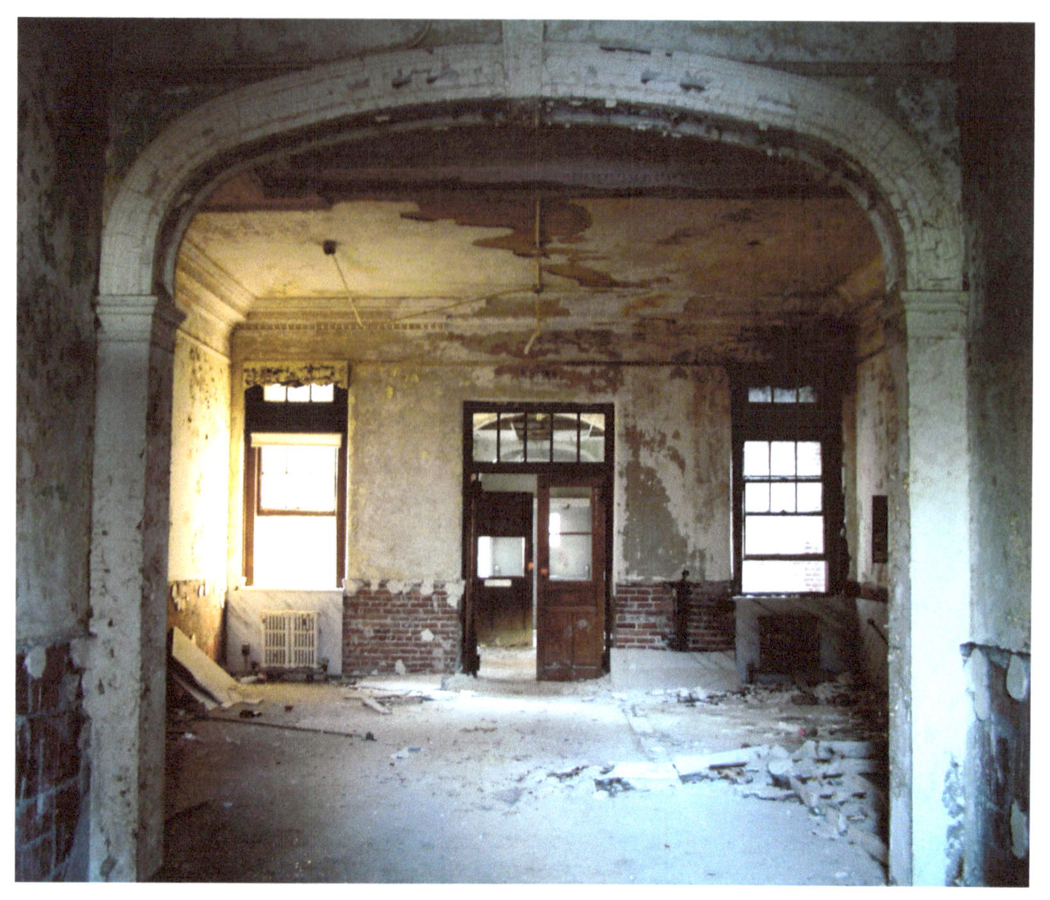

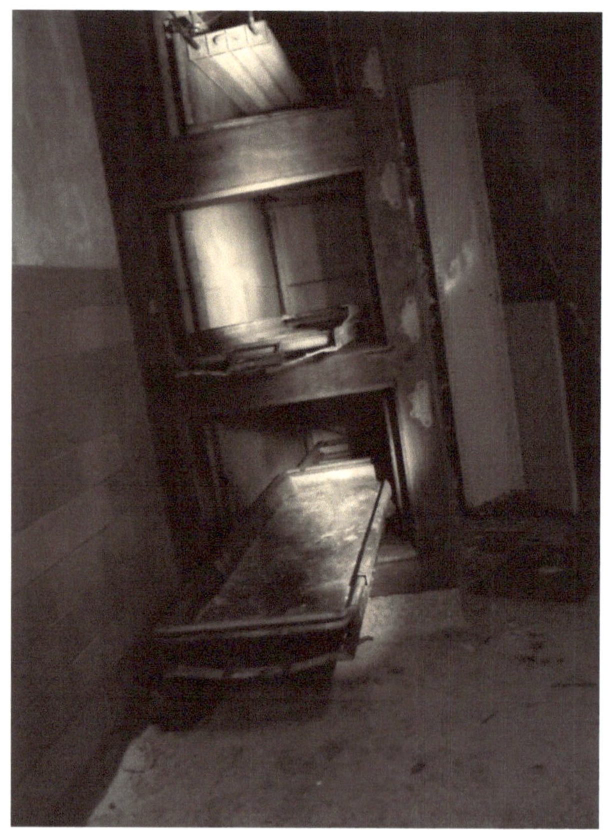

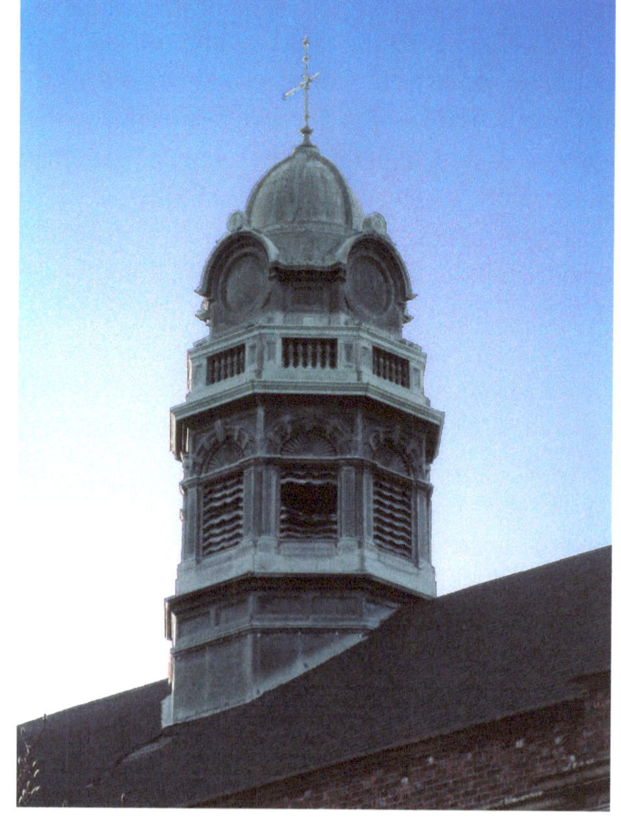

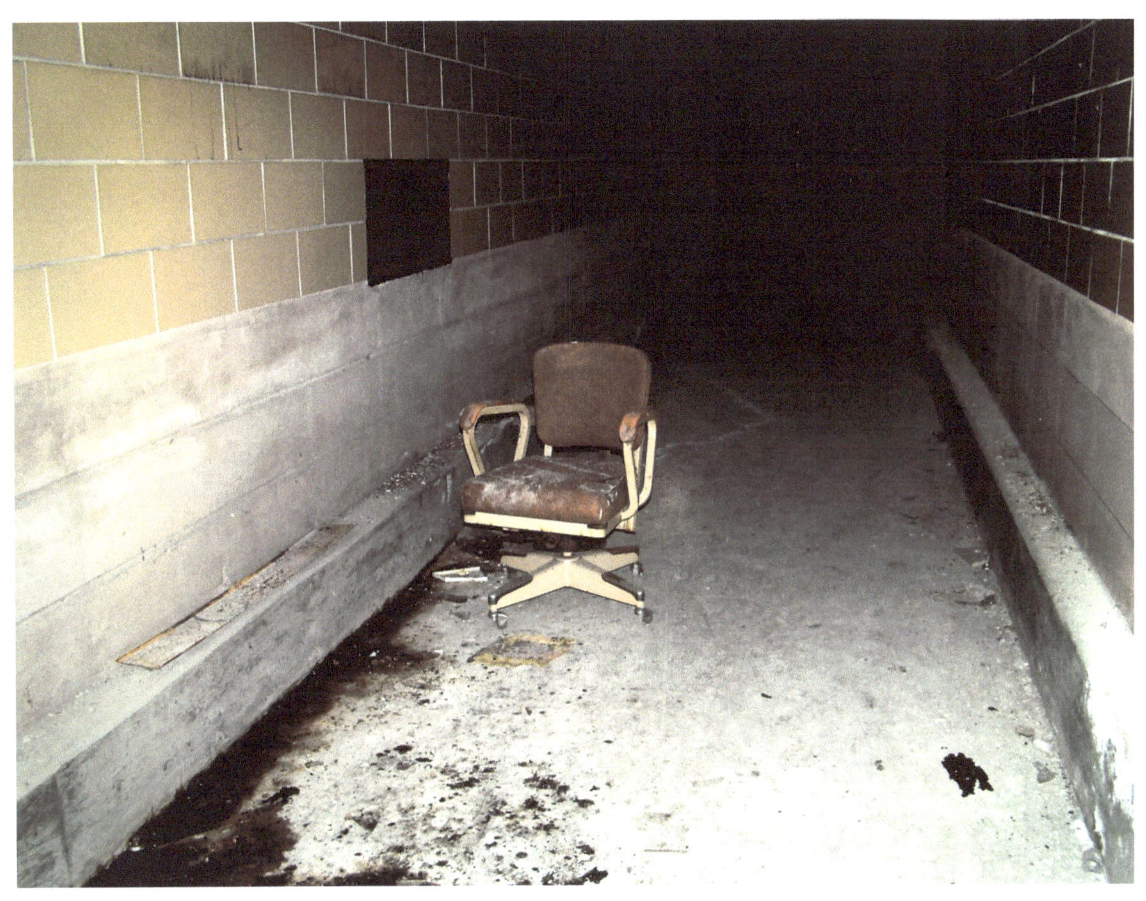

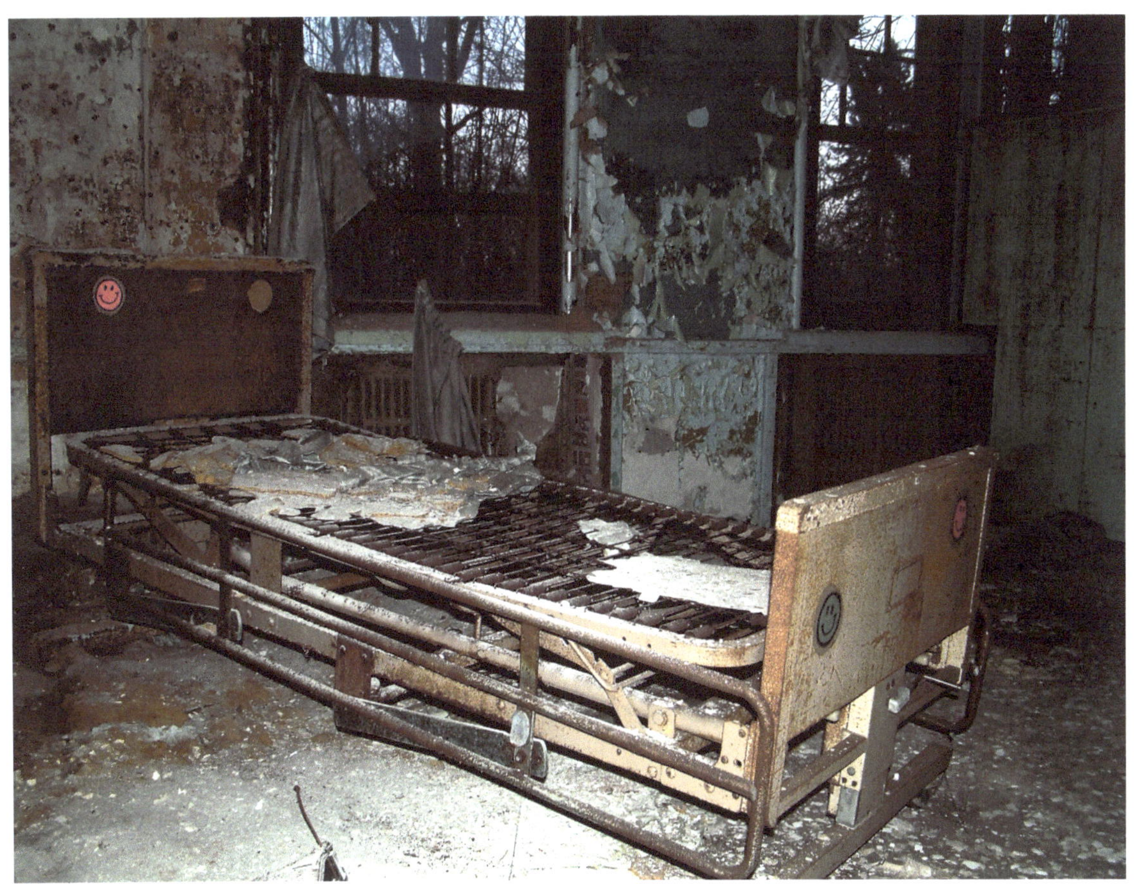

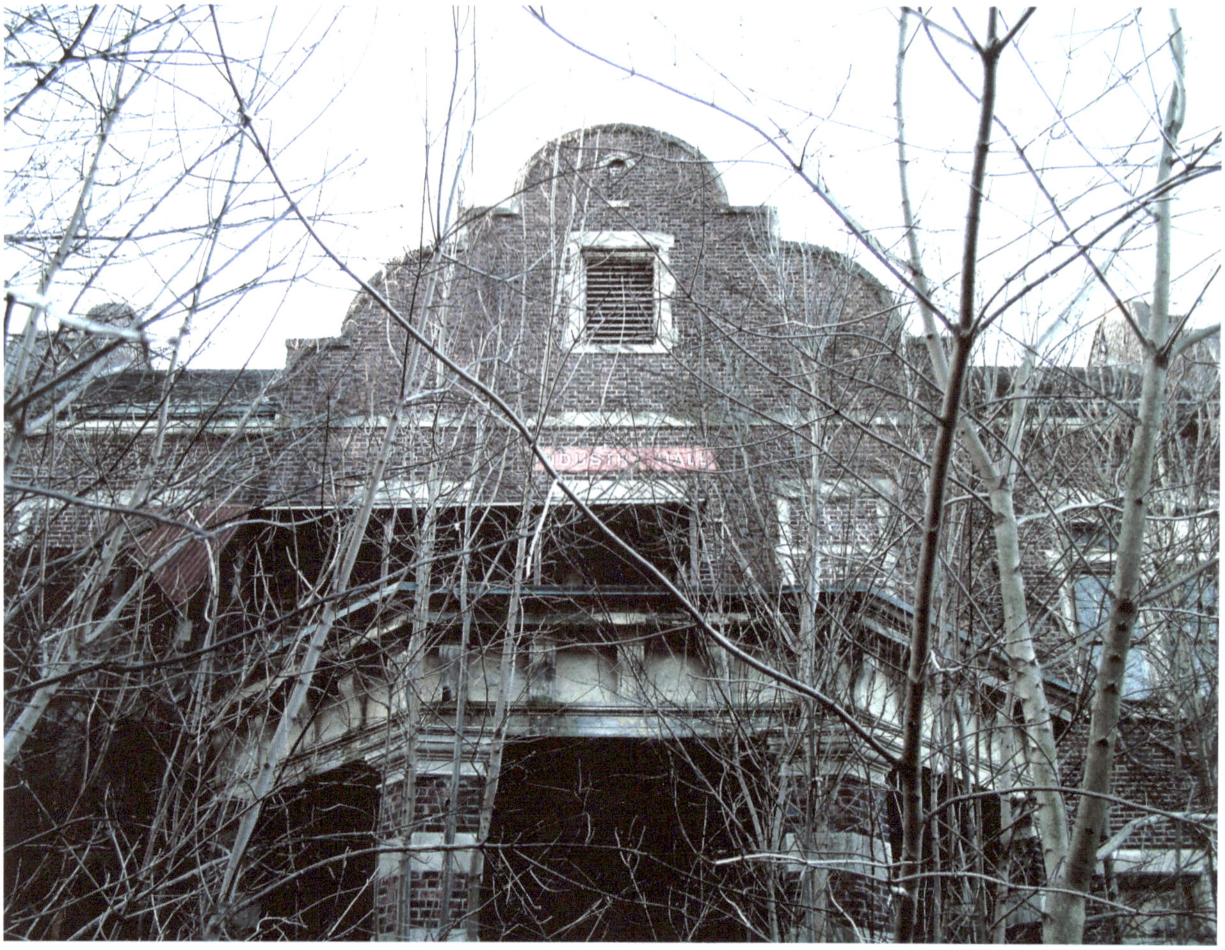

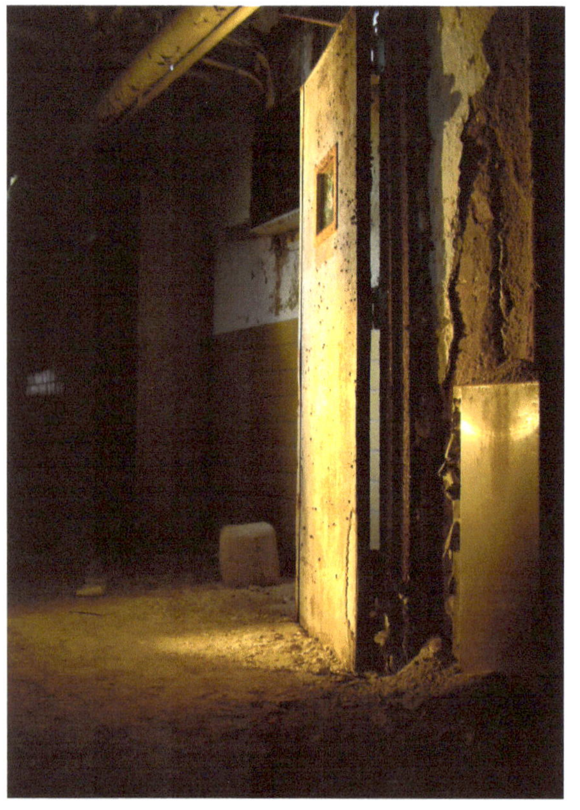

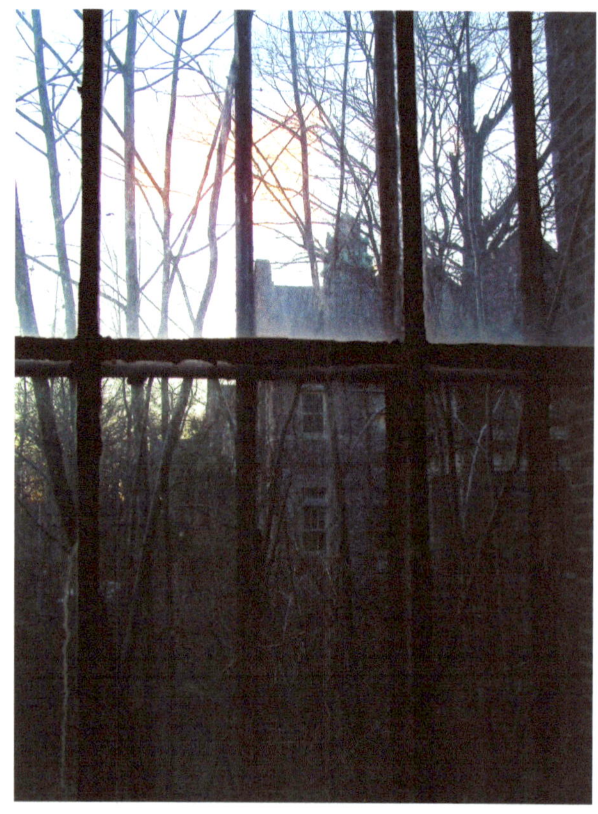

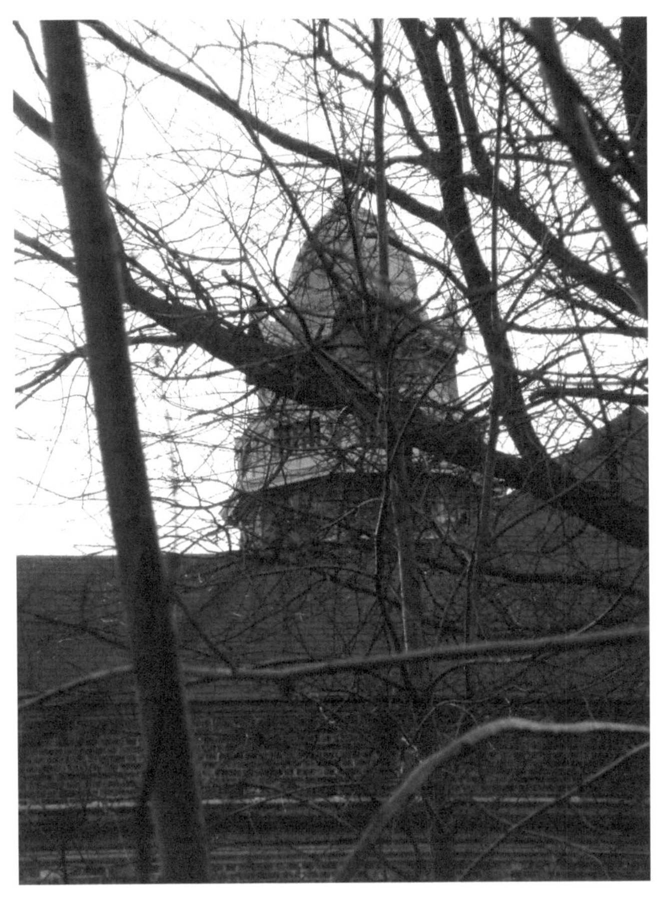

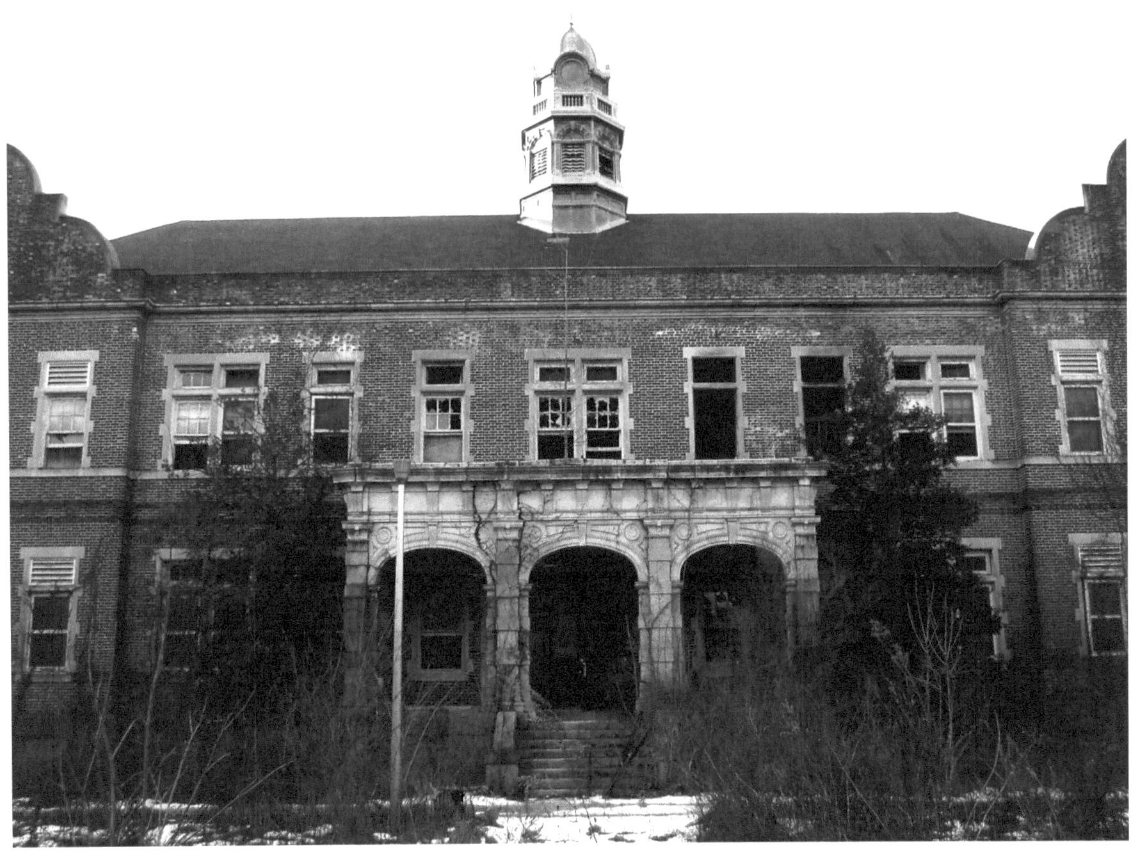

CHAPTER SEVEN

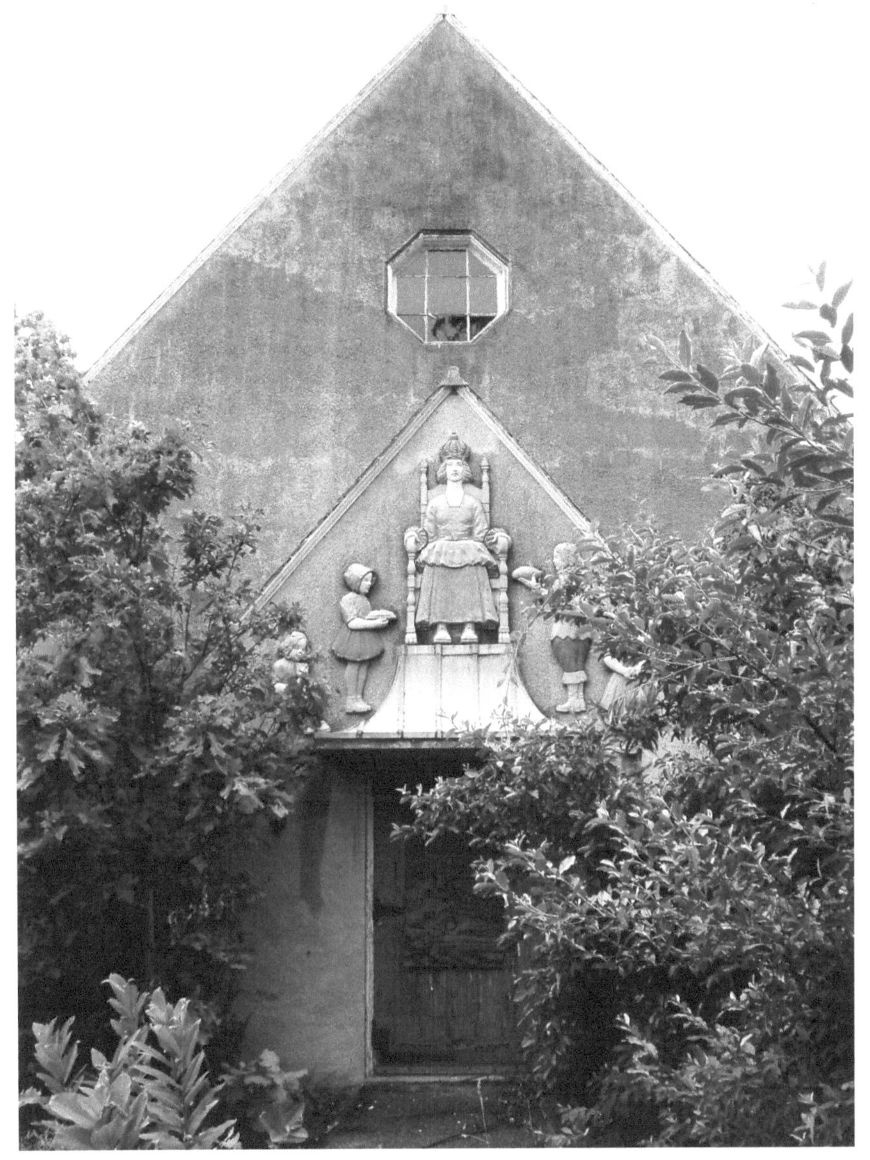

Lancaster Heights Tuberculosis Sanitarium

New England

Lancaster Heights Tuberculosis Sanitarium

Therapeutic Torture

I went to Lancaster with a relatively large group of travelers. There were only four of us, but that's like a mob when you're trying to be inconspicuous in the middle of the day. Billamack was our guide and this was John and Johnny's first abandoned building excursion. I think they got their money's worth with this place. It wasn't nearly as old and sinister as some of the turn of the century asylums, but it was full of medical apparatus. When this place shut down some hospital closure executive thought it imperative to remove all the everyday equipment like chairs, beds, office furniture and supplies. In their haste to cleanse the place of the mundane they left behind x-ray machines, an entire hydrotherapy suite, what appeared to be a fully functional pathology lab and countless other important looking medical equipment. It is possible that some of this equipment, even though it all looked functional, was critically outdated. After all, we did find iron lung machines and, to the best of my knowledge, those went out of fashion with leaded gasoline.

Since we had a guide we were forced to, you guessed it, walk a few miles. It was little drizzly that day, but there wasn't two feet of snow on the ground, it wasn't below freezing and we didn't have to walk uphill in either direction, so I suppose I couldn't complain. This place was on a busy road, so we did have to go through some woods. It was a short walk through the trees and we exited near the oldest building on the property.

There were several buildings in the complex. Two dorms, the newer contemporary hospital building and the oldest one, which resembles a chapel with cupolas and some very strange terracotta wall reliefs. We went past the older building because Billamack had not been in there before and it looked totally boarded up. That building was in a more advanced state of disrepair than the others. Apparently, it closed long before the hospital completely shut down. I noticed this a lot in my travels. Older buildings were abandoned as newer structures were added. These dark and shuttered places often sat right next to the active buildings.

We started with the older of the two dorm buildings. There were no boards on this building and we walked right in. It was in decent condition with no vandalism or graffiti evident. In fact, with a coat of paint, it could be probably be used for something practical rather than sit here and rot, but nobody asked my opinion on the matter so we just looked around inside. We covered the building from the top floor to the basement. Billamack was in search of a strange room he had heard about that contained a huge UFO looking contraption. We found nothing that resembled a spaceship, nor any rooms large enough to contain it. We did find a billiards table, but we were prevented from wasting time on a game or two because we had no balls.

From there, we headed over to the main hospital. We admitted ourselves and began the tour of the building. A brief stop on the first floor and then down to the basement we went. We wandered through huge areas critical to hospital function such as the kitchens, receiving areas and finally a flooded boiler room the size of a football field.

It was dark and murky in the basement and we almost passed right by the door to the pathology laboratory on our way back upstairs. Our flashlights revealed the morgue to be in such excellent condition that it looked as if a body could have been wheeled out moments before we got there. It was the quintessential Frankenstein's lab. There was an autopsy table complete with a tray of tools ready for the first incision. A shelf contained a wide selection of disgusting and unidentifiable substances in large glass jars along with empty glass beakers. Someone had left candles behind so we lit one and examined the room in the flickering light. While unnerving shadows danced across the walls, I brooded over what activity in an abandoned morgue would require candles.

We spent some time taking photographs of the area when someone suggested that we try out the body trays. I've never had much inclination to occupy one of those before it was absolutely necessary, but not wanting to spoil anyone's fun I went along. Johnny climbed in first. Of course, the first thing John did was slide the tray in and close the door. This didn't produce the desired frantic reaction so the door was reopened and the tray, with body, was slid back out. Everyone took a turn and then it was mine. I climbed up onto the tray with some trepidation and someone took a picture. It was a disturbing experience and one I'm not likely to repeat.

Extinguishing the candles, we left the morgue and its deathly gloom and took a stairwell upstairs. Our first stop on the upper floor was the auditorium. Old movie projectors must not have very much value because they were left behind here as in other places I've visited. The rain had intensified and the leaking roof high above us was a virtual waterfall. We exited the theater and continued roaming the floor.

The halls and patient rooms were, for the most part, devoid of anything but a musty smell. We did find several operating theaters, and they were empty too save for huge examination lights mounted to a track the ceiling. These were in such good condition that it was possible to move and aim them smoothly along the dolly system.

On another floor we came across a medical device of unknown purpose. It had a menacing look and appeared better suited to torture than therapy. The thing resembled a rack with pulleys and gears for what looked like a painful, or at least uncomfortable, treatment regiment. It sat upon a large, dark stain that further negated the hint of any rehabilitative purpose.

From there we found a fully equipped x-ray laboratory, a gynecological examination room, a urology suite and a hydrotherapy treatment area. This hydrotherapy room looked different than the archaic predecessors used in the older asylums. There were stainless steel hot tubs and a large chamber that was likely used to exercise patients against a stream of water pressure.

The rest of the hospital seemed empty until we found the room with the iron lungs. They looked like an extremely uncomfortable way to accomplish the normally automatic task of breathing. The patient was required to lay inside a long tube with their head poking through an airtight seal. The machine then supplied the air pressure necessary to compress the chest and force the lungs to move air. I felt pity for the afflicted that were unfortunate enough to require the utility of this contraption.

The day was getting long so we headed out of the main hospital building. We crossed the overgrown area between the buildings and bushwhacked our way towards the older building. We tried several doors that were either locked, nailed or screwed shut. It appeared that this doddering old building was more secure than the others. Until one of us trampled through a particularly weed choked area and found a wide open door. It was obvious at a glance that this antiquated space was crumbling apart at the seams. Doors were hanging by a hinge and the walls were a mess of flaking plaster. There was a basement, but the stairs had tumbled down into the shadowy darkness long ago.

We found a door with a startling image of a giant mosquito painted on its glass window. Beyond the door was a lab that, from the illustration, obviously had something to do with insects. I grimaced at the thought of insect testing in such close proximity to human patients. We passed through the lab, into another room, and came face to face with the "ufo thing" that Billamack was looking for. It was truly an unidentifiable object. It wasn't flying, but was firmly attached to the ceiling. It was twenty feet in diameter and had strange lights protruding from the bottom. After careful deliberation, we still had no idea what the thing was for. It was an oddball feature and looked especially otherworldly in the old building.

Wading out through the overgrown entrance we agreed to call our mission a success and head off the property. As we wended our way along the building we noticed one final eccentricity of this place. Above a door was deep relief sculpture depicting a Queen-like figure surrounded by children with offerings of some type. It was unsettling because the children were downcast and the Queen seemed to stare blindly into the distance. We turned our backs on this macabre presentation and bid farewell to the Lancaster Heights Tuberculosis Sanitarium.

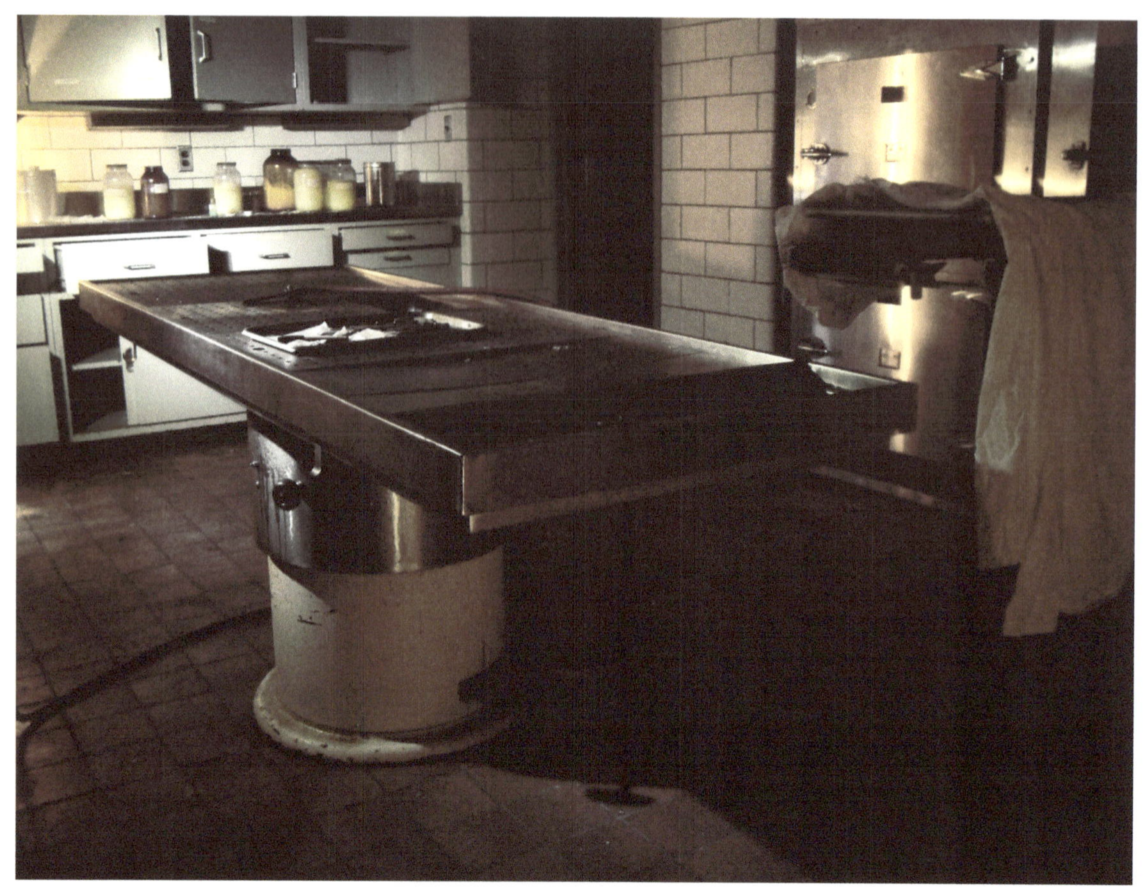

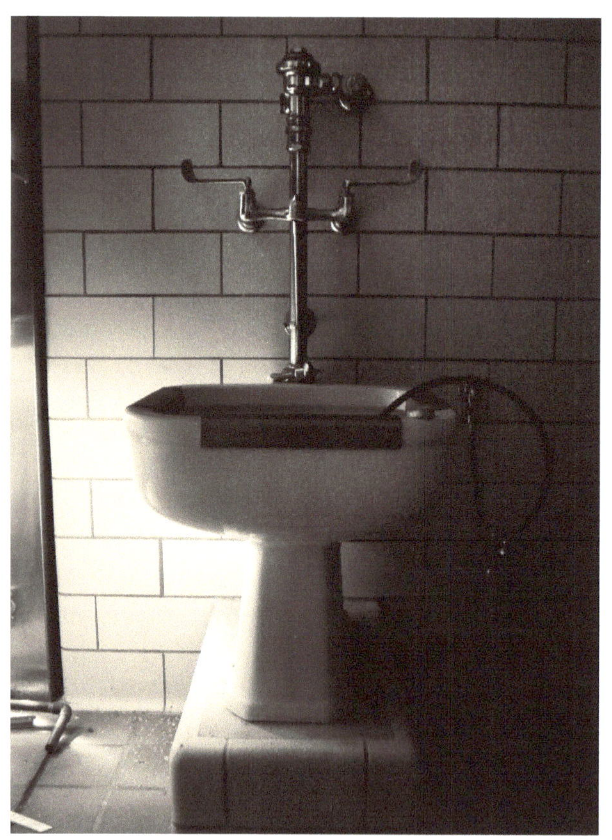

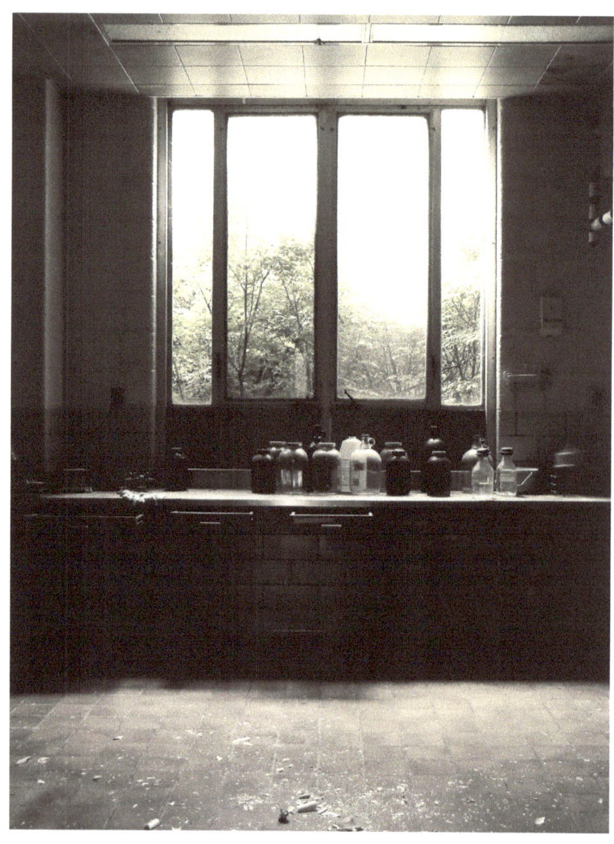

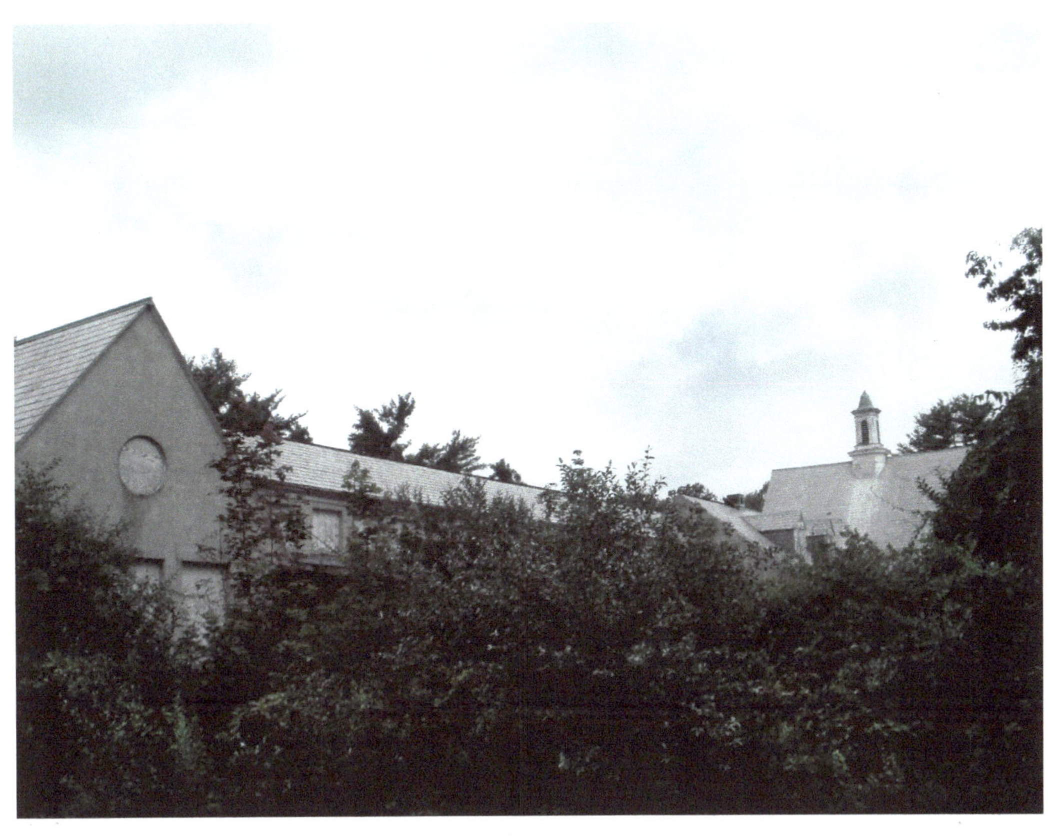

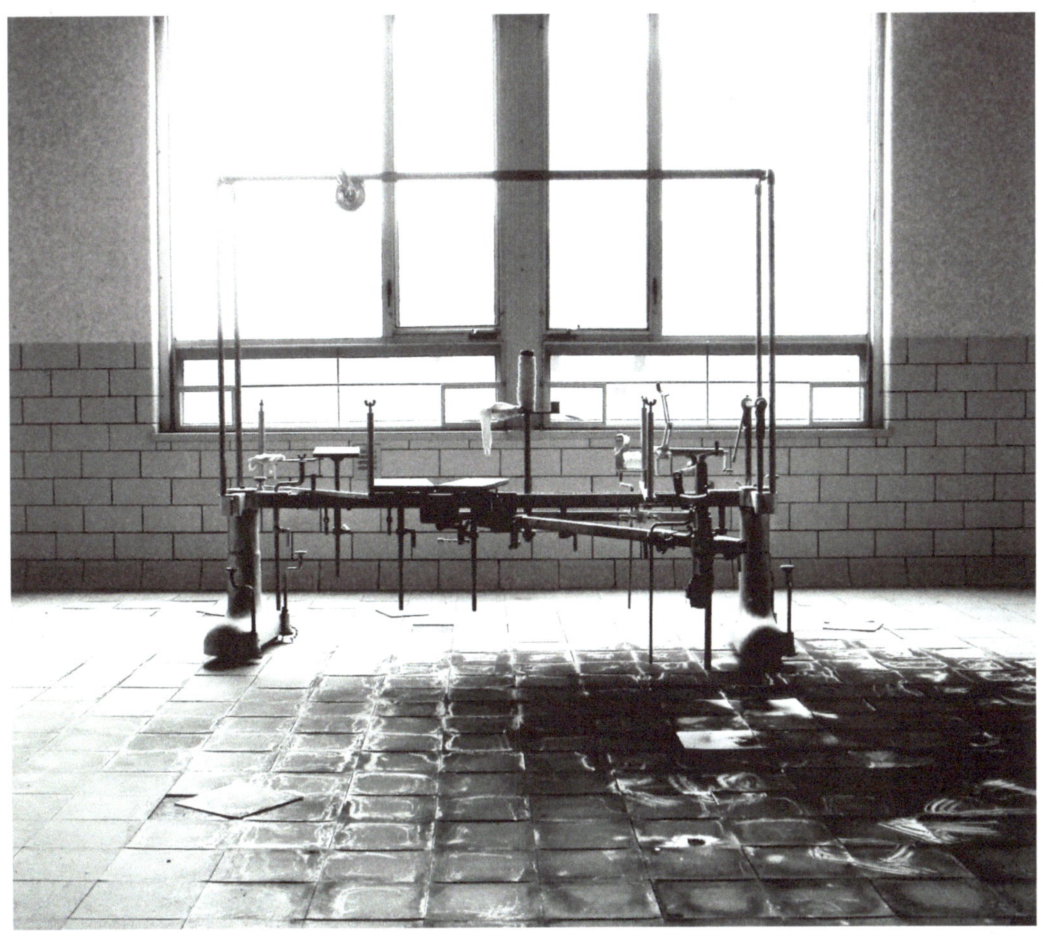

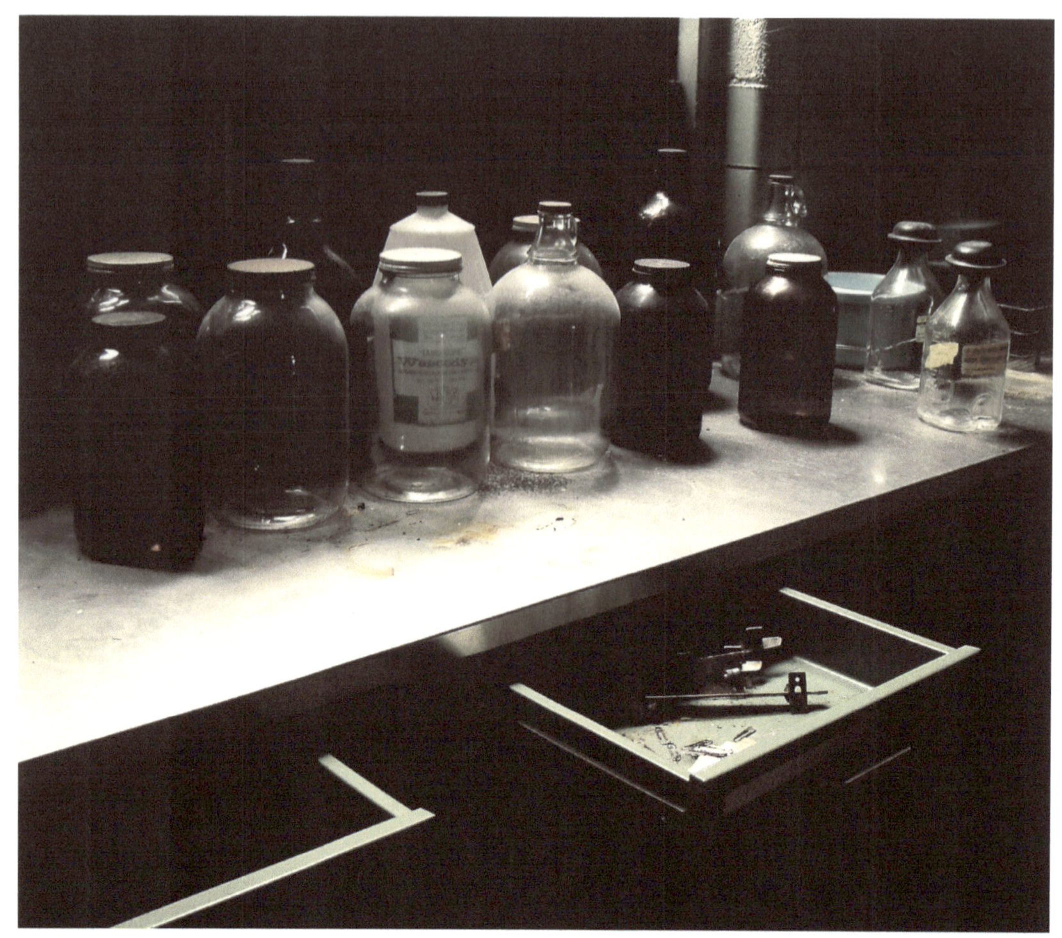

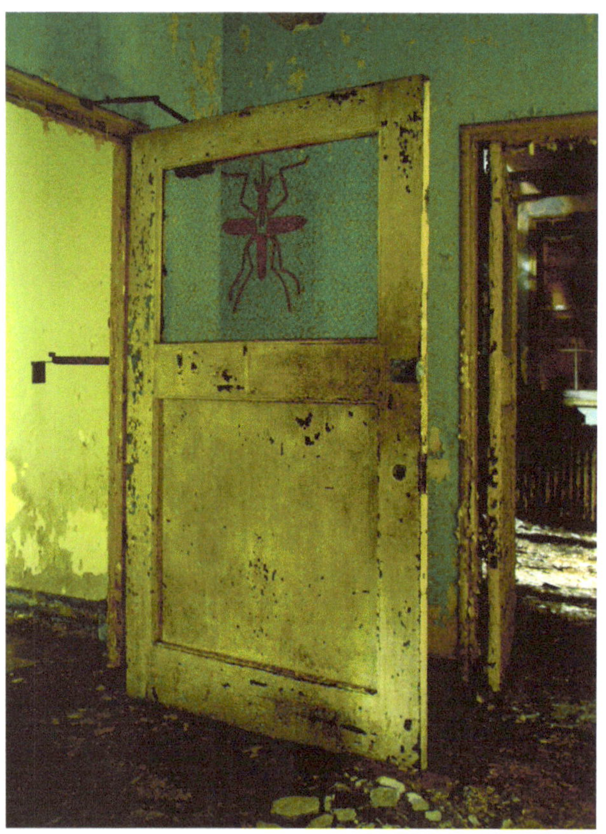

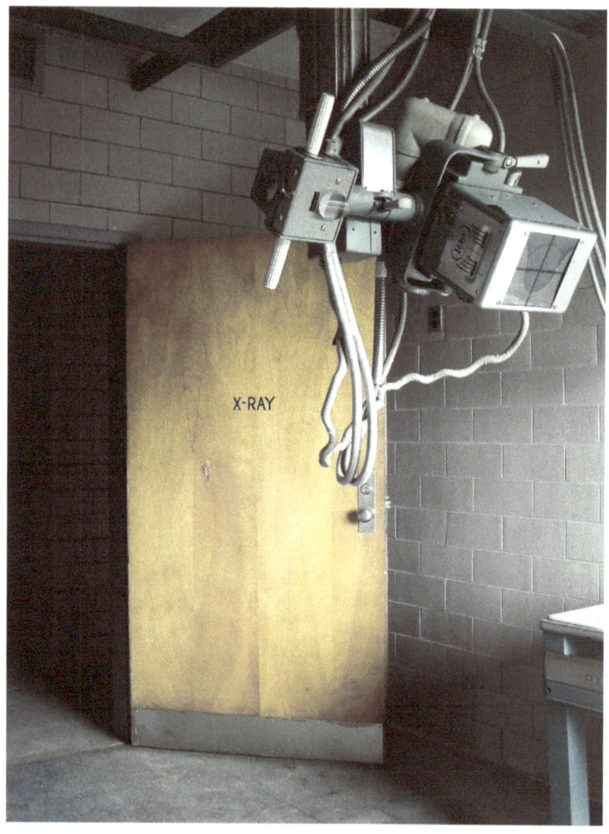
X-RAY

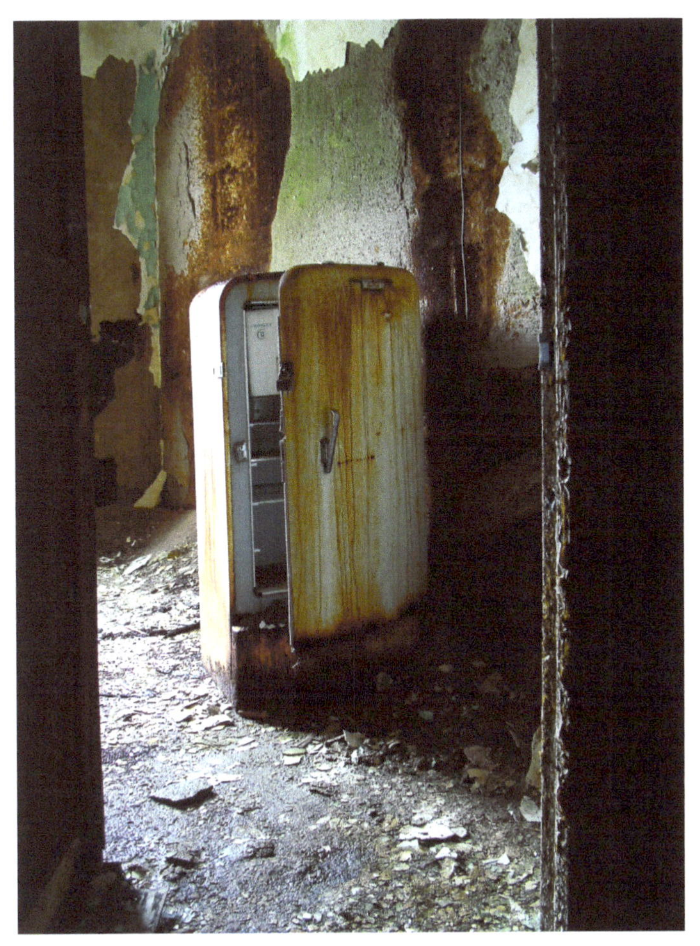

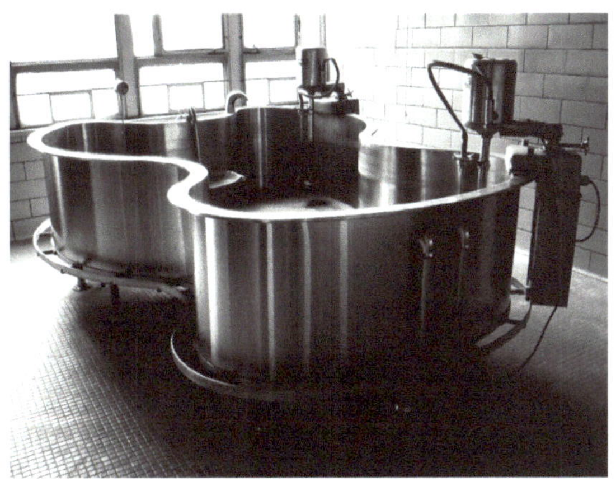

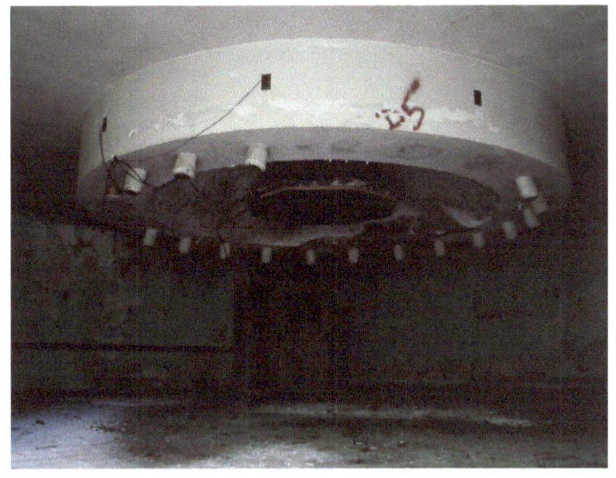

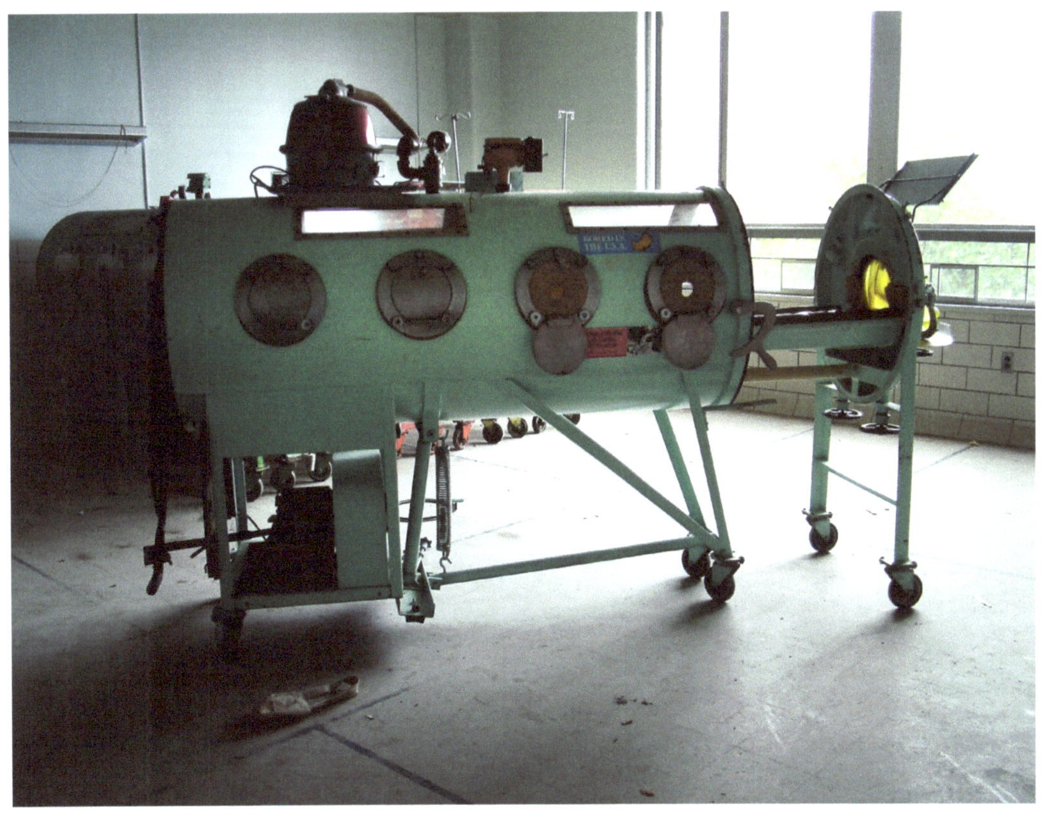

CHAPTER EIGHT

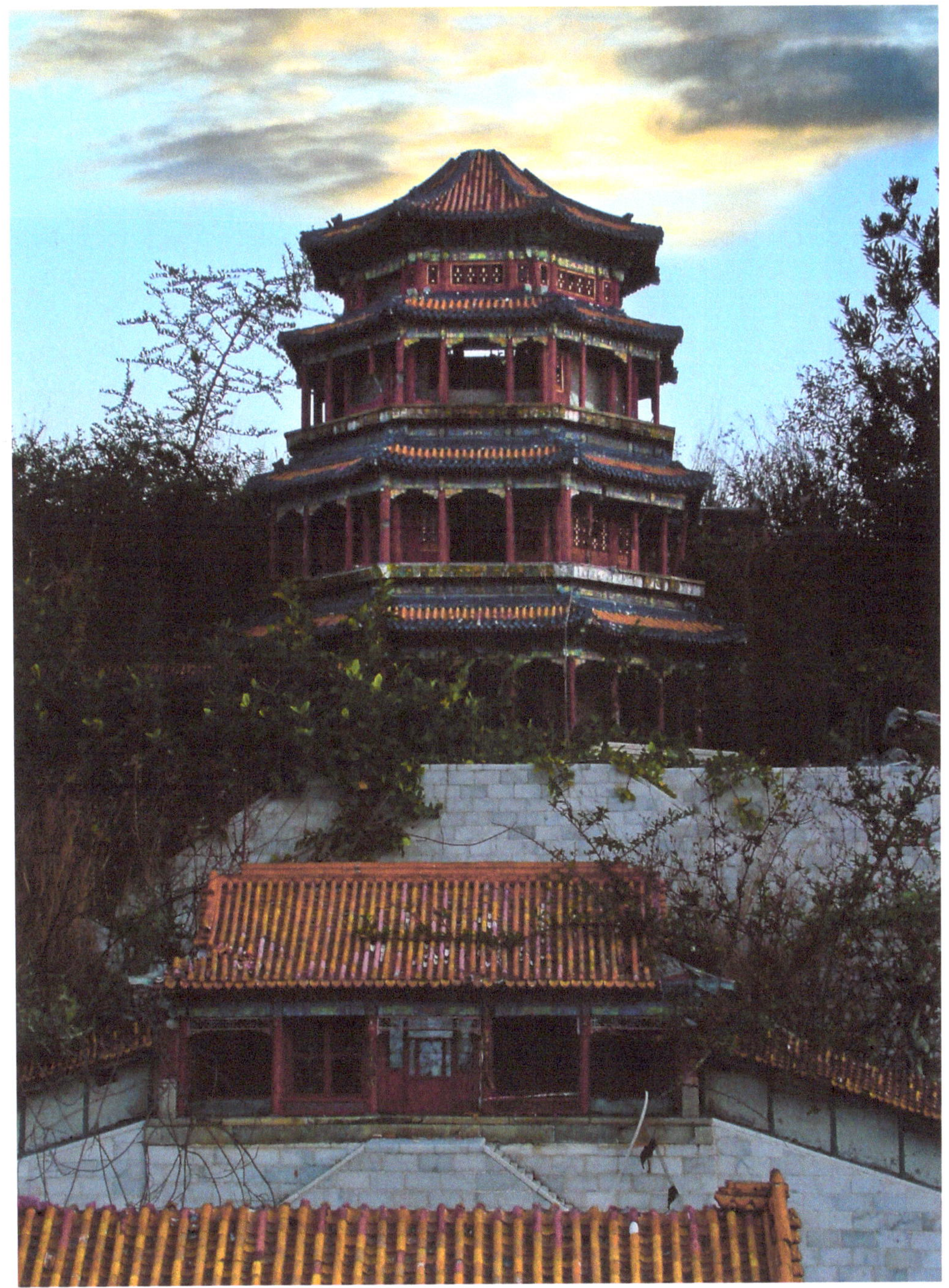

AMAZING ASIA

Florida

Amazing Asia

Crouching Tiger, Hidden White Elephant

Crouching in the Central Florida scrublands, not far from a much more famous theme park, is a hidden theme park of both epic and micro proportions. It is shrouded with international intrigue, clouded by financial ruin and utterly dishonored by vandals. Amazing Asia cost over $100 million dollars to build and it closed after only being open for ten years. While it was built in the U.S., it was literally Made By China because thousands of Asian workers were imported to build this seventy acre miniature version of their homeland. It included a scale model of the Great Wall, The Forbidden City, and a four-story tall Buddha, among other wonders of the Orient in miniature scale. While open, the park was beset by rumors that it was a propaganda machine of Communist China. It was picketed and protested by groups sympathetic to Tibetan and Taiwanese causes and finally suffered catastrophic financial losses that reportedly dwarfed even the massive initial price tag. Closed for good in 1993, with most of it's grandiose displays auctioned off, what's left of the park now forlornly meditates its fate ensconced behind its walls and iron gates. Luckily for us, it's front gates were left wide open. As we pulled into the parking lot one Saturday afternoon, a small group of us were delighted to find that there was no parking fee, no long lines and no admission tickets necessary to tour what was left of Amazing Asia. The former proprietors were even considerate enough to leave behind stacks of brochures and park maps, although we could only find Spanish language versions. It was a good thing too, because the park covers a sprawling, overgrown seventy acres. We started our tour in "Chinatown" which was a fairly bland collection of shops and restaurants. Quite a few of the stores still had merchandise left behind along with cash registers and other commercial equipment. When we visited, the park had been closed for over a decade and was heavily vandalized. Still, there was an amazing array of goods left behind. A visit the park the day after it closed must have been exactly as if it was open. Minus the tourists, of course. That day, we were the only tourists in sight and the park seemed embarrassed by its tawdry condition. The theater showed signs of a fire and crude graffiti was everywhere. I was starting to think this adventure was a waste of time until we exited the commercial area and glimpsed the first miniature building. As I mentioned before, most of the displays were previously auctioned off, but many were permanently built into the grounds. We stared in amazement at a six foot tall replica of an ornate Pagoda. The detail was breathtaking. Each roof tile was individually applied. The doors and windows were functional and had glazing within their frames and stairwells inside had tiny banisters attached. It was if a Lilliputian construction crew actually built the thing, brick-by-brick, from the ground up. We moved on and saw a giant mountainous structure looming in the distance. As we got closer, a sign told us that this was a replica of The Stone Forest, which is considered the First of the Seven Wonders of the World. The scaled down mountains led to the labyrinthine Zhiyun Cave. By now it was starting to get dark and the wending paths of the caves took on a gloomy, sinister feel. When we emerged from the caves, we were greeted by a 1/8 scale Buddha. The real Buddha must be truly epic, because his little American brother was forty feet tall. He smiled peacefully at us through splatters of spray paint and paintball stains. Considering his size, rubbing his belly probably would have brought lifetimes of luck, but we had other sites to see, so no one chose to scale his massive girth for a rub. The place is full of winding paths and even with map in hand, we were soon lost among the overgrown displays. Some directional signs remained, but not enough to give us a point of reference. We wandered in large, looping circles for a bit, only aware of our misdirection by seeing the same displays over and over. Finally, we struck off through what looked like a field and stumbled on The Forbidden City. Of course, someone in our group had to do the Godzilla thing and quietly rampage the City. I told him that Godzilla was in Japan, not China, but who can argue with someone pretending to be a six-foot nuclear lizard? His rampage waned (not that he would have, but there was nothing left to destroy; sadly the display had been smashed by vandals) and we moved on. Our next bit of amazement came when we saw The Great Wall on a small hill. Again, we were taken by the amazing detail. I later learned that this model was constructed of seven million individual one inch bricks and was over a half mile long. The amount of man-hours necessary to lay that many tiny bricks is staggering. After the Wall, the other remnants of the displays paled by comparison. Until we stumbled on an underground cave. We peered into the gloomy entrance with our flashlights and wondered if we should proceed. Vagrants are always a risk in abandoned places and an underground cave would also make a nice, safe place for animals to bunk down. Of course, our curiosity got the best of us and down we went. What we found was a wasteland of potsherds and terra-cotta rubble. I bent down and picked up a human hand. Nearby was a horse's hoof. The it dawned on me; This was a model of the Terra-Cotta Warriors which was unearthed in China in 1974. Again, the vandals had beat us here and destroyed this once amazing reproduction. The detail of the shards and pieces that were left spoke of the extreme talent of the artisan's hand. It must have been simply breathtaking prior to it's destruction. The depth of ignorance it takes to destroy something of such craftsmanship and detail never ceases to amaze me. From what I could tell from the remains, it looked as if the the figures in the display were each about four feet tall and included individual warriors, warriors on horseback and even horse-drawn battle carts. From their sad current condition and the amount of rubble, it seemed as is someone had spent an awfully long amount of time with a baseball bat to fell these once proud warriors. Depressed by the pointless destruction, we exited the cave and finished our tour. Along the way we saw a completely burned out wooden pavilion of unknown purpose along the path. I suppose if there was a fire in the park, the fire department would have a hard time wending their hoses through this maze of weed choked paths. It may be prudent to not risk lives for this abandoned mess and finally just let it burn. We then stumbled upon a huge entertainment pavilion that our brochure indicated once held shows of dancers, martial artists and animals. The night was getting long so we decided to find our way out the Orient for the night. This proved easier said than done because of the sheer scale of the place. We wandered around for a bit more until we finally found a breach in the outer wall and exited Amazing Asia for the night.

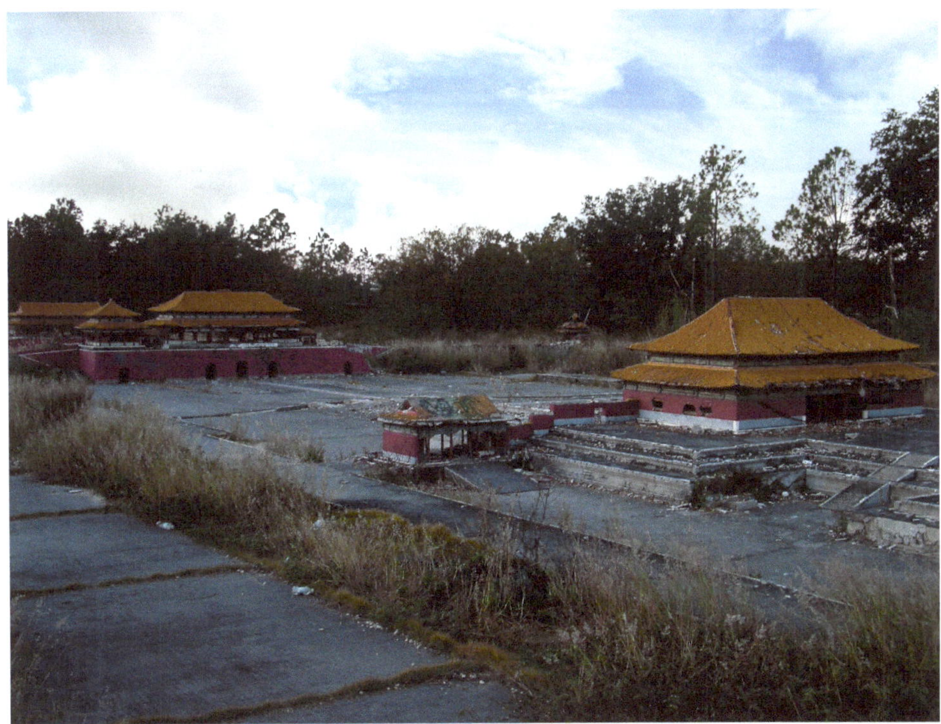

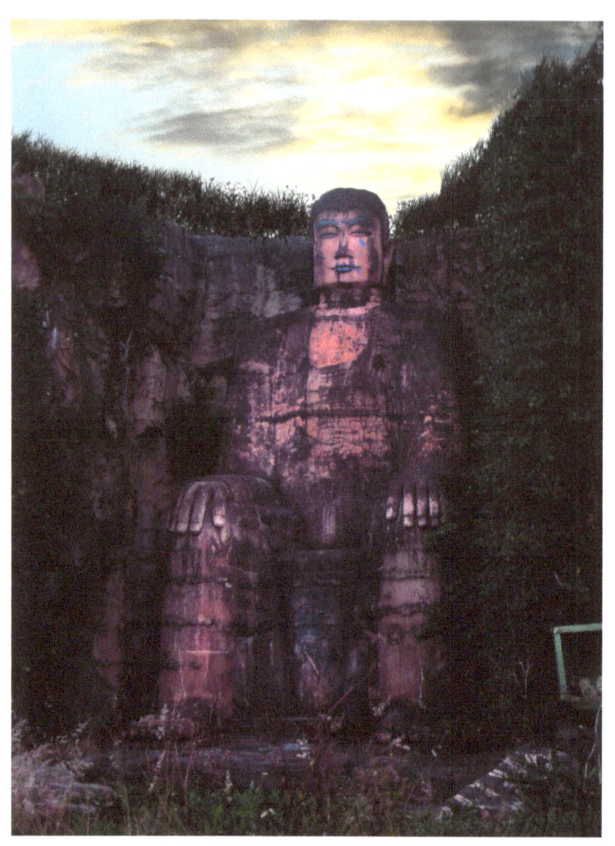

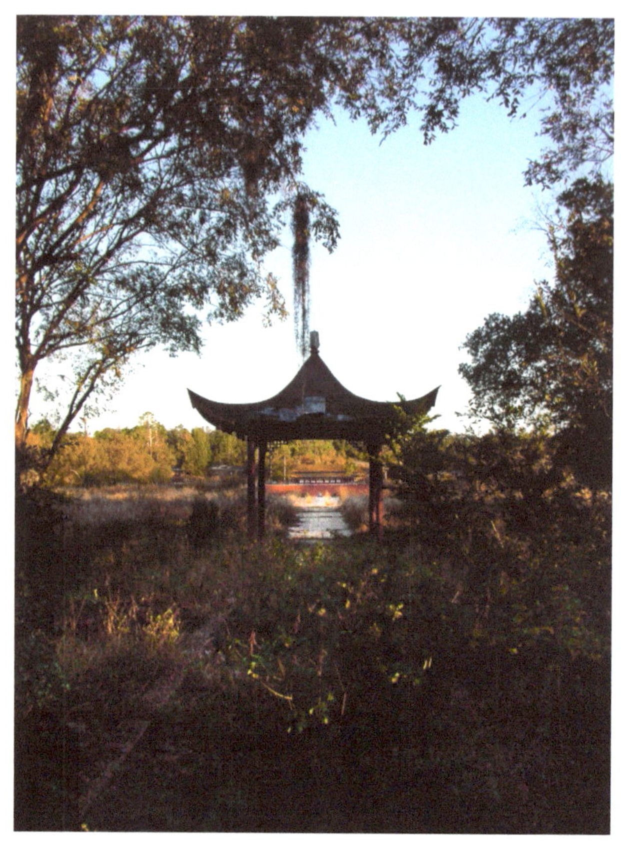

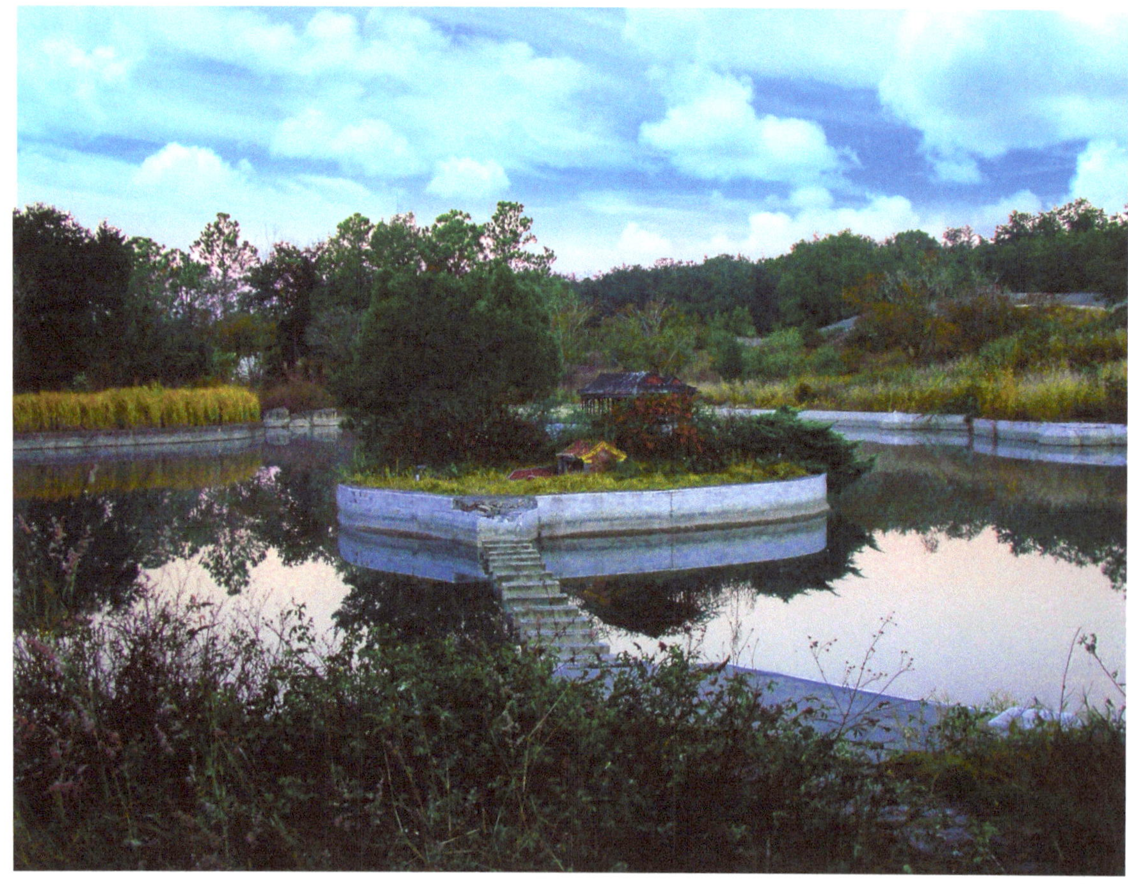

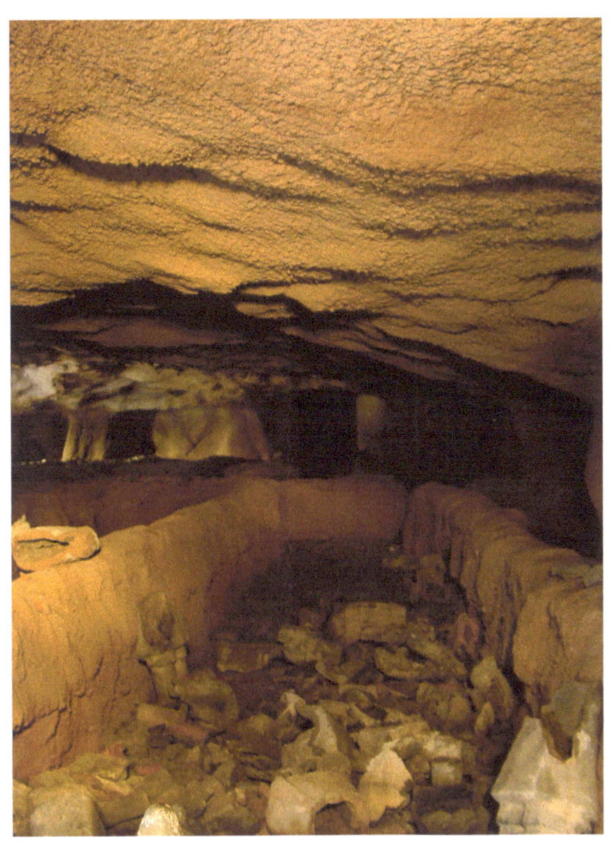

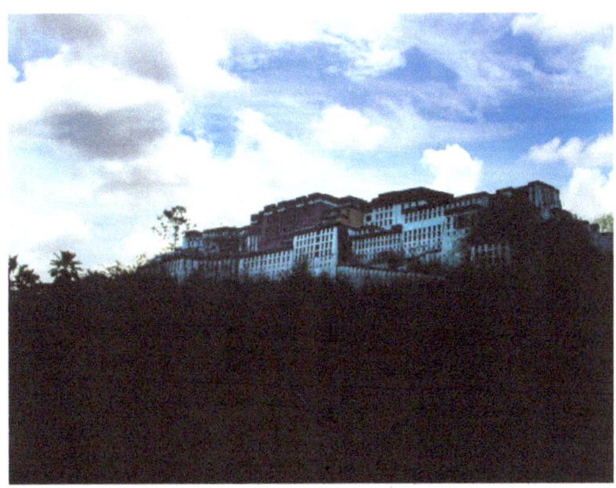

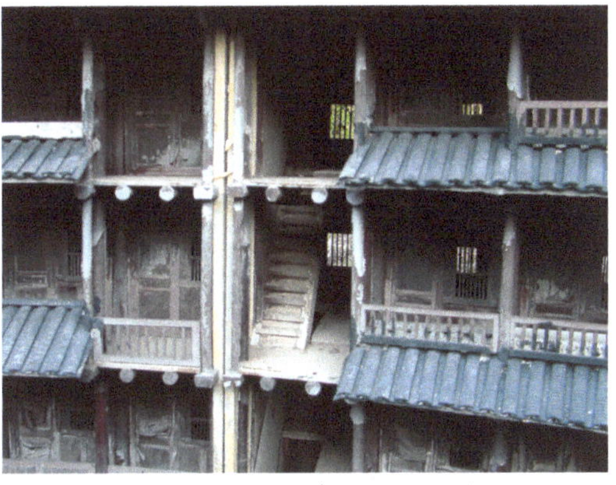

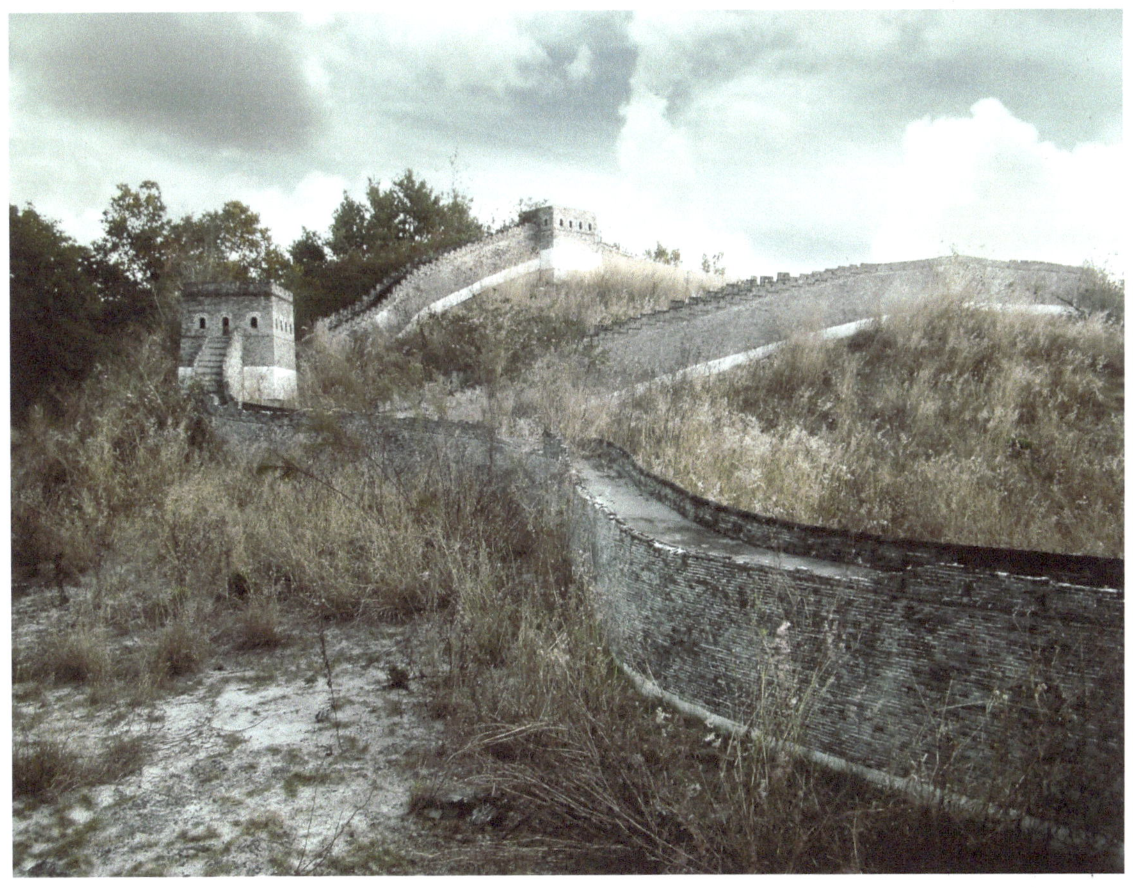

CHAPTER NINE

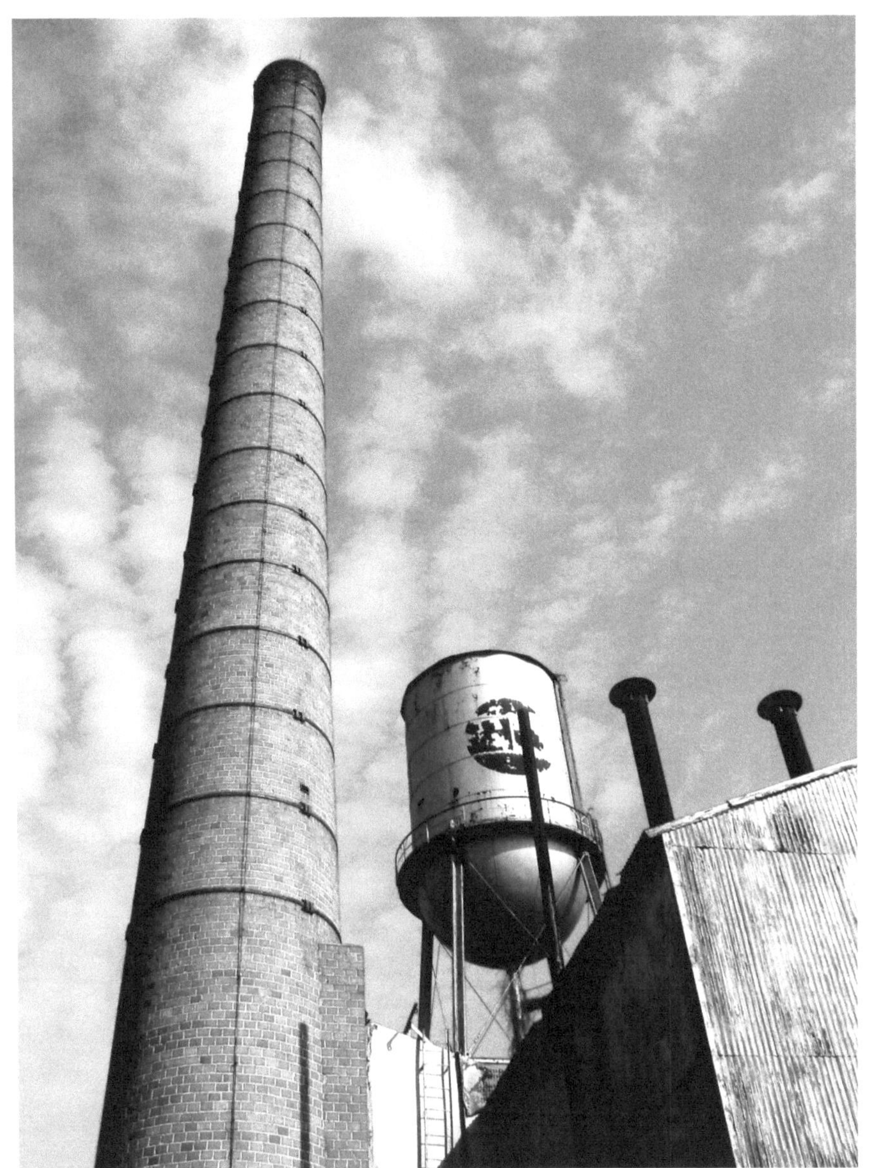

The Rat Factory

Florida

The Rat Factory

A Good Place To Die

I was heading to an art show with fellow artist Steele and his daughter Syd. Steele prides himself on knowing the most obscure possible route to any given destination. We were about five miles east of nowhere when we stumbled upon this foundry. As we drove past, I asked if they wanted to go back and have a closer look. They knew of my fascination with the abandoned so they agreed.

We pulled up and saw a for sale sign and realized that it wasn't technically abandoned. Acting like we were in the market for an old run down factory we got out and began taking pictures. It was a utilitarian structure consisting of a redbrick smokestack attached to one side of a rusting metal building with a matching rusty water tower. The stack is what caught my eye so we examined that first. It was large and seemed almost too tall for the scale of the building. After crawling in through an opening in the side of the stack, I looked up and saw a passage leading into the building. It was accessed by an old metal ladder that looked like it would crumble to the touch. Steele wanted to climb it and get inside but I thought it wasn't a safe idea.

A quick walk around the other side of the building revealed that the rusty ladder wasn't necessary at all. The huge rolling doors on this side were open enough for us to pass through. Since we were in the role of prospective buyers, we thought we would be remiss in not inspecting the interior.

We were treated with a time capsule of aged industrial equipment. Much of it was unidentifiable by us, but we did glean that this used to be a foundry. There was huge brick blast furnace in the center that rose at least three stories, maybe more. A metal catwalk surrounded it and Steele promptly climbed up and wandered around. This, of course, made Syd and myself nervous. The last thing we wanted to do was carry Steele out on a makeshift stretcher and attempt to find a hospital in the middle of a rural area. He finally climbed down and we poked around snapping pictures.

The floor crunched under our feet and we finally noticed the cause. The entire place was blanketed with rat skeletons. It seemed every available surface was littered with the little bones. Some were ground into an off white dust, and some were mostly fragments, which is why we didn't notice them at first. In the less trafficked areas, like behind and inside the furnace, there were fully intact specimens. I've encountered the occasional dead animal in abandoned places but never anything like this. To this day, we have no idea why so many rats were attracted to that factory. The only thing we could reason was that the place was empty so long it became an erstwhile rat graveyard. Perhaps there was some rodent psychic connection and they knew to go there and die. I have no other answer and all I can say is that it was weird and creepy and little revolting.

Steele and I spent a little while longer in there while Syd waited outside. She was not too keen on the whole rat graveyard concept and went outside for a breath of fresh air. We quickly finished up and left.

I haven't been back that way so I have no idea what became of the Rat Factory. For all I know, it still sings its siren song and calls the elderly and infirm rat population to their final resting place.

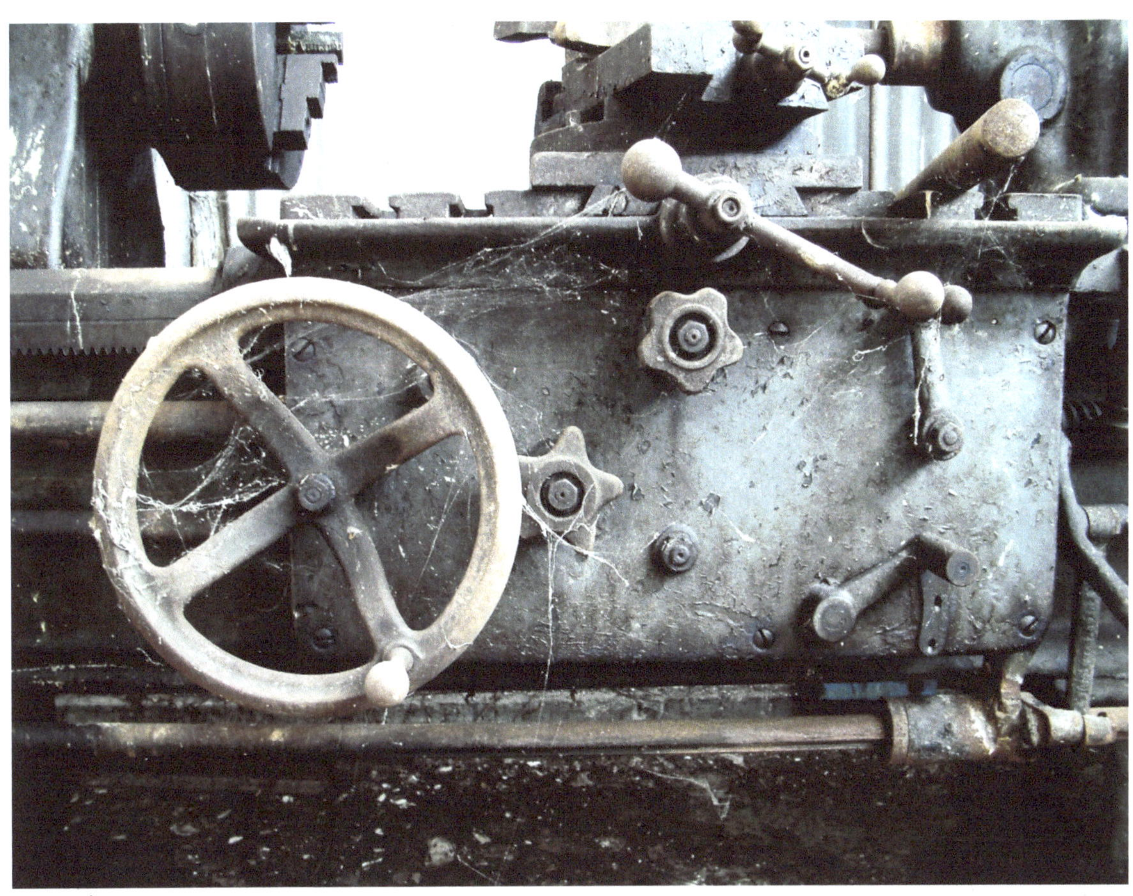

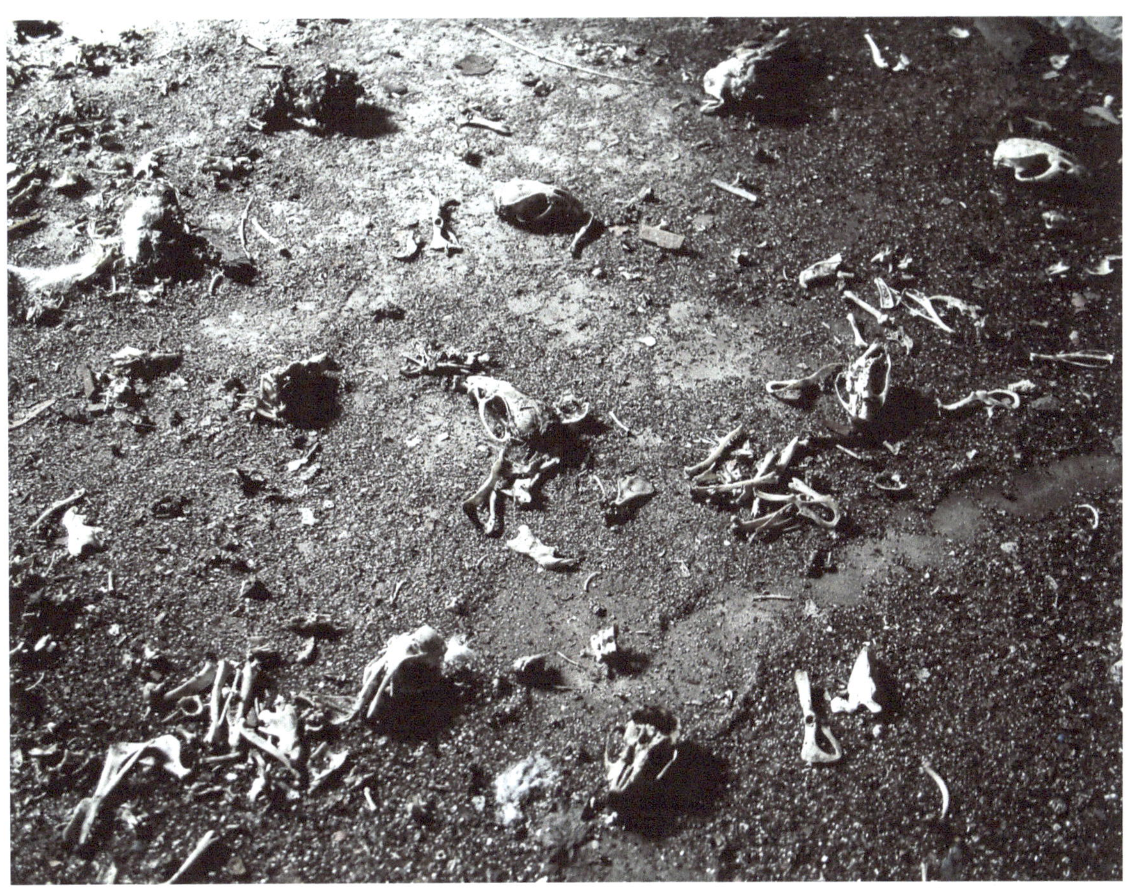

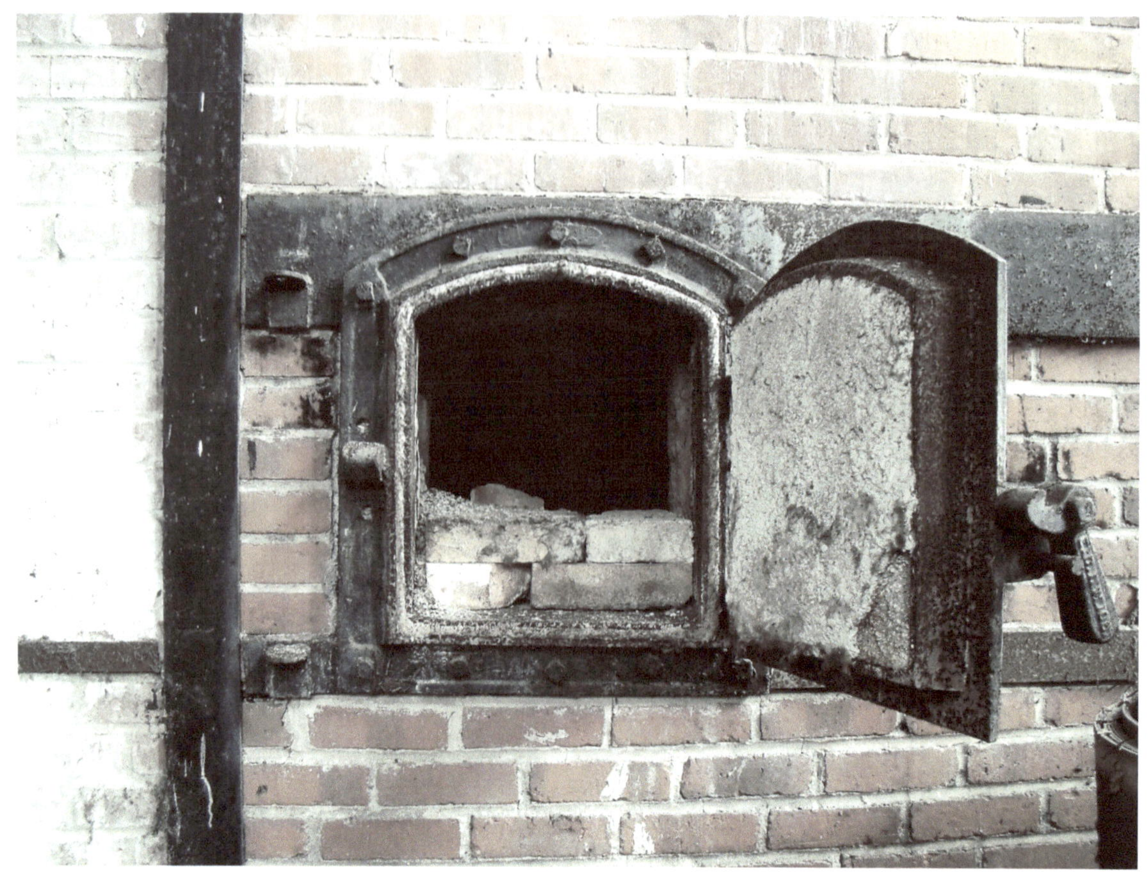

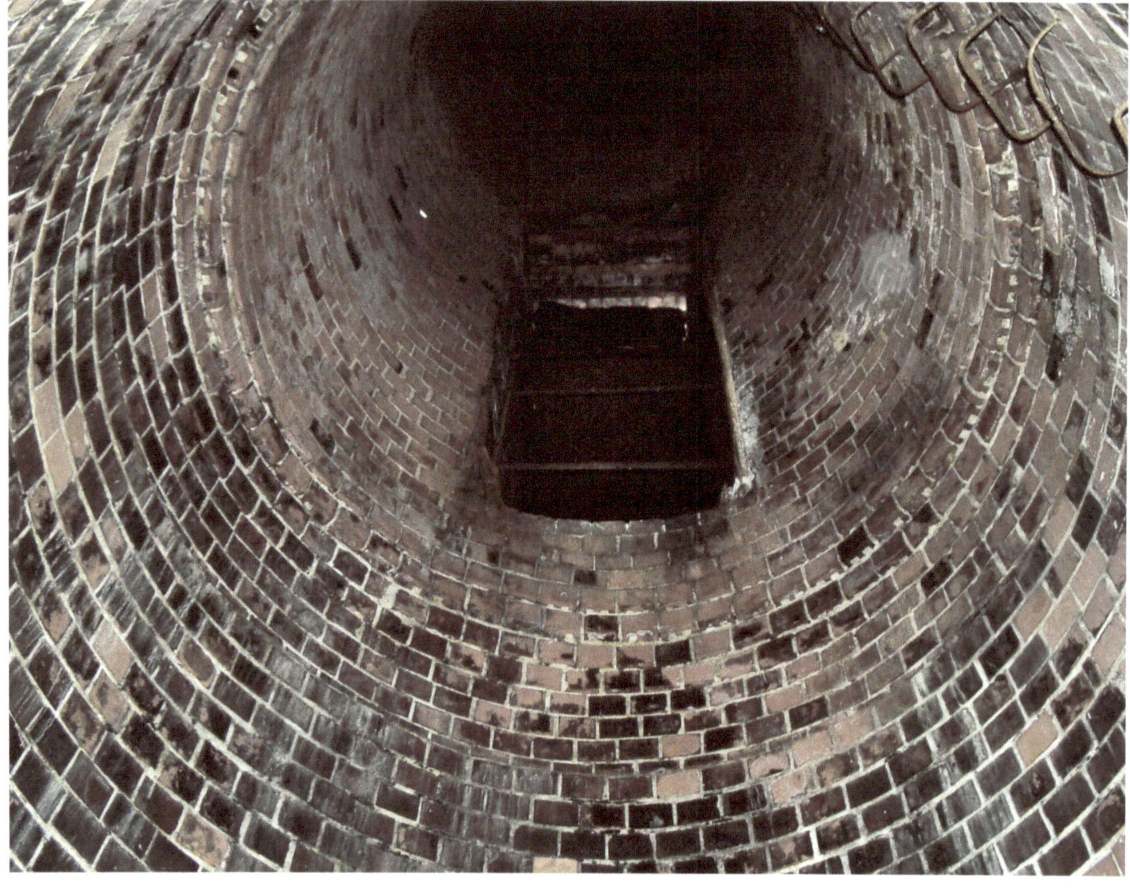

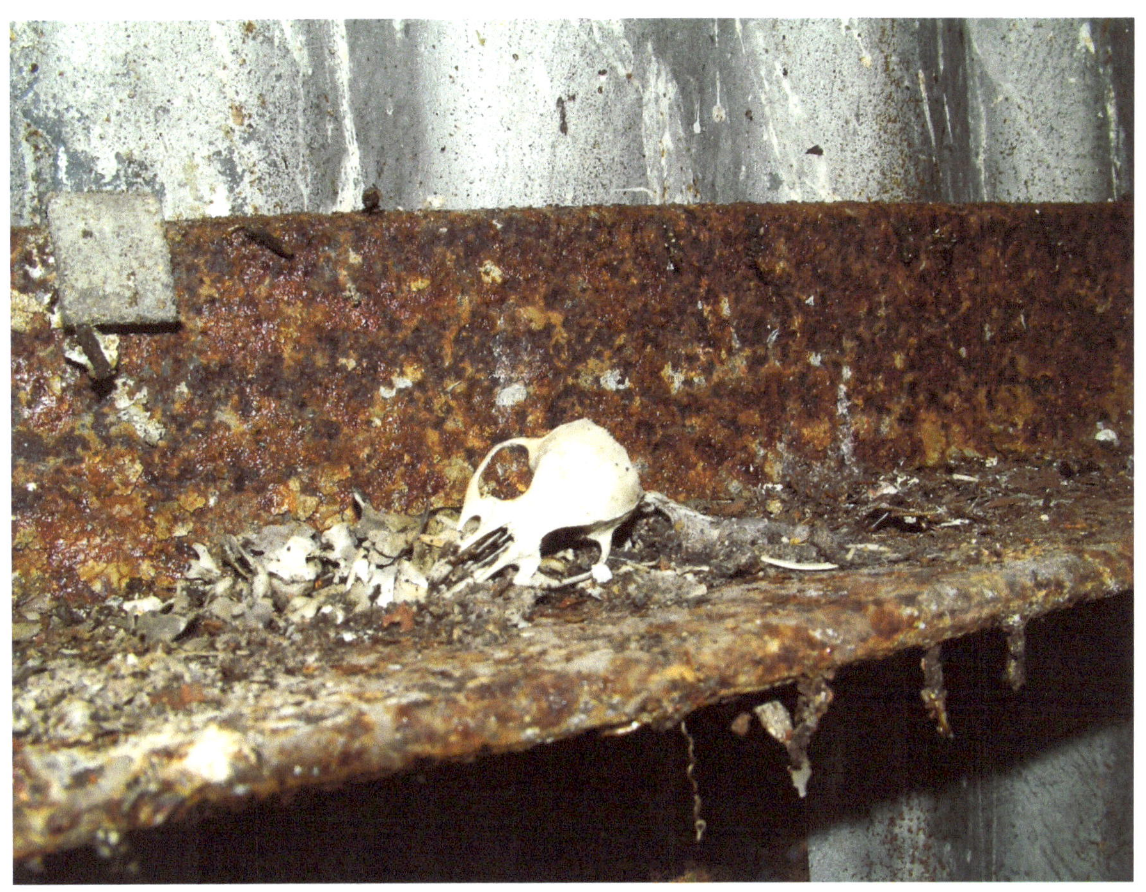

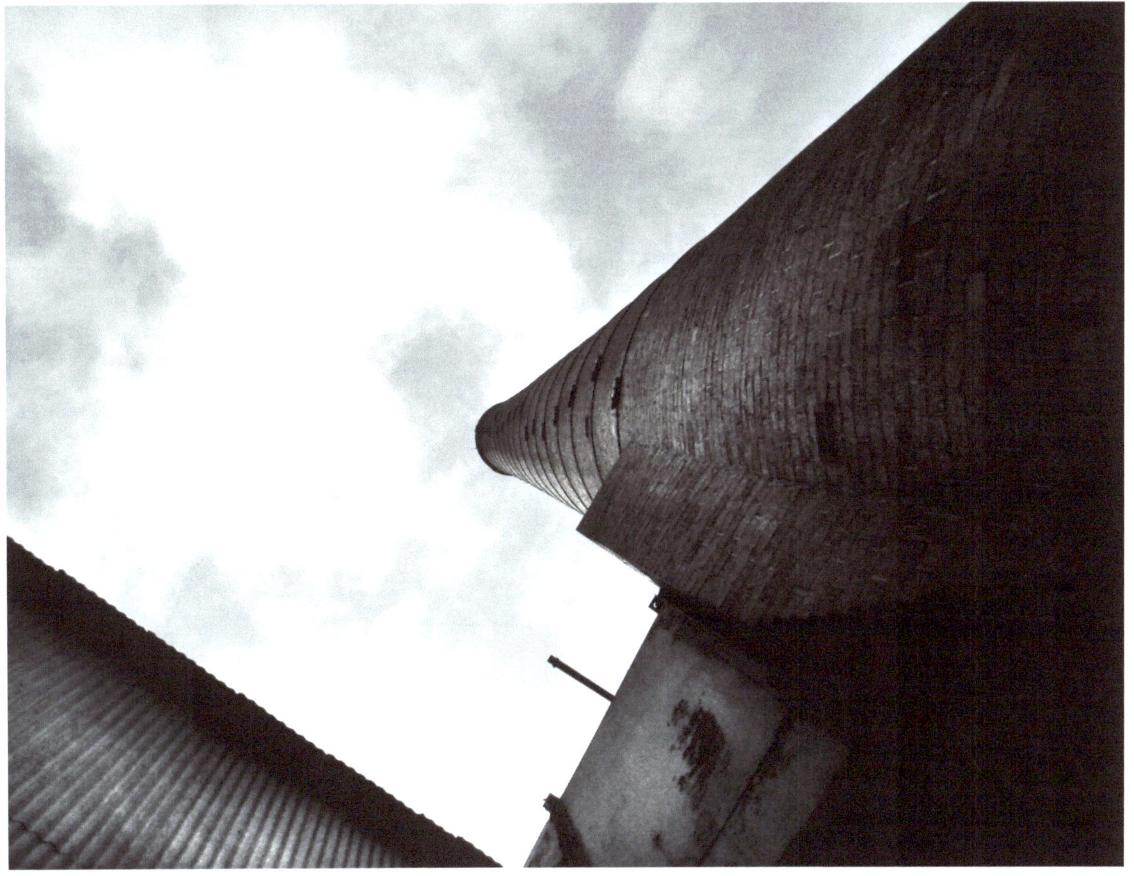

Sightseeing

Outside tours only. These sites were unaccessible at the time or not interesting enough to risk entering.
Several will be visited on future Day Trips.

CHAPTER TEN

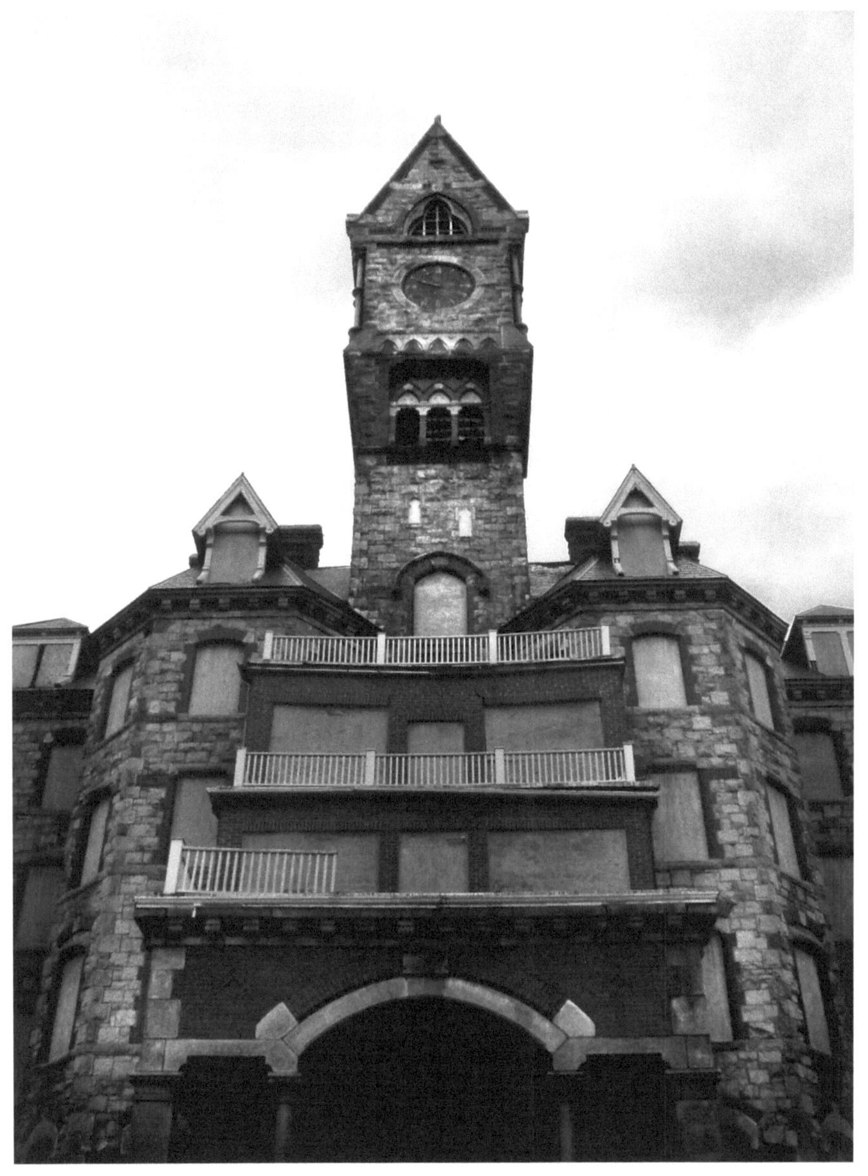

WORCESTER LUNATIC ASYLUM

Massachusetts

Worcester Lunatic Asylum

A Madhouse Designed by A Madman

I tried to convince Billamack and his crew to join me for a visit to Worcester Lunatic Asylum after we toured Metropolitan State Hospital. They all had other plans, so I headed out on my own. I arrived at the entrance to the modern, active psychiatric center that borders the older buildings and drove up the road leading to the complex.

Before I got to the older Kirkbride Building, its distinctive clock tower loomed above the trees. The Gothic architecture was chilling to say the least. As I got closer, some trick of construction made the clock tower seem to loom out over the road. I pulled the car into an area appropriately labeled "clock tower parking." I got out and gazed up at one of the most bizarre asylums I have ever seen. It looked like the architect couldn't decide what material to make this thing out of. Most of it was rough-hewn gray granite, other parts were smooth granite and other parts were red brick. There were wooden railings and delicate window treatments mixed with the hard, cold stone. The clock tower seemed scaled all wrong for the size of the building, which had octagon, square and round features. It looked like a madman designed this madhouse. If ever a building resembled it's intended purpose it was this one. It was almost comically weird.

Add to this crazy mishmash hawks perched menacingly on top of the tower and bats fluttering out the broken windows and you have a horror castle of epic proportions. This place lived up to its grim appearance over the years by stockpiling the criminally insane in sub standard conditions. There were rumors of shackles in the cellar, mass showers, and a prison-like environment along with all the other so called treatments of the era.

Hydrotherapy was among one of these supposed cures. The process originally consisted of lashing a patient in a tub under a canvas tarp with only their head sticking out. Ice-cold water was then poured under the tarp and the "lunatics" then spent hours wallowing in their own excrement all the while screaming from the agony of the freezing water. The idea of the treatment was two fold: it was believed that mental illness was, in part, caused by "overheating" of the brain. Cooling the patient would solve that problem. The other purpose was to distract the troubled mind so that it couldn't focus on its insanity. The treatment obviously didn't affect the intended result and most patients came out of this torture worse than when they went in.

The other revolutionary treatment practiced here, and at other asylums, was the lobotomy. This involved hammering a long ice pick into the frontal lobe of the patient's brain through a tear duct in the corner of the eye socket. The pick was then wiggled around, destroying brain tissue. There is extensive study showing that this procedure had amazing results in some patients. In others, it simply turned the patient permanently and irrevocably catatonic. In a way, I suppose it served its purpose. If a mental patient prone to violence could be reduced to a drooling zombie he couldn't hurt himself or anyone else.

The lobotomy was looked upon with horror in modern times and by the 1950's most states had banned its use. The Massachusetts General Hospital of Boston performed this operation all the way up to the 1980's. Massachusetts seemed to be the asylum capitol of the U.S. and it's appropriate that they would hold on to this archaic mix of treatment and torture for so long.

I wandered around taking pictures of the building with thoughts of these horrors capering about in my mind. The overcast and quiet Sunday afternoon provided the perfect mood of despair. The close proximity of the active mental institution added to general feeling of insanity that pervaded this campus and I wondered what the current patients thought when they looked out their windows at this creepy place.

Worcester has been abandoned for decades and in 1991 it suffered a devastating fire. Huge sections of the original Kirkbride wings are gone, giving it a disconnected look. At least back then, the city officials appreciated the structure for historical value and took efforts to stabilize the building. Stone from the burned sections were used to seal up the gaping holes in an attempt to protect the building from the elements. I wonder if that effort would be taken if the building burned today. The rash of demolitions and redevelopment being perpetrated at other historic asylums tells me probably not.

I knew from other experienced travelers that it was difficult, but not impossible to get in. However, I didn't really have an intention of trying to enter any of the buildings that day. The hospital next door surely had a security patrol. I had to catch a flight home later that afternoon and I didn't want to be delayed by an ambitious guard. I made note of the layout and saved this creepshow for another day.

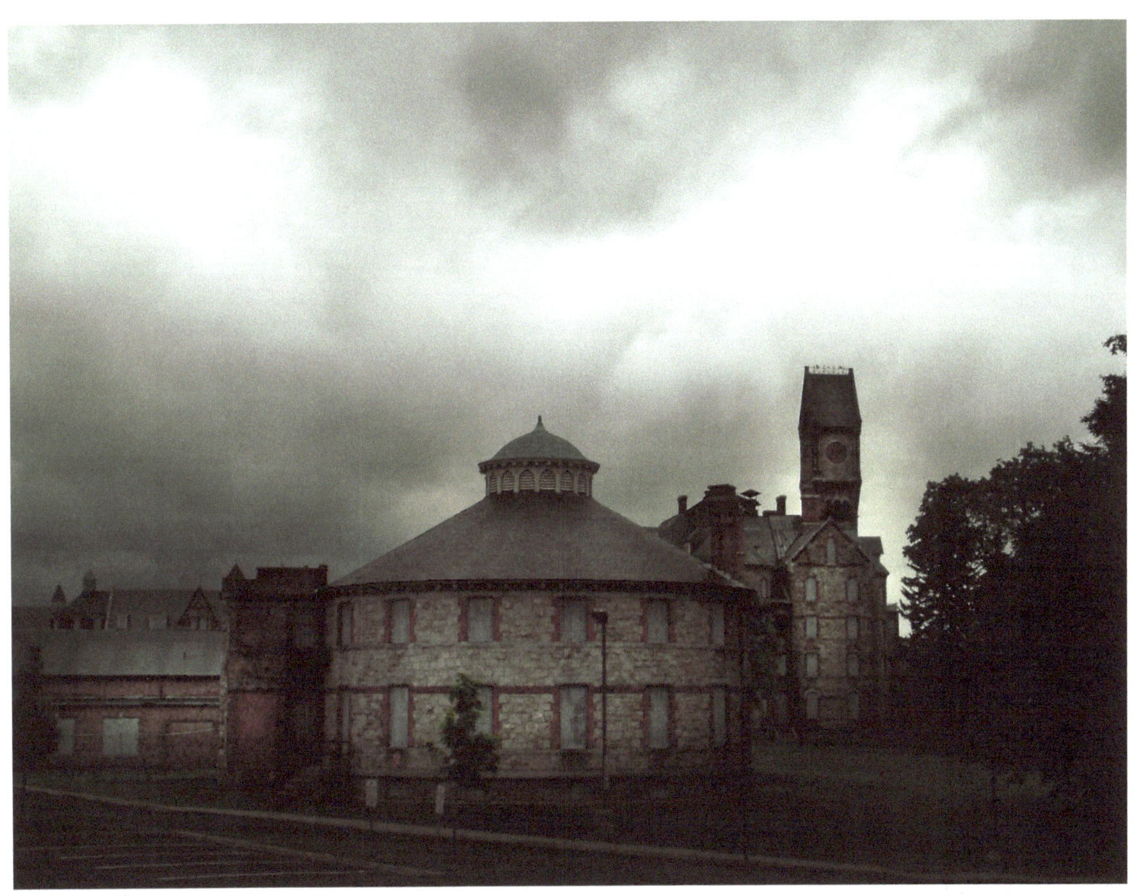

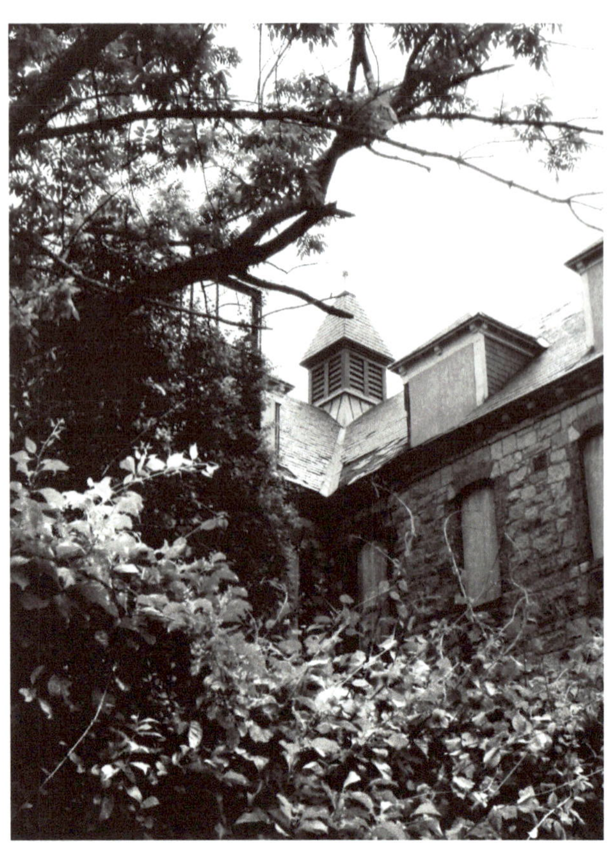

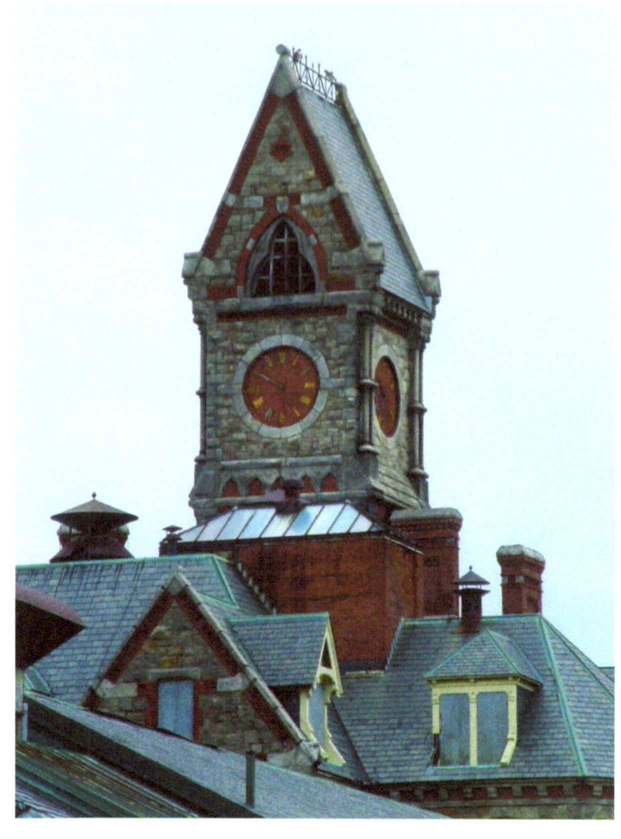

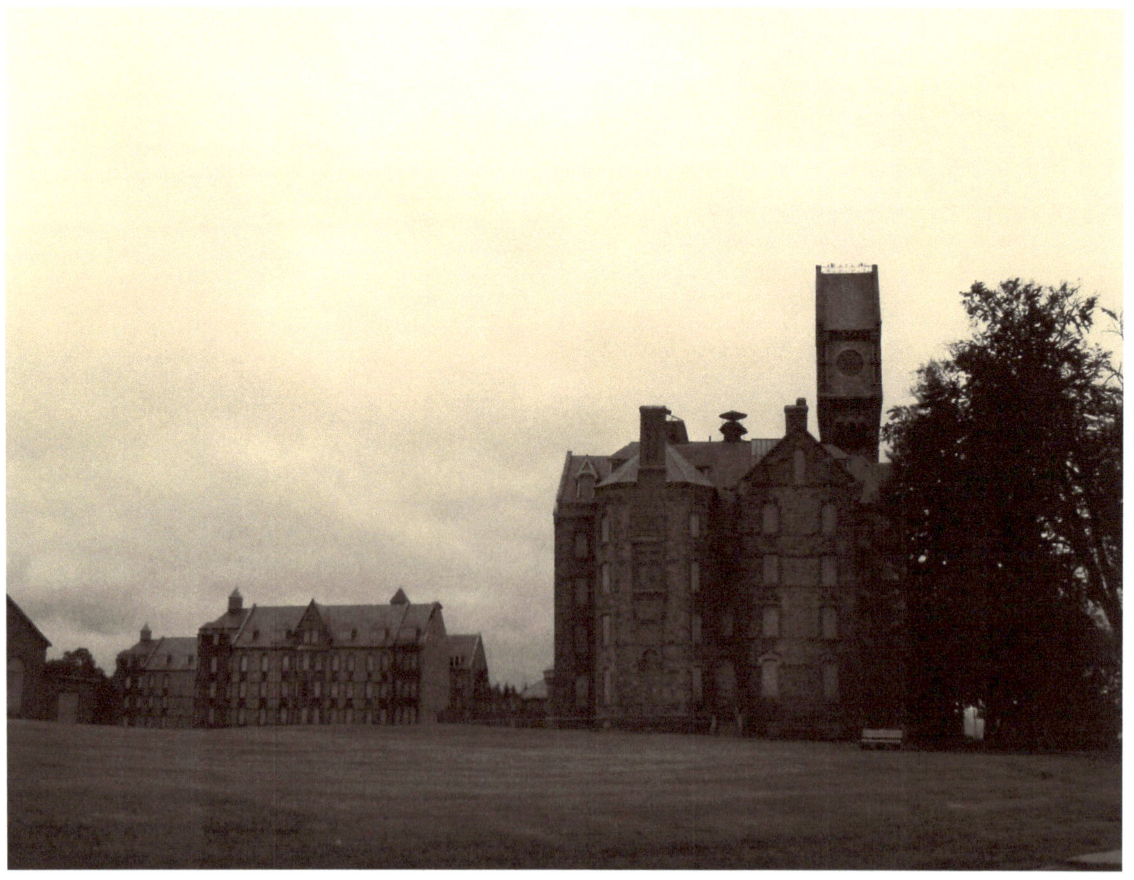

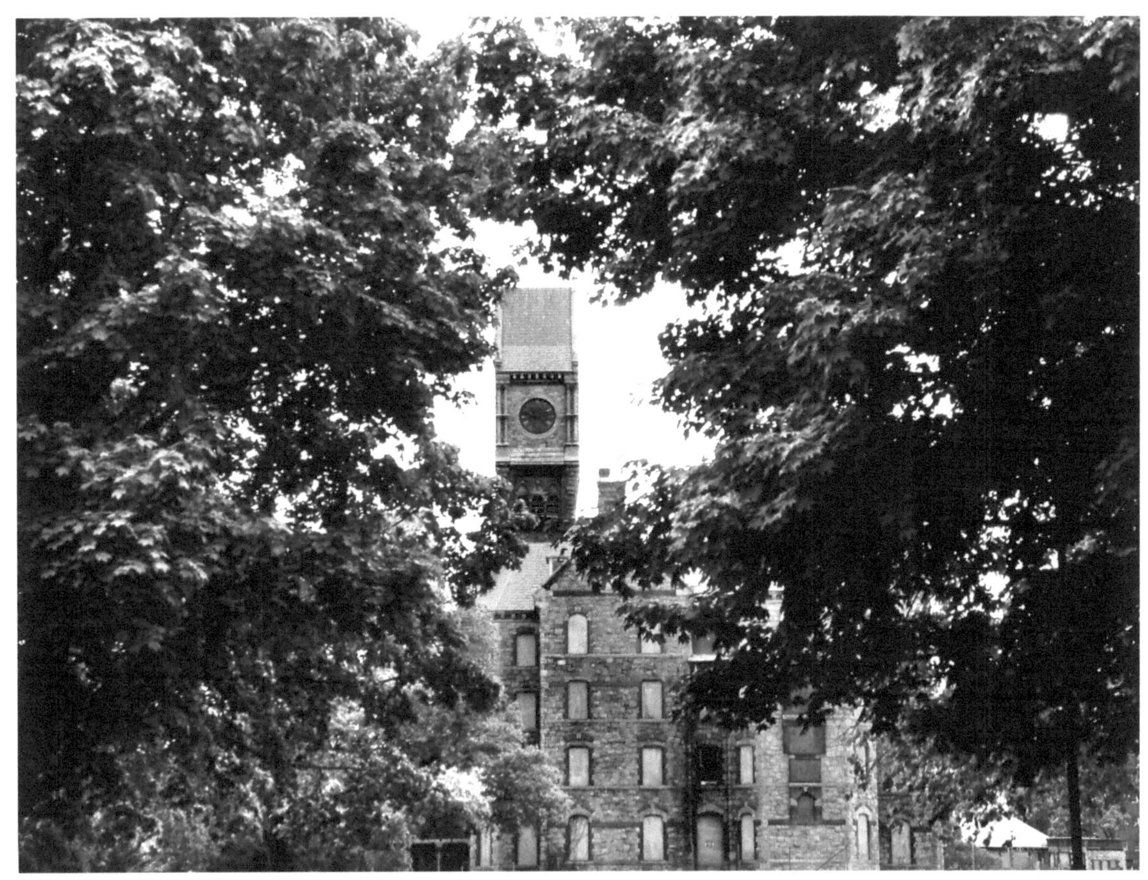

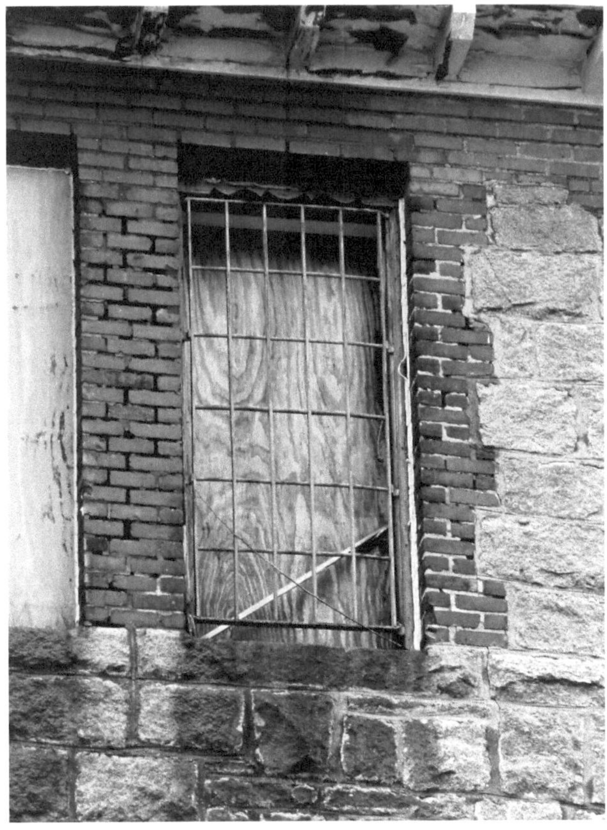

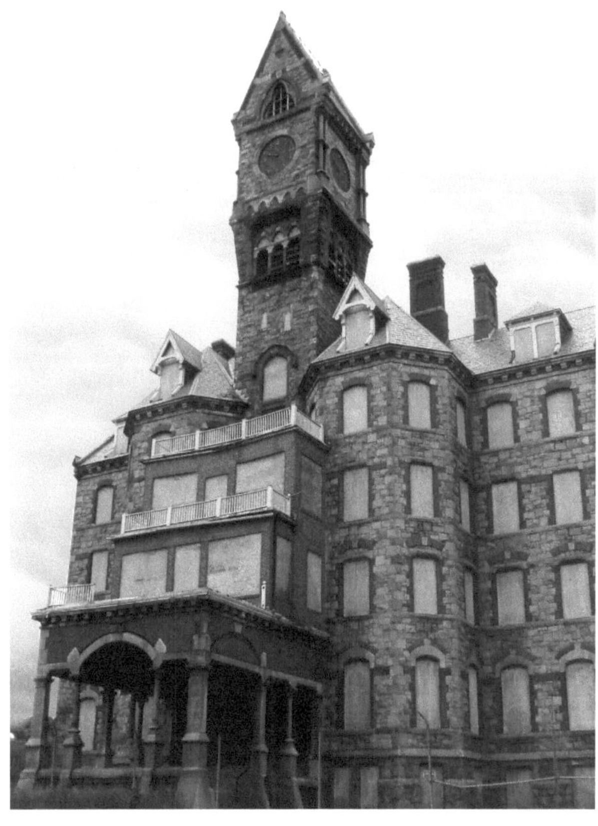

CHAPTER ELEVEN

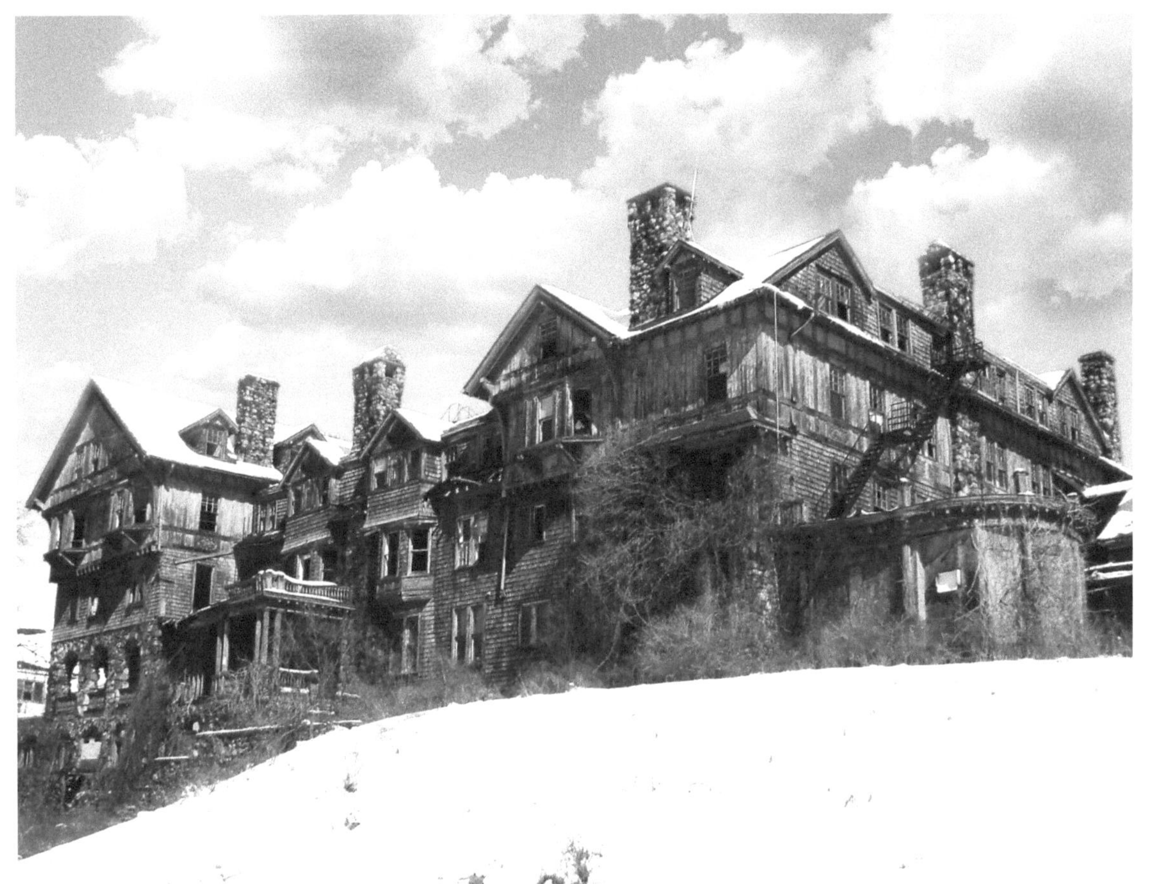

BENNETT SCHOOL

New York

Bennett School

Charmingly Dreary

If Danvers State Hospital was America's Scariest Building then The Bennett School ran a close second. I had occasion to visit this charmingly dreary structure with Bobio the same day that we went to Riverside Psychiatric Center. It sits in an idyllic little upstate town, crouching by the road like something straight out of a B movie. When set designers need a haunted house this is where they should come for ideas. It's definitely photogenic in a patently dilapidated way. So much so that it made the cover for this book.

The bizarre placement is the first thing that I noticed. It's nestled on a slight rise between newer town homes and, of all things, a daycare center. I think the children must dread outside playtime with this hulking beast staring down at them through its broken windows. I'm sure its even worse on windy days as pieces of it are likely to fall off in a clatter of splintery old wood. It's a bit surprising that thing is standing at all given its condition.

Of course, it wasn't always like this. Built in 1893, it was originally known as Halcyon Hall and it was an exclusive upstate retreat for the wealthy. In its heyday, captains of industry and the politically powerful strolled the columned porticos and gazed out the turreted windows at miles of virgin wood. Despite its advanced state of decomposition, you can easily see that it was once quite a grand place. It boasted its own art gallery, library and even electric lights run by it own generators - quite the marvel in the late 19th century. Regardless of grandiosity, the owners miscalculated the need for a one hundred and twenty five-room resort in the woods. It closed a mere eight years after opening

It sat empty until 1907, when an enterprising schoolmistress purchased it and christened it The Bennett Finishing School for Girls. Under this moniker it polished generations of debutantes. Education in the proper forms of etiquette gave way to higher education in 1938 and it became a junior college. By the 1970s it was beginning to become architecturally outdated and in need of serious renovations. Single gender schools were also becoming socially outdated and enrollment dropped off. Changing to coed failed to generate new blood and the consequent financial disaster was the death knell of the school and ultimately the building. The Bennett finally closed its doors in 1977 and school was out forever.

Our arrival sometime in the mid-morning and the proximity to the residential neighborhood made entry very risky. Add to that the boarded windows and doors and we found it to be nearly impossible. I say nearly because we did find a way in. It unfortunately led us into a room that was sealed from the rest of the building. We could have probably penetrated further into the structure but we were parked right out front and the trooper at Riverside was still fresh in our minds. A concerned citizen warning us of the dangers inside the building had already approached us. We assured him we only wanted to take pictures and, of course, as soon as he left we went in. We found that the inside didn't match the exterior architecture. There were many additions to the school over the years and this was one of them.

We kept hearing cars go by on the residential road outside and started getting nervous. We figured it was only a matter of time before a car with lights on top came by. Another run-in with a State Trooper wasn't on our agenda so we made our exit. We remained for a while longer and walked around outside in the deep snow taking exterior pictures. Despite the risks, I was still trying to determine if there was another way into the older portion of the building. I wasn't quite ready to give up, but the Bennett School wasn't accepting admissions that day. I left with a promise to be back but I don't know if that will come to be. The previously convoluted paths of title ownership and tax deeds that kept this structure upright for decades were unraveling. Like so many other great historical locations, the legal wrangling would leave this once proud building unprotected from the developers and their bland visions of shopping malls and condominiums.

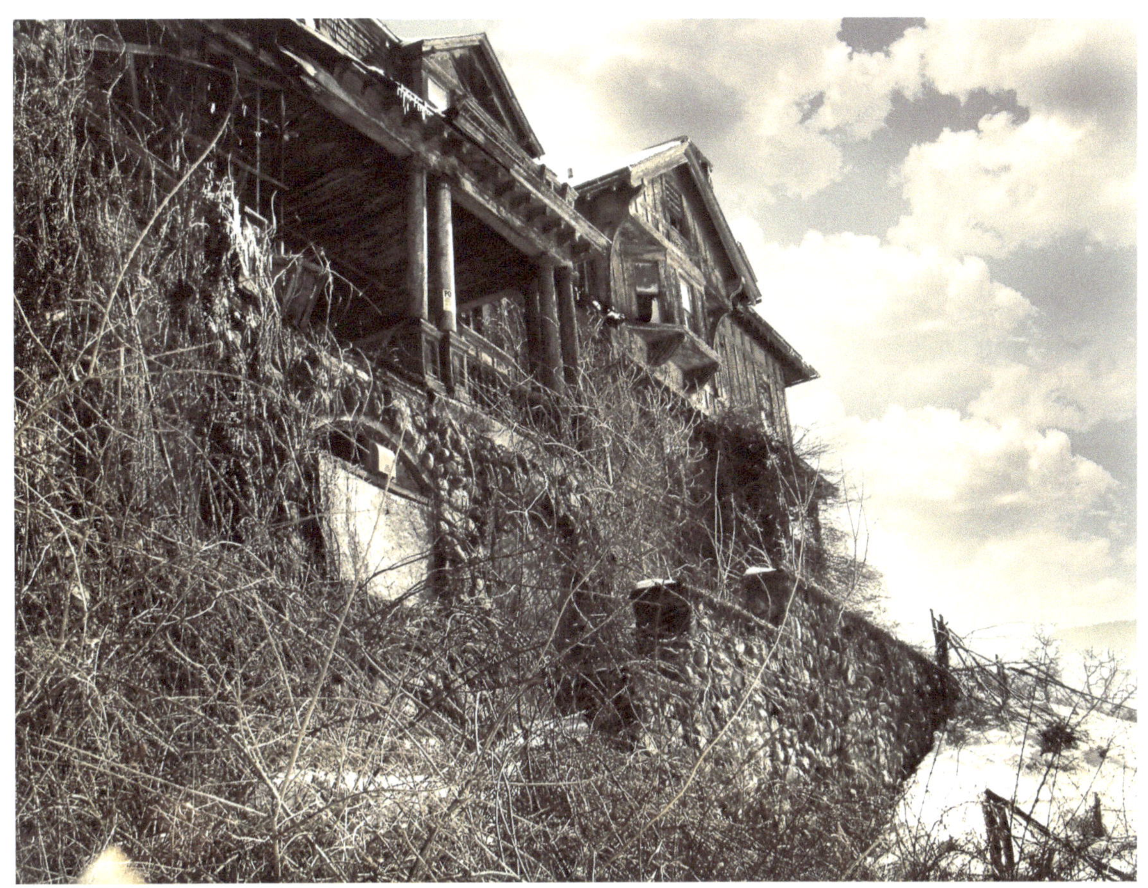

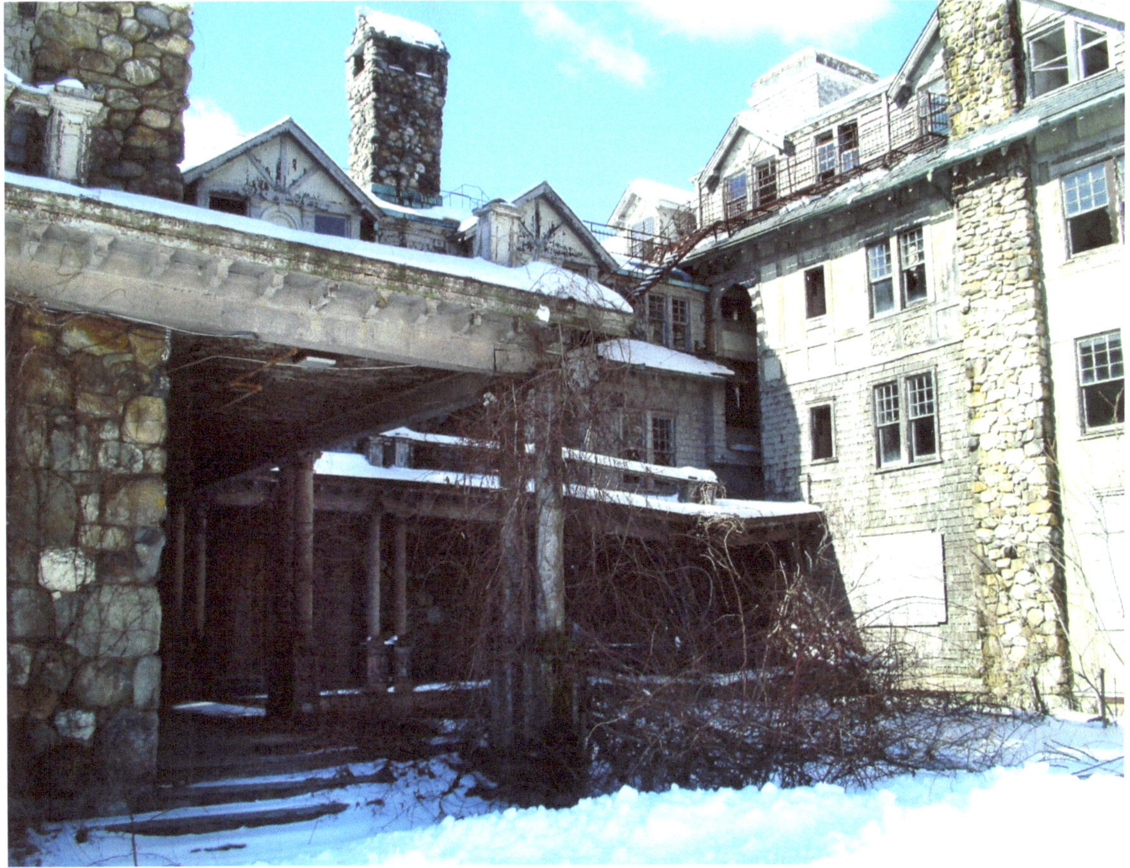

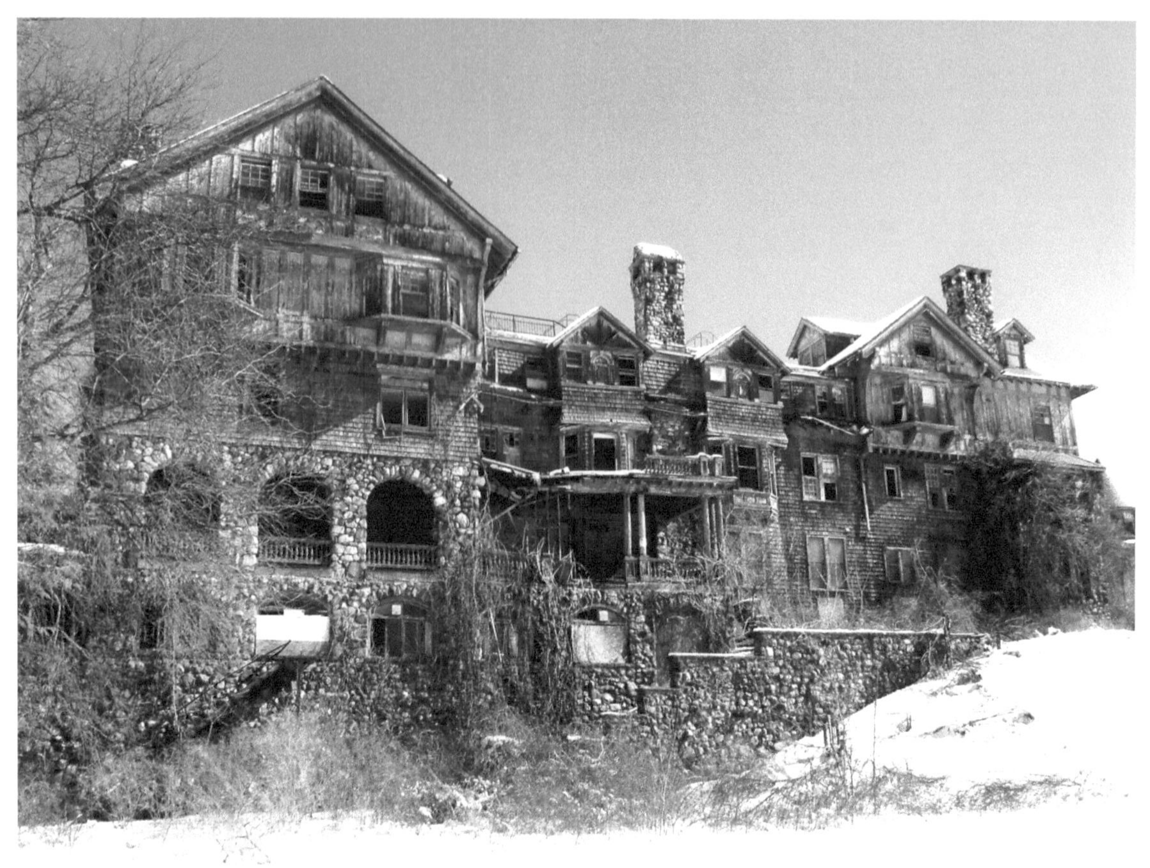

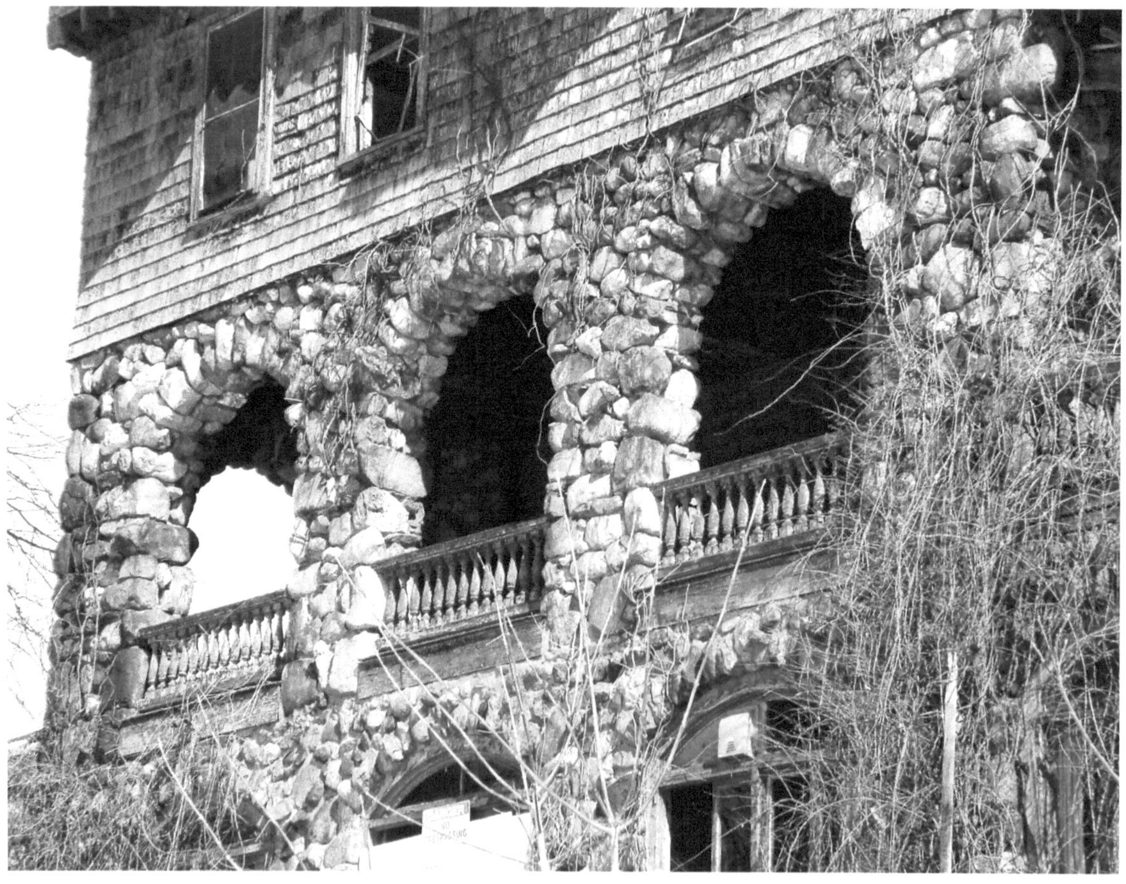
NO

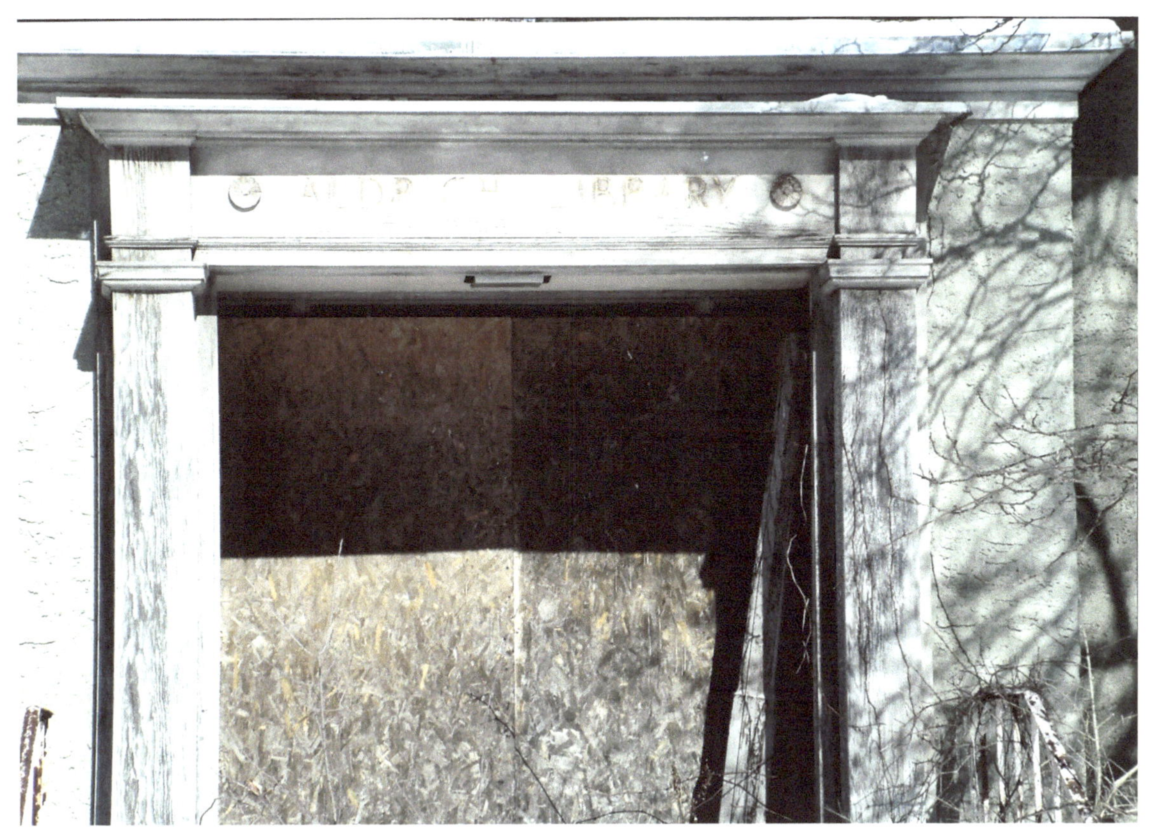

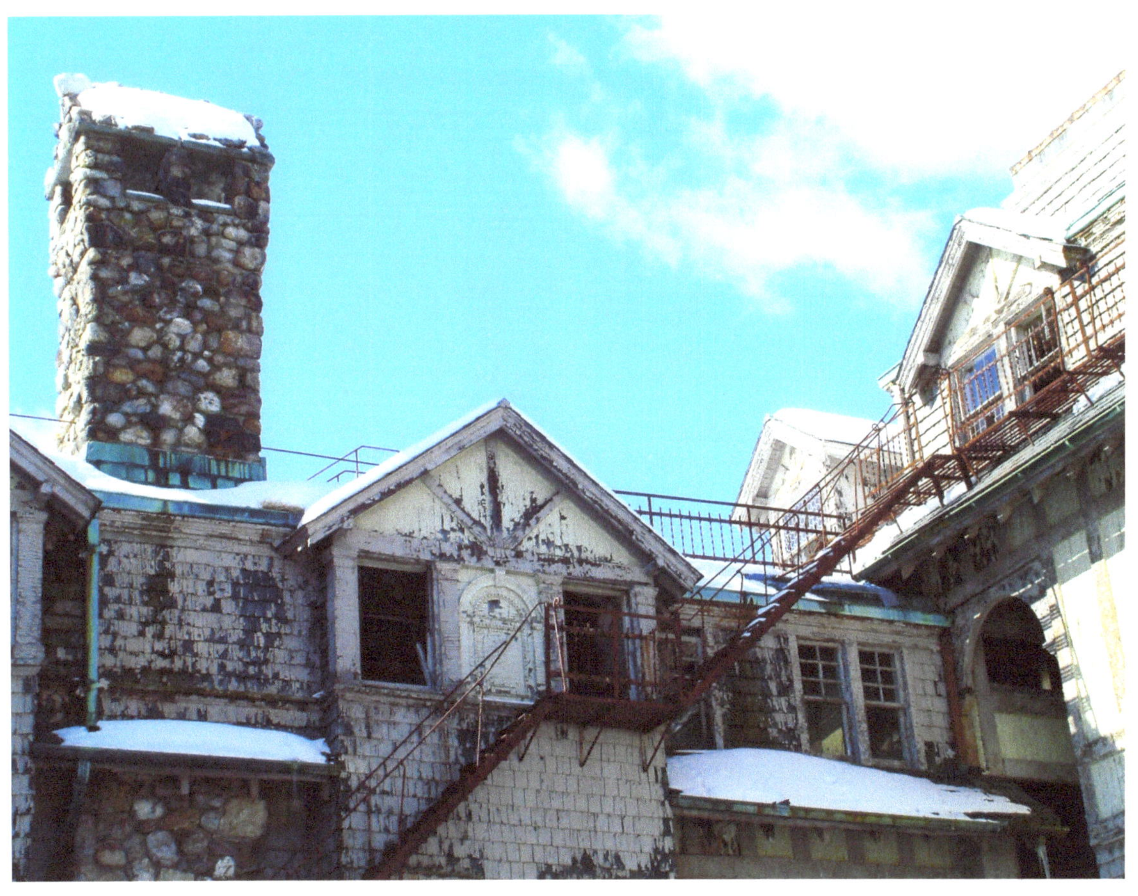

CHAPTER TWELVE

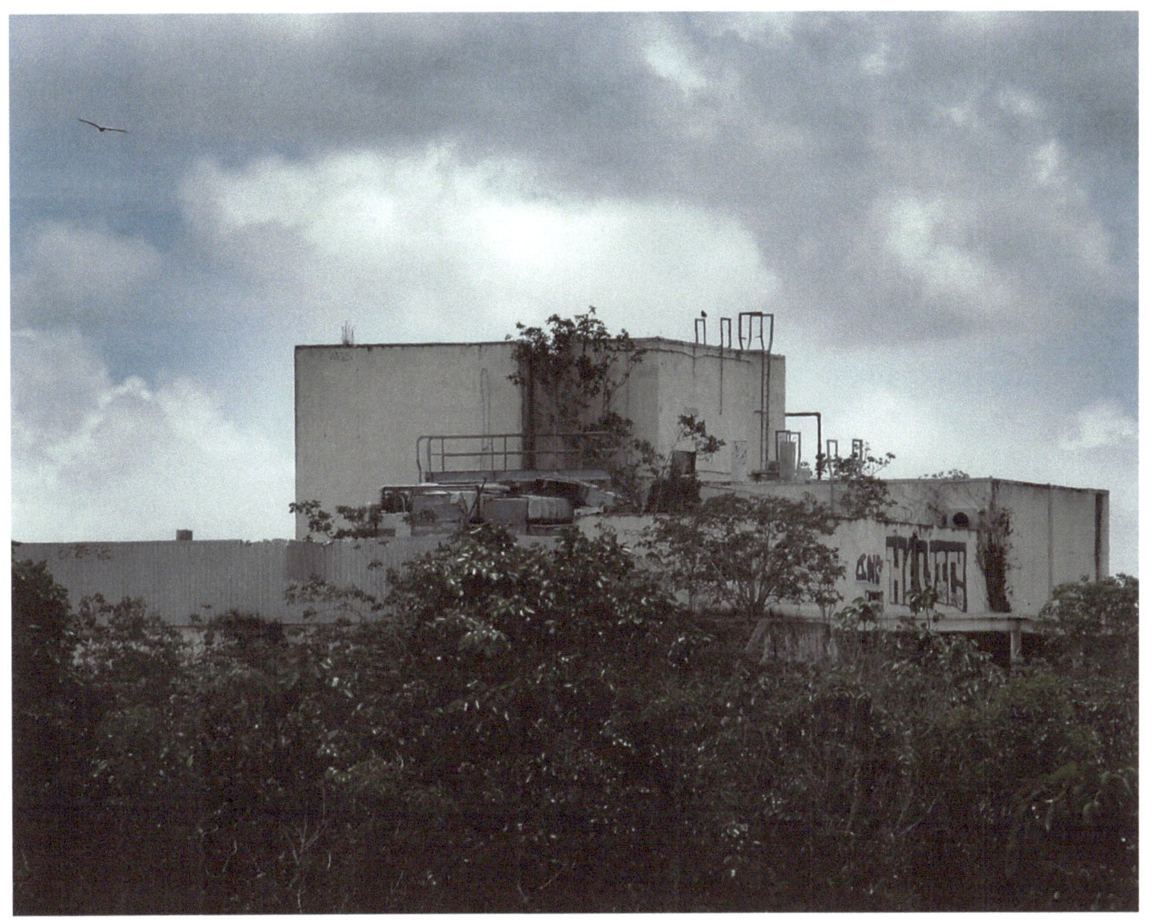

THE SWAMP ROCKET

Florida

The Swamp Rocket

It's a Long Way to the Moon

Florida is known for it's thousands of square miles of swampland. It's a mushy, insect-infested realm of alligators, cypress trees and impassable mangroves. Full of unexpected, harsh beauty, it's absolutely the last place you would expect to stumble upon a moon rocket. Back in the early 1960's, at the height of the Space Race, Florida swampland was cheap and plentiful. It was actually a perfect place to build huge facility for the purpose of building and testing the world's largest solid rocket. Deep in no man's land and far from any human habitation, the massive rocket could be test fired without accidentally incinerating any of the locals. Unfortunately, Florida is also known for hurricanes. In 1992 a monster storm named Andrew blew through the state and so severely damaged this facility that it was finally abandoned after 30 years of operation. The rocket was doomed long before then anyway because after three test fires, it was shelved in favor of the liquid rocket that finally sent our Astronauts to the moon.

I was on my way to Key West for a relaxing a weekend with my girlfriend, Stevie, and I had, of course, planned a side trip to see the facility. I knew from research that the site was not guarded and was secured only by the vast distance that it stood from civilization. In fact, the site is buried ten miles in the swamp. Our GPS unit, which has no real sense of direction, finally guided us to the desolate road leading to the facility after an hour of bumper to bumper South Florida traffic. There was faded sign indicating that this was a "Wildlife and Environmental Area". We thought that photographing wildlife would be a good cover for our true intentions. As we sat there pondering our next move, we saw a car coming up the road, so we acted as if we were checking our map until they were gone. We didn't actually have a map. Who uses maps anymore? We have amazingly advanced technological devices to help us get lost now. Nonetheless, the ruse worked quite well. The car had a sign on it that indicated that occupants were some type of engineers. We thought that engineers were a bit out place in the in the swamp, but they were not security, so we waited until they moved on and we proceeded down the road. After about a quarter mile, the presence of engineers suddenly made sense as we encountered a construction crew standing around, pretending to perform some important tasks by the side of the road. They stared us down as we went by, but we continued on. After we passed the workers, there was nothing to see but endless miles of swaying cattails and swamp grass in all directions. The only sign of civilization was only the seemingly endless ribbon of faded blacktop stretching off into the vanishing point. About three miles in, we were abruptly denied further access by a yellow steel barrier. The sign on the barrier simply said "No Authorized Vehicles Beyond This Point". There was a short road just before the gate to the left that led to an ominous looking razor wire fence, so we pulled off the main road, parked and got out. I pulled out my camera and snapped a few pictures of the impassable razor-wired gate. The gate didn't appear lead to anywhere or guard anything more than the seas of swamp grass waving in the stiff breeze. I then used my camera to zoom off into the distance and spied a complex of overgrown buildings. They looked like our target, but were impossibly far away. We couldn't drive to them, but we could walk. That is, if we felt like trekking what looked like at least five miles through the swamp. Disappointed that this was as far as we would go, we busied ourselves with taking pictures of the local flora and fauna. Just then I was looking down the road in the direction that we came and saw a truck approaching. This did not bode well for us because there was no apparent reason for anyone to be on this road; including us. The origin and intentions of the truck driver were unknown. They could be security, or construction workers curious about our curiosity or something more sinister. Either way we thought it prudent to get in our car and prepare to head for safety. The truck was moving faster than I anticipated and he was upon us before we could make a hasty exit. As the truck screeched to a halt, blocking our exit, I noticed it was an official state vehicle. Our fears of sinister intentions were allayed, but it also meant our jaunt was over. Or so I thought. The driver, who resembled Juan Valdez of Colombian coffee fame, exited the vehicle and began to open the gate, completely ignoring us. I considered our long drive and the reason we were in this God-forsaken place for a moment and then threw caution to the wind. I exited our vehicle and approached the driver. The ersatz

Juan had no coffee, but he did have something much more valuable: information about the rocket. After an awkward greeting he asked what exactly we were doing there. I told him that I heard there was a rocket somewhere out here.

He said "Oh, that thing is long gone."

I knew this was not true so I pressed him and said I traveled halfway across the state to see it.

He replied "Really?"

I nodded in the affirmative. He peered at me through narrowed eyes and finally said

"Ok, follow me".

I jumped back in our car and we followed him through the gate. He stopped a short distance beyond the gate, got out and went back to re-lock it. I looked at Stevie and we both realized that now we were in the custody of some guy that looked like Juan Valdez, deep in the swamp with no way to exit other than by foot. It was a bit nerve racking, but when he got back in his truck and moved on, we followed. About a mile down the road he stopped again. Again we looked at each other with dread and wondered what this unscheduled stop could mean. Juan got out, walked out in front of his truck and busied himself with some unknown task. As I put the car in reverse, ready to make a quick exit, he walked up to us with a small turtle in his hand that had been crossing the road. He showed us the reptile, mugged for a few pictures and then carefully placed it off the road in the tall grass. Juan took his responsibility to the wildlife and environment seriously. I briefly wondered if he would be as enthusiastic if an eight foot alligator was crossing the road. He got back in his truck and moved on. After another few miles we started to see massive buildings of indeterminate purpose off to our left. There was yet another metal gate and we both stopped while he unlocked it. I got out, snapped a few pictures and asked Juan if he needed some help. He grunted in the negative and told me that these buildings were off limits. While you could conceivably walk the lonely miles down this road, there was indeed a fence and no trespassing signs posted all around this complex of buildings. Apparently, the rocket was not hidden in any of these buildings because after opening the gate, we piled back in our vehicles and headed back down the road. That is, after our guide re-locked this gate. Now there were two locked gates between us and the rest of the world. The desolate landscape rolled by and we finally came to another road to our left. Off in the distance a large building stood all alone. We turned down the road and as we got closer I realized just how massive the building was. Distance plays tricks with your perception and, while this building looked big from afar, close up it was massive. It was at least five stories tall and constructed of a bland, utilitarian sheet metal construction. It basically resembled a huge shed. As we approached, Juan veered off to the right and took us down a driveway that led through a garage-like building. It seemed a strange detour considering the building was right in front of us. Later, we realized the purpose of the detour. The lot surrounding the huge shed was bisected by rails upon which the massive building would slide to reveal the rocket. Those rails buried in the asphalt would wreak havoc on tires. We pulled up to the massive shed building and got out. Juan led us around the side and beamed as he told us the rocket was in there. Apparently, Juan was quite proud of his secret in the swamp. The doors of the building were open, but covered with chain link fencing topped with barbed wire. He held back a section of chain link while we squeezed through. It was a tight fit and a bit tricky to avoid the barbed wire, but we made it through. We were rewarded with a giant empty shed. In the center of the floor was huge circle of rusted steel. As we walked closer it became apparent that the steel circle was a huge door. It was welded shut and riddled with rusty holes. I kneeled and took a closer look through the rust holes and was thoroughly amazed to be looking at a rocket of epic scale twenty one foot in diameter stretching down one hundred and fifty feet into the earth. Inside the echoing hangar, Juan opened up and regaled us with facts and tales about the rocket and it's facility. He seemed genuinely happy to have someone who cared about his rocket as much as he did. I rarely have a tourguide on my adventures, but Juan's enthusiasm and knowledge definitely enhanced the experience. I've seen some pretty amazing abandoned things in my travels, but seeing that rocket crouched in its silo, in nearly pristine condition, as if ready to fire at any moment, was simply awe-inspiring and worth the trip.

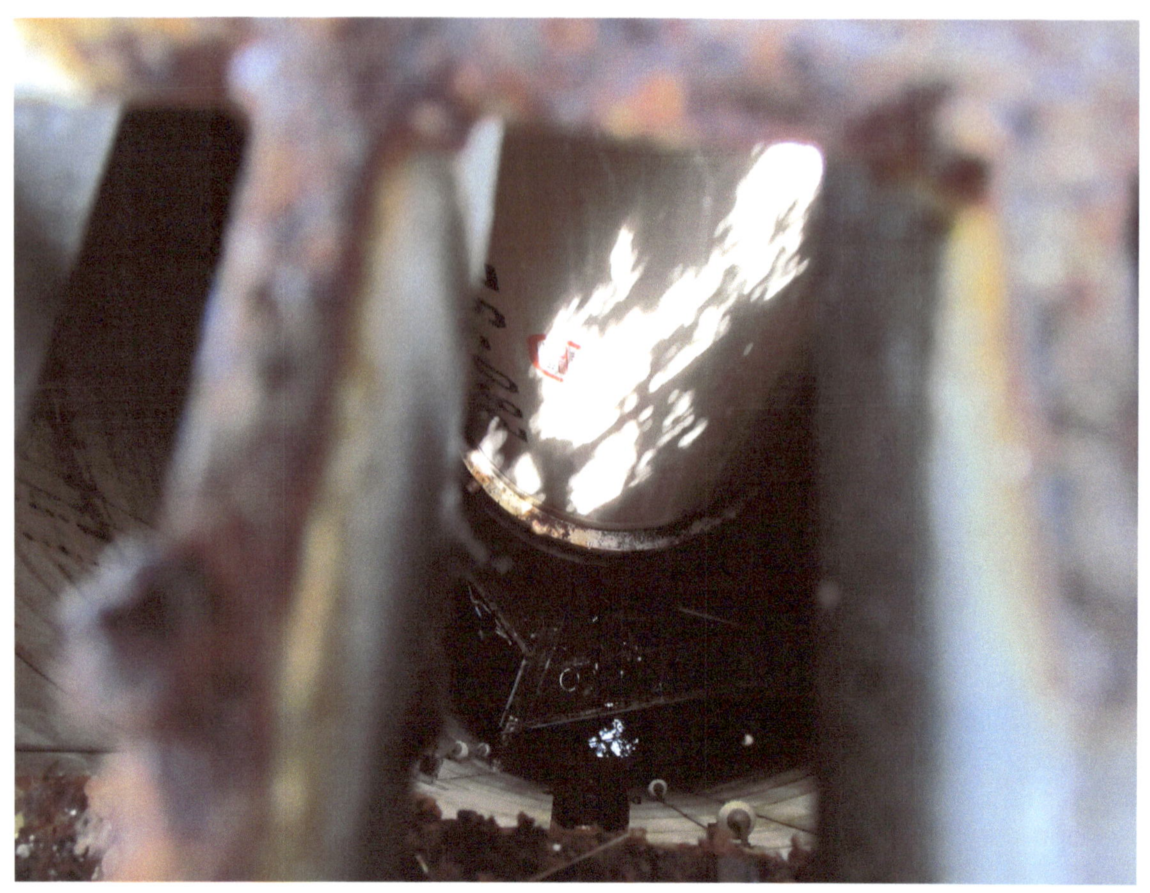

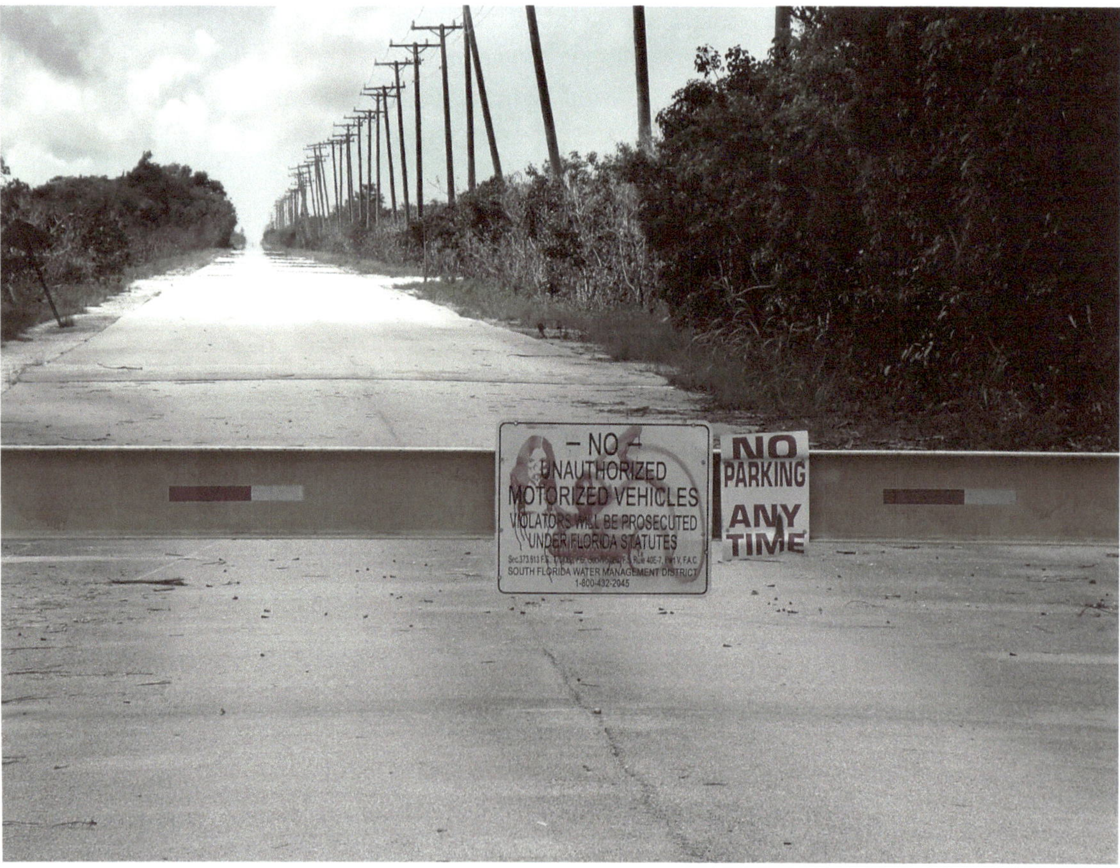
– NO –
UNAUTHORIZED
MOTORIZED VEHICLES
VIOLATORS WILL BE PROSECUTED
UNDER FLORIDA STATUTES
SOUTH FLORIDA WATER MANAGEMENT DISTRICT
1-800-432-2045
NO
PARKING
ANY
TIME

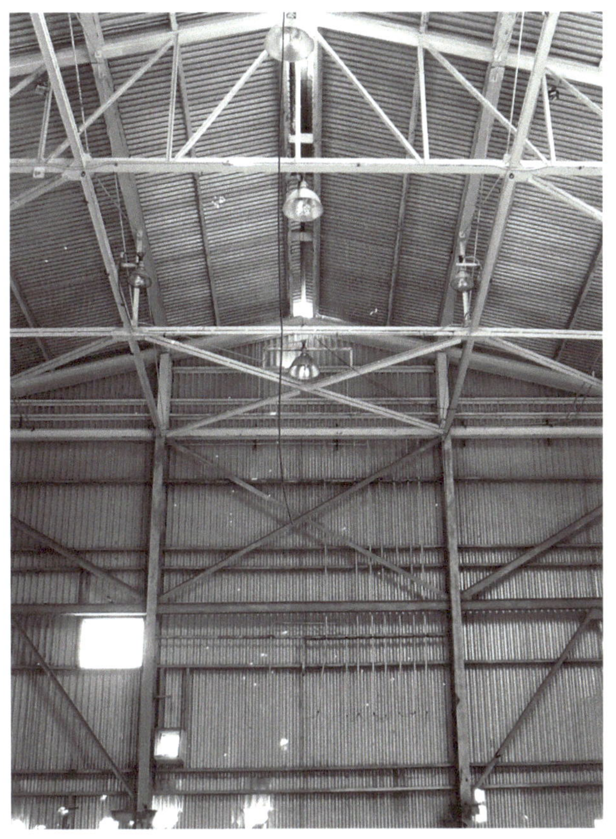

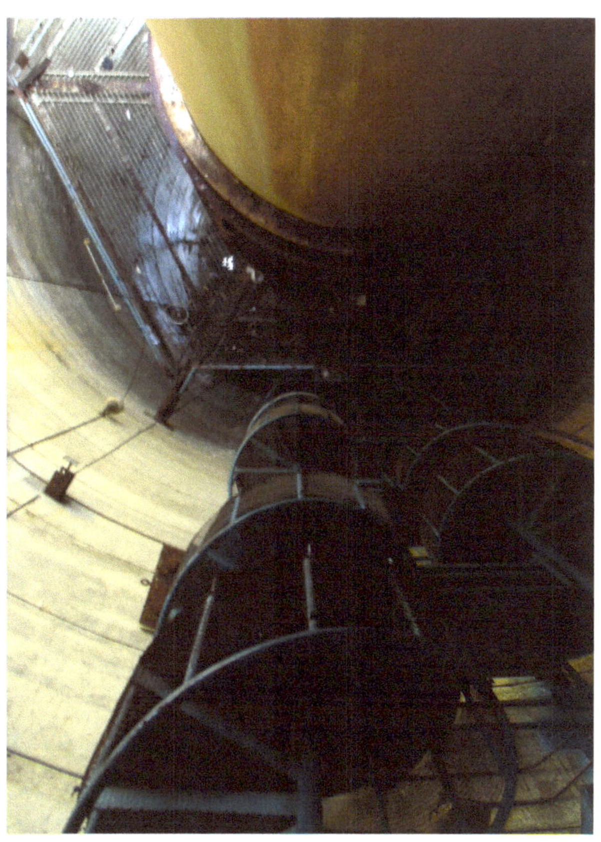

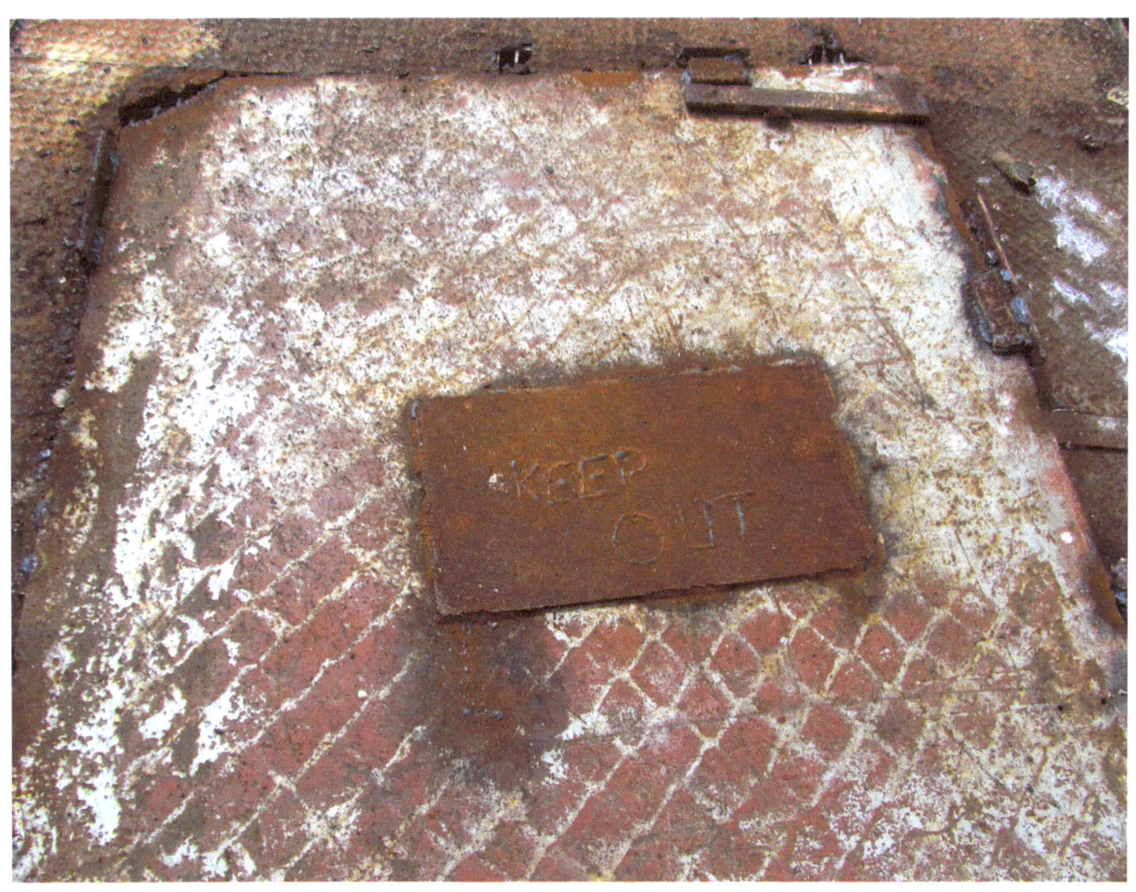
KEEP
OUT

CHAPTER THIRTEEN

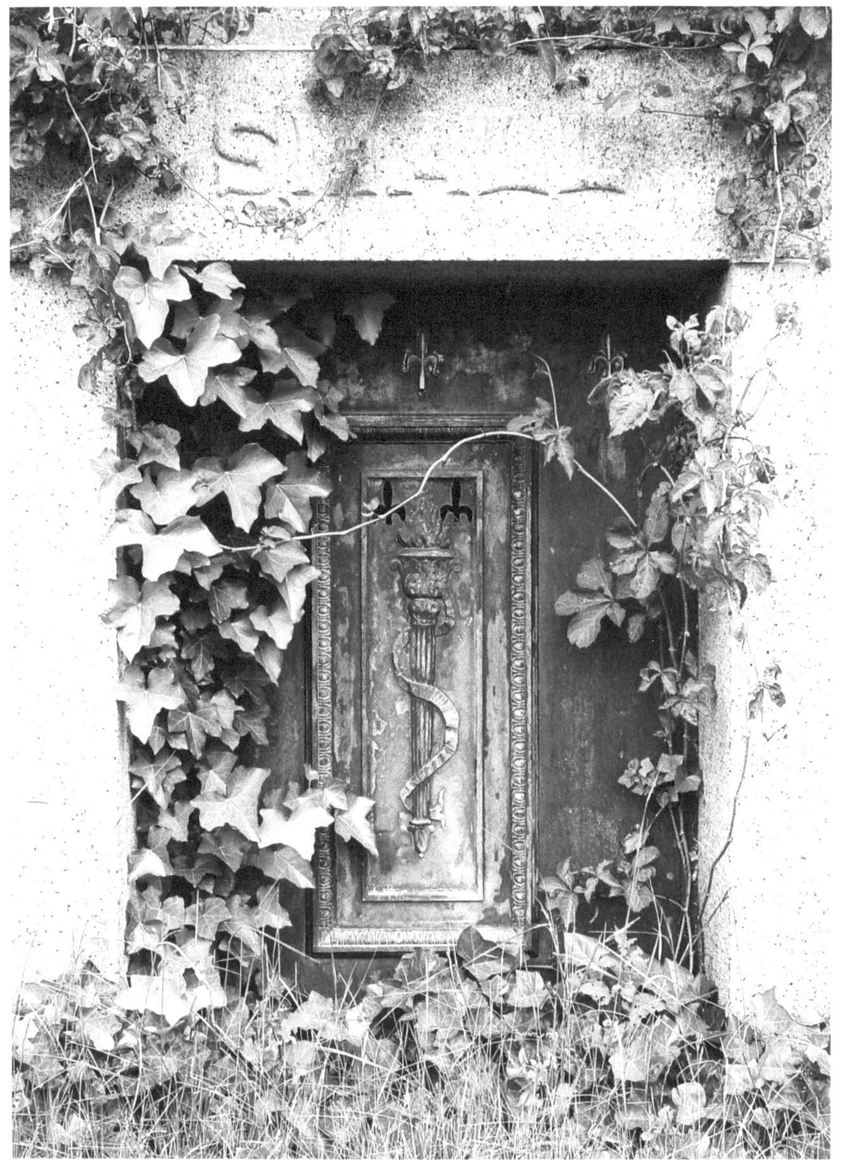

CAPE COD CEMETERIES

Massachusetts

CAPE COD CEMETERIES

Empty Graves

I had occasion to visit two cemeteries on Cape Cod. One in Provincetown, the other in Wellfleet. Neither is abandoned, but some of those resting there probably are. There are headstones dating back to the early 1800's and it's quite possible that there is no one left to mourn the interred.

The Provincetown Cemetery is on one of the highest elevations in town and is a peaceful place of quiet and reflection. There are elaborate crypts within the ground that harken back to a very different age. There are markers that simply say Mother or Father. Others have flowery inscriptions, one sadly describing a nine year old, adorning the vaults. Some vaults have steel mesh doors and if you have the desire, you can gaze in upon the wooden caskets. The vicious Cape winters have not been kind to these caskets and the wood has cracked and splintered. A glimpse of the inhabitants is visible through some of the cracks. It felt it was a little disrespectful to photograph these structures but then I remembered that some people liked to take rubbings of headstones. Somehow that seems worse than taking pictures. The crypts and their settings were so beautiful I put my trepidations aside.

Wellfeet Cemetery is less groomed and has more of a feeling of being abandoned. The summer wildflowers were tall when I was there and some of the headstones leaned at crazy angles. I spotted a tree there, surrounded with graves, that brought to mind The Legend of Sleepy Hollow. No particular reason for this, there were no headless there as far as I know, it just gave me that impression. The buzzing symphony of insects accompanied my walk among the tombstones when I was shocked to happen upon an open crypt. I peek into the dim interior revealed that it was being used to store tools. I wondered why they didn't just build a shed. I also wondered what on earth they did with whoever was interred there.

The echoes of the past drift through these old and quiet places. Standing there, you can imagine a day when men of the sea risked their lives to put a fresh catch on the table. The sea was a bountiful and merciless mistress in those days, as she still is today. When she took brave, seasoned men in her cold and wet embrace, she rarely let go. If you ever visit the cemeteries of Cape Cod and see a tombstone marked "Captain" know that it is likely empty.

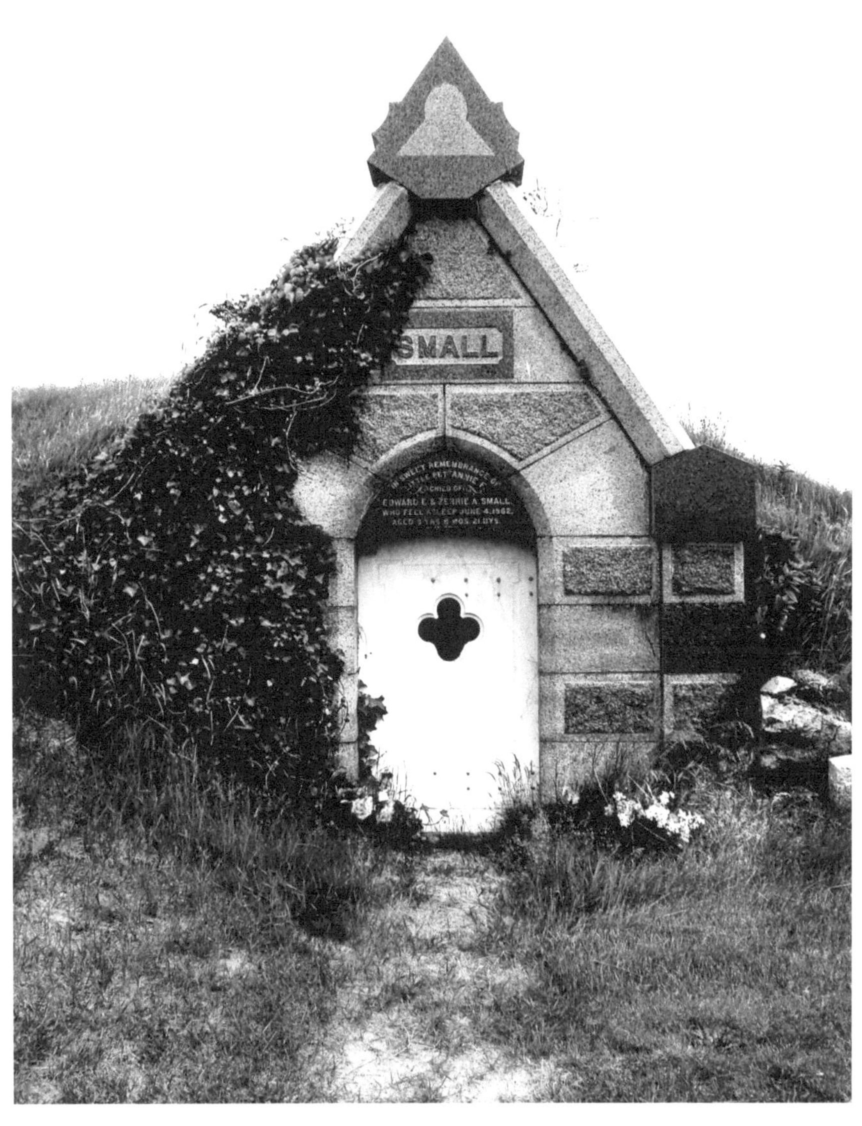
SMALL

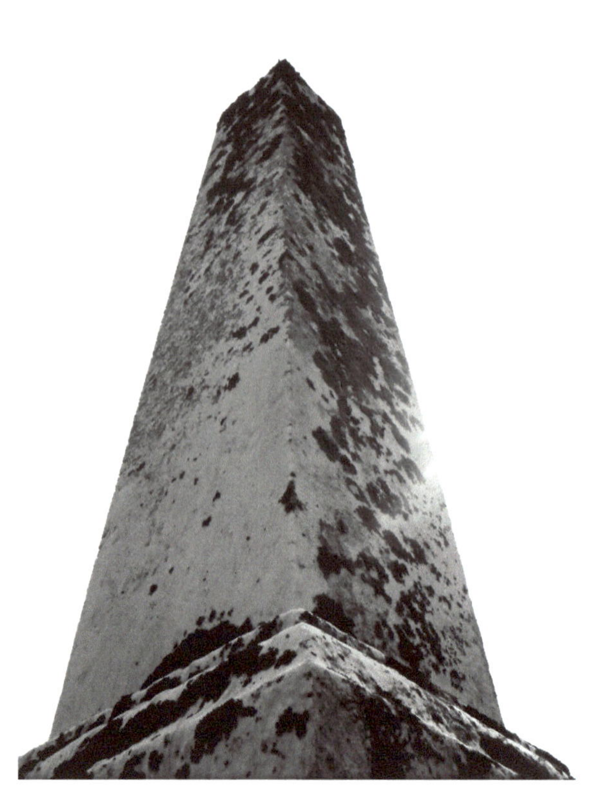

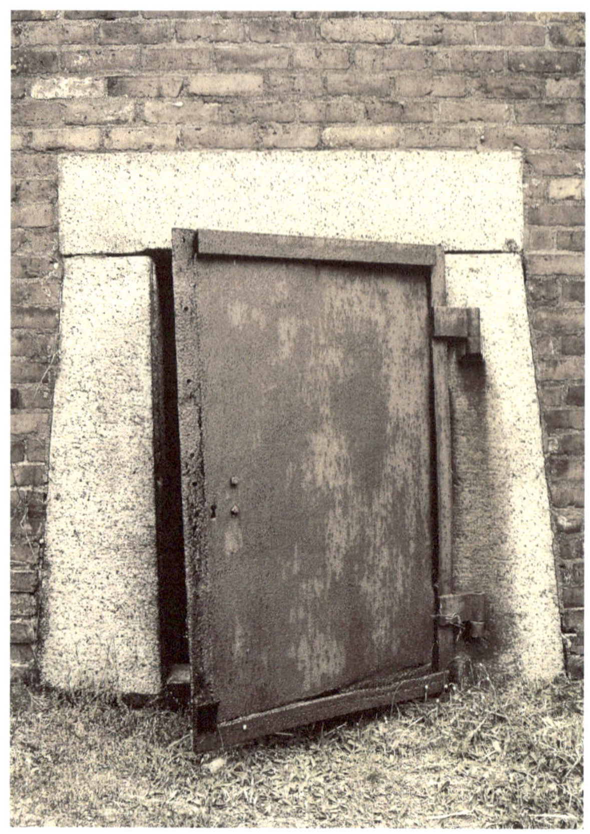

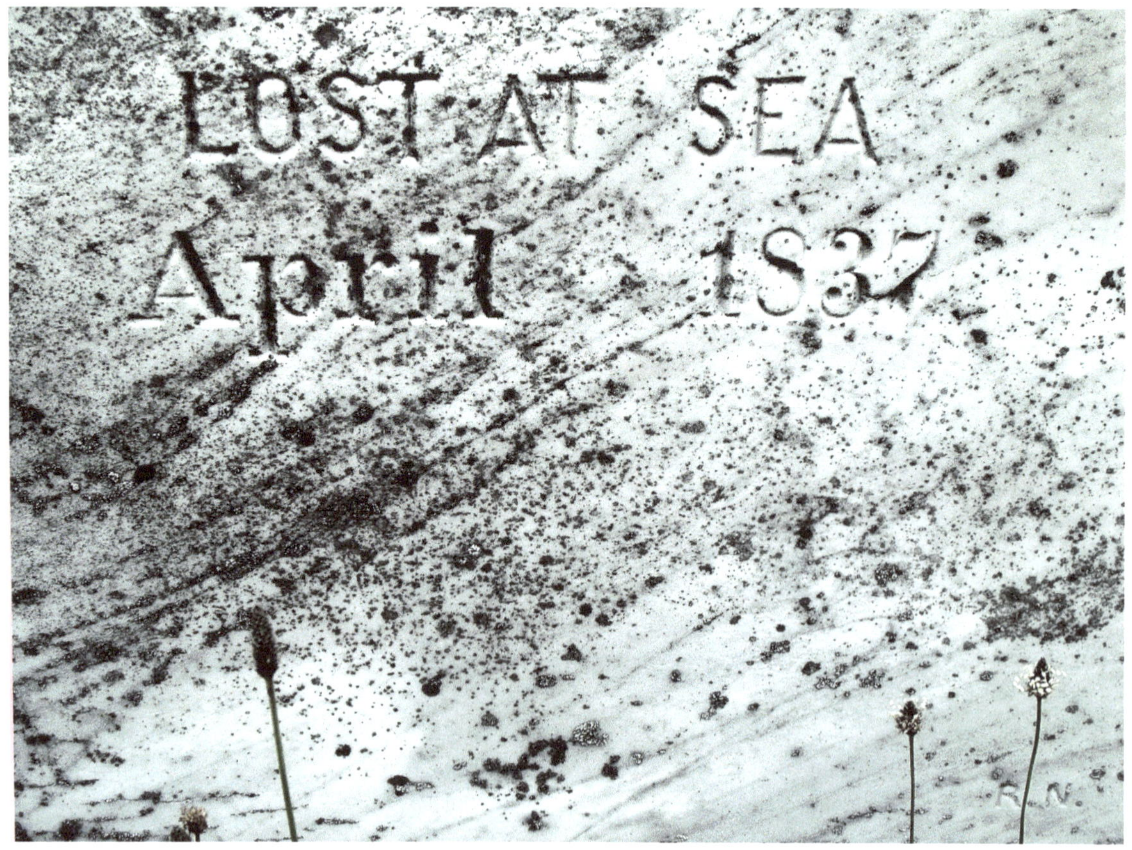
LOST AT SEA
April 1837

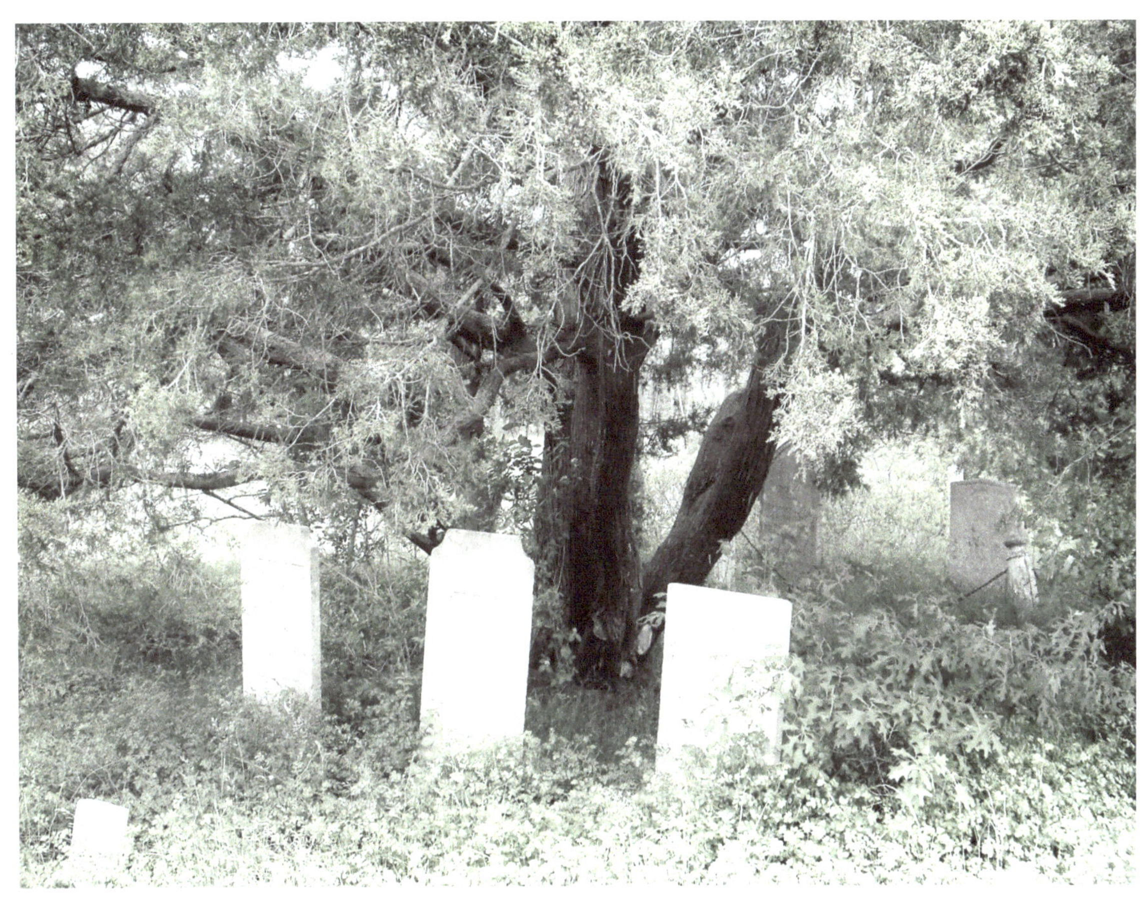

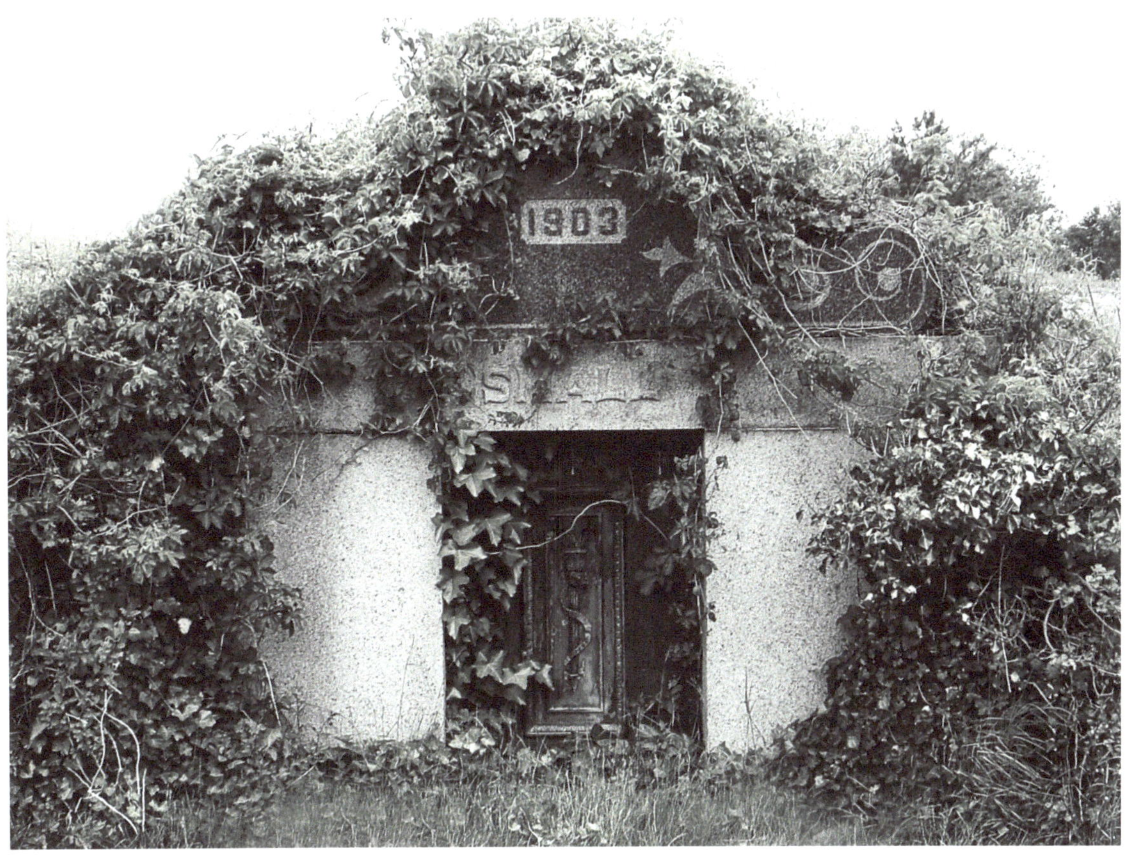
1903

Departures

I hope you enjoyed traveling with me to the bizarre, the frightening, the extraordinary and the forbidden. I suspect that you must have or you wouldn't be reading this right now. Unless you're the kind of person that just has to read the ending of a book first. My Grandmother always did that and I never quite understood why. I asked her once and she told me it was because she wanted to know how the book ended. Of course. Why didn't I think of that? But why must you know the ending *first*? I never got an answer to that one.

If you came here first in your quest for the ending, you're out of luck because my travels will never end. This book is only the beginning. I am already researching the next stops on my endless quest for the forgotten. You're welcome to travel with me in spirit and as soon as I return I will be sure to tell you all about it.

This project grew from pictures taken at the various locations. It started out as a photography book and took on a life of it's own, developing into what you now hold in your hands. This book would not have been possible without the help and support of my friends and family, who were not only my principal proofreaders, but believe in just about everything I do, no matter how crazy it seems, and for that I am grateful. It also would not have been possible without the valuable assistance of Bobio, Xav, Billamack, Ryguy, Johnny Hooch, Little John, Webb, Steele, Syd, Greywolf, MmT, Mike Dijital of D5, and all the other kindred souls who I pressed for information and pressed into accompanying me on my travels. My eternal thanks go out to all of you.

October 2011
Somewhere in Florida, U.S.A.

About The Author

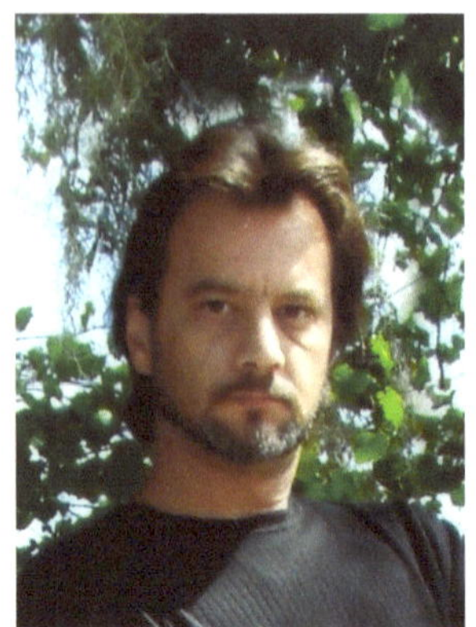

Abandoned buildings and the industrial landscape were woven into the fabric of this author, artist, photographer and musician at an early age. Growing up in Philadelphia exposed Fred Szabries to superlative architecture along with the inevitable urban decay. This contrasted landscape has shaped his professional career as an artist and is reflected in his masterful use of industrial materials such as aluminum and steel. Since beginning his art career in 1992, he has attracted an international audience with his signature style. His work is avidly sought by art connoisseurs worldwide and can be found in prestigious collections, both corporate and private. This is his first book. He lives in Florida with his son. You can visit his websites at szabries.com or TheForbiddenTourist.com

www.ingramcontent.com/pod-product-compliance
Lightning Source LLC
LaVergne TN
LVHW070127110826
845147LV00002B/201